50% OFF
Online PERT Prep Course!

By Mometrix

Dear Customer,

We consider it an honor and a privilege that you chose our PERT Study Guide. As a way of showing our appreciation and to help us better serve you, we are offering **50% off our online PERT Prep Course**. Many PERT courses are needlessly expensive and don't deliver enough value. With our course, you get access to the best PERT prep material, and **you only pay half price**.

We have structured our online course to perfectly complement your printed study guide. The PERT Prep Course contains **in-depth lessons** that cover all the most important topics, **180+ video reviews** that explain difficult concepts, over **350 practice questions** to ensure you feel prepared, and more than **350+ digital flashcards**, so you can study while you're on the go.

Online PERT Prep Course

Topics Included:

- Mathematics
  - o Numbers and Operations
  - o Proportions and Ratios
  - o Polynomial Algebra
- Reading
  - o Persuasion and Rhetoric
  - o Plot and Story Structure
- Writing
  - o Parts of Speech
  - o Agreement and Sentence Structure
  - o Writing Style and Form

Course Features:

- PERT Study Guide
  - o Get content that complements our best-selling study guide.
- Full-Length Practice Tests
  - o With over 350 practice questions, you can test yourself again and again.
- Mobile Friendly
  - o If you need to study on the go, the course is easily accessible from your mobile device.
- 350+ PERT Flashcards
  - o Our course includes a flashcard mode with over 350+ content cards to help you study.

To receive this discount, visit us at mometrix.com/university/pert/ or simply scan this QR code with your smartphone. At the checkout page, enter the discount code: **pert50off**

If you have any questions or concerns, please contact us at support@mometrix.com.

FREE Study Skills Videos/DVD Offer

Dear Customer,

Thank you for your purchase from Mometrix! We consider it an honor and a privilege that you have purchased our product and we want to ensure your satisfaction.

As part of our ongoing effort to meet the needs of test takers, we have developed a set of Study Skills Videos that we would like to give you for FREE. These videos cover our *best practices* for getting ready for your exam, from how to use our study materials to how to best prepare for the day of the test.

All that we ask is that you email us with feedback that would describe your experience so far with our product. Good, bad, or indifferent, we want to know what you think!

To get your FREE Study Skills Videos, you can use the **QR code** below, or send us an **email** at studyvideos@mometrix.com with *FREE VIDEOS* in the subject line and the following information in the body of the email:

- The name of the product you purchased.
- Your product rating on a scale of 1-5, with 5 being the highest rating.
- Your feedback. It can be long, short, or anything in between. We just want to know your impressions and experience so far with our product. (Good feedback might include how our study material met your needs and ways we might be able to make it even better. You could highlight features that you found helpful or features that you think we should add.)

If you have any questions or concerns, please don't hesitate to contact me directly.

Thanks again!

Sincerely,

Jay Willis
Vice President
jay.willis@mometrix.com
1-800-673-8175

PERT
Study Guide

PERT Exam
Secrets Book

Full-Length Practice Test

**Step-by-Step
Video Tutorials**

3rd Edition

Written and edited by Matthew Bowling

Printed in the United States of America

This paper meets the requirements of ANSI/NISO Z39.48-1992 (Permanence of Paper).

Mometrix offers volume discount pricing to institutions. For more information or a price quote, please contact our sales department at sales@mometrix.com or 888-248-1219.

Paperback
ISBN 13: 978-1-5167-2003-3
ISBN 10: 1-5167-2003-2

DEAR FUTURE EXAM SUCCESS STORY

First of all, **THANK YOU** for purchasing Mometrix study materials!

Second, congratulations! You are one of the few determined test-takers who are committed to doing whatever it takes to excel on your exam. **You have come to the right place.** We developed these study materials with one goal in mind: to deliver you the information you need in a format that's concise and easy to use.

In addition to optimizing your guide for the content of the test, we've outlined our recommended steps for breaking down the preparation process into small, attainable goals so you can make sure you stay on track.

We've also analyzed the entire test-taking process, identifying the most common pitfalls and showing how you can overcome them and be ready for any curveball the test throws you.

Standardized testing is one of the biggest obstacles on your road to success, which only increases the importance of doing well in the high-pressure, high-stakes environment of test day. Your results on this test could have a significant impact on your future, and this guide provides the information and practical advice to help you achieve your full potential on test day.

Your success is our success

We would love to hear from you! If you would like to share the story of your exam success or if you have any questions or comments in regard to our products, please contact us at **800-673-8175** or **support@mometrix.com**.

Thanks again for your business and we wish you continued success!

Sincerely,
The Mometrix Test Preparation Team

> **Need more help? Check out our flashcards at:**
> **http://MometrixFlashcards.com/PERT**

TABLE OF CONTENTS

Introduction

Thank you for purchasing this resource! You have made the choice to prepare yourself for a test that could have a huge impact on your future, and this guide is designed to help you be fully ready for test day. Obviously, it's important to have a solid understanding of the test material, but you also need to be prepared for the unique environment and stressors of the test, so that you can perform to the best of your abilities.

For this purpose, the first section that appears in this guide is the **Secret Keys**. We've devoted countless hours to meticulously researching what works and what doesn't, and we've boiled down our findings to the four most impactful steps you can take to improve your performance on the test. We start at the beginning with study planning and move through the preparation process, all the way to the testing strategies that will help you get the most out of what you know when you're finally sitting in front of the test.

We recommend that you start preparing for your test as far in advance as possible. However, if you've bought this guide as a last-minute study resource and only have a few days before your test, we recommend that you skip over the first two Secret Keys since they address a long-term study plan.

If you struggle with **test anxiety**, we strongly encourage you to check out our recommendations for how you can overcome it. Test anxiety is a formidable foe, but it can be beaten, and we want to make sure you have the tools you need to defeat it.

Review Video Directory

As you work your way through this guide, you will see numerous review video links interspersed with the written content. If you would like to access all of these review videos in one place, click on the video directory link found on the bonus page: **mometrix.com/bonus948/pert**

1

Secret Key #1 – Plan Big, Study Small

There's a lot riding on your performance. If you want to ace this test, you're going to need to keep your skills sharp and the material fresh in your mind. You need a plan that lets you review everything you need to know while still fitting in your schedule. We'll break this strategy down into three categories.

Information Organization

Start with the information you already have: the official test outline. From this, you can make a complete list of all the concepts you need to cover before the test. Organize these concepts into groups that can be studied together, and create a list of any related vocabulary you need to learn so you can brush up on any difficult terms. You'll want to keep this vocabulary list handy once you actually start studying since you may need to add to it along the way.

Time Management

Once you have your set of study concepts, decide how to spread them out over the time you have left before the test. Break your study plan into small, clear goals so you have a manageable task for each day and know exactly what you're doing. Then just focus on one small step at a time. When you manage your time this way, you don't need to spend hours at a time studying. Studying a small block of content for a short period each day helps you retain information better and avoid stressing over how much you have left to do. You can relax knowing that you have a plan to cover everything in time. In order for this strategy to be effective though, you have to start studying early and stick to your schedule. Avoid the exhaustion and futility that comes from last-minute cramming!

Study Environment

The environment you study in has a big impact on your learning. Studying in a coffee shop, while probably more enjoyable, is not likely to be as fruitful as studying in a quiet room. It's important to keep distractions to a minimum. You're only planning to study for a short block of time, so make the most of it. Don't pause to check your phone or get up to find a snack. It's also important to **avoid multitasking**. Research has consistently shown that multitasking will make your studying dramatically less effective. Your study area should also be comfortable and well-lit so you don't have the distraction of straining your eyes or sitting on an uncomfortable chair.

 The time of day you study is also important. You want to be rested and alert. Don't wait until just before bedtime. Study when you'll be most likely to comprehend and remember. Even better, if you know what time of day your test will be, set that time aside for study. That way your brain will be used to working on that subject at that specific time and you'll have a better chance of recalling information.

Finally, it can be helpful to team up with others who are studying for the same test. Your actual studying should be done in as isolated an environment as possible, but the work of organizing the information and setting up the study plan can be divided up. In between study sessions, you can discuss with your teammates the concepts that you're all studying and quiz each other on the details. Just be sure that your teammates are as serious about the test as you are. If you find that your study time is being replaced with social time, you might need to find a new team.

2

Secret Key #2 – Make Your Studying Count

You're devoting a lot of time and effort to preparing for this test, so you want to be absolutely certain it will pay off. This means doing more than just reading the content and hoping you can remember it on test day. It's important to make every minute of study count. There are two main areas you can focus on to make your studying count.

Retention

It doesn't matter how much time you study if you can't remember the material. You need to make sure you are retaining the concepts. To check your retention of the information you're learning, try recalling it at later times with minimal prompting. Try carrying around flashcards and glance at one or two from time to time or ask a friend who's also studying for the test to quiz you.

To enhance your retention, look for ways to put the information into practice so that you can apply it rather than simply recalling it. If you're using the information in practical ways, it will be much easier to remember. Similarly, it helps to solidify a concept in your mind if you're not only reading it to yourself but also explaining it to someone else. Ask a friend to let you teach them about a concept you're a little shaky on (or speak aloud to an imaginary audience if necessary). As you try to summarize, define, give examples, and answer your friend's questions, you'll understand the concepts better and they will stay with you longer. Finally, step back for a big picture view and ask yourself how each piece of information fits with the whole subject. When you link the different concepts together and see them working together as a whole, it's easier to remember the individual components.

Finally, practice showing your work on any multi-step problems, even if you're just studying. Writing out each step you take to solve a problem will help solidify the process in your mind, and you'll be more likely to remember it during the test.

Modality

Modality simply refers to the means or method by which you study. Choosing a study modality that fits your own individual learning style is crucial. No two people learn best in exactly the same way, so it's important to know your strengths and use them to your advantage.

For example, if you learn best by visualization, focus on visualizing a concept in your mind and draw an image or a diagram. Try color-coding your notes, illustrating them, or creating symbols that will trigger your mind to recall a learned concept. If you learn best by hearing or discussing information, find a study partner who learns the same way or read aloud to yourself. Think about how to put the information in your own words. Imagine that you are giving a lecture on the topic and record yourself so you can listen to it later.

For any learning style, flashcards can be helpful. Organize the information so you can take advantage of spare moments to review. Underline key words or phrases. Use different colors for different categories. Mnemonic devices (such as creating a short list in which every item starts with the same letter) can also help with retention. Find what works best for you and use it to store the information in your mind most effectively and easily.

3

Secret Key #3 – Practice the Right Way

Your success on test day depends not only on how many hours you put into preparing, but also on whether you prepared the right way. It's good to check along the way to see if your studying is paying off. One of the most effective ways to do this is by taking practice tests to evaluate your progress. Practice tests are useful because they show exactly where you need to improve. Every time you take a practice test, pay special attention to these three groups of questions:

- The questions you got wrong
- The questions you had to guess on, even if you guessed right
- The questions you found difficult or slow to work through

This will show you exactly what your weak areas are, and where you need to devote more study time. Ask yourself why each of these questions gave you trouble. Was it because you didn't understand the material? Was it because you didn't remember the vocabulary? Do you need more repetitions on this type of question to build speed and confidence? Dig into those questions and figure out how you can strengthen your weak areas as you go back to review the material.

 Additionally, many practice tests have a section explaining the answer choices. It can be tempting to read the explanation and think that you now have a good understanding of the concept. However, an explanation likely only covers part of the question's broader context. Even if the explanation makes perfect sense, **go back and investigate** every concept related to the question until you're positive you have a thorough understanding.

As you go along, keep in mind that the practice test is just that: practice. Memorizing these questions and answers will not be very helpful on the actual test because it is unlikely to have any of the same exact questions. If you only know the right answers to the sample questions, you won't be prepared for the real thing. **Study the concepts** until you understand them fully, and then you'll be able to answer any question that shows up on the test.

It's important to wait on the practice tests until you're ready. If you take a test on your first day of study, you may be overwhelmed by the amount of material covered and how much you need to learn. Work up to it gradually.

On test day, you'll need to be prepared for answering questions, managing your time, and using the test-taking strategies you've learned. It's a lot to balance, like a mental marathon that will have a big impact on your future. Like training for a marathon, you'll need to start slowly and work your way up. When test day arrives, you'll be ready.

Start with the strategies you've read in the first two Secret Keys—plan your course and study in the way that works best for you. If you have time, consider using multiple study resources to get different approaches to the same concepts. It can be helpful to see difficult concepts from more than one angle. Then find a good source for practice tests. Many times, the test website will suggest potential study resources or provide sample tests.

Secret Key #4 – Have a Plan for Guessing

When you're taking the test, you may find yourself stuck on a question. Some of the answer choices seem better than others, but you don't see the one answer choice that is obviously correct. What do you do?

The scenario described above is very common, yet most test takers have not effectively prepared for it. Developing and practicing a plan for guessing may be one of the single most effective uses of your time as you get ready for the exam.

In developing your plan for guessing, there are three questions to address:

- When should you start the guessing process?
- How should you narrow down the choices?
- Which answer should you choose?

When to Start the Guessing Process

Unless your plan for guessing is to select C every time (which, despite its merits, is not what we recommend), you need to leave yourself enough time to apply your answer elimination strategies. Since you have a limited amount of time for each question, that means that if you're going to give yourself the best shot at guessing correctly, you have to decide quickly whether or not you will guess.

Of course, the best-case scenario is that you don't have to guess at all, so first, see if you can answer the question based on your knowledge of the subject and basic reasoning skills. Focus on the key words in the question and try to jog your memory of related topics. Give yourself a chance to bring the knowledge to mind, but once you realize that you don't have (or you can't access) the knowledge you need to answer the question, it's time to start the guessing process.

It's almost always better to start the guessing process too early than too late. It only takes a few seconds to remember something and answer the question from knowledge. Carefully eliminating wrong answer choices takes longer. Plus, going through the process of eliminating answer choices can actually help jog your memory.

Summary: Start the guessing process as soon as you decide that you can't answer the question based on your knowledge.

5

How to Narrow Down the Choices

The next chapter in this book (**Test-Taking Strategies**) includes a wide range of strategies for how to approach questions and how to look for answer choices to eliminate. You will definitely want to read those carefully, practice them, and figure out which ones work best for you. Here though, we're going to address a mindset rather than a particular strategy.

Your odds of guessing an answer correctly depend on how many options you are choosing from.

Number of options left	5	4	3	2	1
Odds of guessing correctly	20%	25%	33%	50%	100%

You can see from this chart just how valuable it is to be able to eliminate incorrect answers and make an educated guess, but there are two things that many test takers do that cause them to miss out on the benefits of guessing:

- Accidentally eliminating the correct answer
- Selecting an answer based on an impression

We'll look at the first one here, and the second one in the next section.

To avoid accidentally eliminating the correct answer, we recommend a thought exercise called **the $5 challenge**. In this challenge, you only eliminate an answer choice from contention if you are willing to bet $5 on it being wrong. Why $5? Five dollars is a small but not insignificant amount of money. It's an amount you could afford to lose but wouldn't want to throw away. And while losing

$5 once might not hurt too much, doing it twenty times will set you back $100. In the same way, each small decision you make—eliminating a choice here, guessing on a question there—won't by itself impact your score very much, but when you put them all together, they can make a big difference. By holding each answer choice elimination decision to a higher standard, you can reduce the risk of accidentally eliminating the correct answer.

The $5 challenge can also be applied in a positive sense: If you are willing to bet $5 that an answer choice *is* correct, go ahead and mark it as correct.

Summary: Only eliminate an answer choice if you are willing to bet $5 that it is wrong.

6

Which Answer to Choose

You're taking the test. You've run into a hard question and decided you'll have to guess. You've eliminated all the answer choices you're willing to bet $5 on. Now you have to pick an answer. Why do we even need to talk about this? Why can't you just pick whichever one you feel like when the time comes?

The answer to these questions is that if you don't come into the test with a plan, you'll rely on your impression to select an answer choice, and if you do that, you risk falling into a trap. The test writers know that everyone who takes their test will be guessing on some of the questions, so they intentionally write wrong answer choices to seem plausible. You still have to pick an answer though, and if the wrong answer choices are designed to look right, how can you ever be sure that you're not falling for their trap? The best solution we've found to this dilemma is to take the decision out of your hands entirely. Here is the process we recommend:

Once you've eliminated any choices that you are confident (willing to bet $5) are wrong, select the first remaining choice as your answer.

Whether you choose to select the first remaining choice, the second, or the last, the important thing is that you use some preselected standard. Using this approach guarantees that you will not be enticed into selecting an answer choice that looks right, because you are not basing your decision on how the answer choices look.

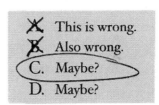

This is not meant to make you question your knowledge. Instead, it is to help you recognize the difference between your knowledge and your impressions. There's a huge difference between thinking an answer is right because of what you know, and thinking an answer is right because it looks or sounds like it should be right.

Summary: To ensure that your selection is appropriately random, make a predetermined selection from among all answer choices you have not eliminated.

Test-Taking Strategies

This section contains a list of test-taking strategies that you may find helpful as you work through the test. By taking what you know and applying logical thought, you can maximize your chances of answering any question correctly!

It is very important to realize that every question is different and every person is different: no single strategy will work on every question, and no single strategy will work for every person. That's why we've included all of them here, so you can try them out and determine which ones work best for different types of questions and which ones work best for you.

Question Strategies

⊘ READ CAREFULLY

Read the question and the answer choices carefully. Don't miss the question because you misread the terms. You have plenty of time to read each question thoroughly and make sure you understand what is being asked. Yet a happy medium must be attained, so don't waste too much time. You must read carefully and efficiently.

⊘ CONTEXTUAL CLUES

Look for contextual clues. If the question includes a word you are not familiar with, look at the immediate context for some indication of what the word might mean. Contextual clues can often give you all the information you need to decipher the meaning of an unfamiliar word. Even if you can't determine the meaning, you may be able to narrow down the possibilities enough to make a solid guess at the answer to the question.

⊘ PREFIXES

If you're having trouble with a word in the question or answer choices, try dissecting it. Take advantage of every clue that the word might include. Prefixes can be a huge help. Usually, they allow you to determine a basic meaning. *Pre-* means before, *post-* means after, *pro-* is positive, *de-* is negative. From prefixes, you can get an idea of the general meaning of the word and try to put it into context.

⊘ HEDGE WORDS

Watch out for critical hedge words, such as *likely*, *may*, *can*, *sometimes*, *often*, *almost*, *mostly*, *usually*, *generally*, *rarely*, and *sometimes*. Question writers insert these hedge phrases to cover every possibility. Often an answer choice will be wrong simply because it leaves no room for exception. Be on guard for answer choices that have definitive words such as *exactly* and *always*.

⊘ SWITCHBACK WORDS

Stay alert for *switchbacks*. These are the words and phrases frequently used to alert you to shifts in thought. The most common switchback words are *but*, *although*, and *however*. Others include *nevertheless*, *on the other hand*, *even though*, *while*, *in spite of*, *despite*, and *regardless of*. Switchback words are important to catch because they can change the direction of the question or an answer choice.

8

⊘ FACE VALUE

When in doubt, use common sense. Accept the situation in the problem at face value. Don't read too much into it. These problems will not require you to make wild assumptions. If you have to go beyond creativity and warp time or space in order to have an answer choice fit the question, then you should move on and consider the other answer choices. These are normal problems rooted in reality. The applicable relationship or explanation may not be readily apparent, but it is there for you to figure out. Use your common sense to interpret anything that isn't clear.

Answer Choice Strategies

⊘ ANSWER SELECTION

The most thorough way to pick an answer choice is to identify and eliminate wrong answers until only one is left, then confirm it is the correct answer. Sometimes an answer choice may immediately seem right, but be careful. The test writers will usually put more than one reasonable answer choice on each question, so take a second to read all of them and make sure that the other choices are not equally obvious. As long as you have time left, it is better to read every answer choice than to pick the first one that looks right without checking the others.

⊘ ANSWER CHOICE FAMILIES

An answer choice family consists of two (in rare cases, three) answer choices that are very similar in construction and cannot all be true at the same time. If you see two answer choices that are direct opposites or parallels, one of them is usually the correct answer. For instance, if one answer choice says that quantity x increases and another either says that quantity x decreases (opposite) or says that quantity y increases (parallel), then those answer choices would fall into the same family. An answer choice that doesn't match the construction of the answer choice family is more likely to be incorrect. Most questions will not have answer choice families, but when they do appear, you should be prepared to recognize them.

⊘ ELIMINATE ANSWERS

Eliminate answer choices as soon as you realize they are wrong, but make sure you consider all possibilities. If you are eliminating answer choices and realize that the last one you are left with is also wrong, don't panic. Start over and consider each choice again. There may be something you missed the first time that you will realize on the second pass.

⊘ AVOID FACT TRAPS

Don't be distracted by an answer choice that is factually true but doesn't answer the question. You are looking for the choice that answers the question. Stay focused on what the question is asking for so you don't accidentally pick an answer that is true but incorrect. Always go back to the question and make sure the answer choice you've selected actually answers the question and is not merely a true statement.

⊘ EXTREME STATEMENTS

In general, you should avoid answers that put forth extreme actions as standard practice or proclaim controversial ideas as established fact. An answer choice that states the "process should be used in certain situations, if…" is much more likely to be correct than one that states the "process should be discontinued completely." The first is a calm rational statement and doesn't even make a definitive, uncompromising stance, using a hedge word *if* to provide wiggle room, whereas the second choice is far more extreme.

9

⊘ BENCHMARK

As you read through the answer choices and you come across one that seems to answer the question well, mentally select that answer choice. This is not your final answer, but it's the one that will help you evaluate the other answer choices. The one that you selected is your benchmark or standard for judging each of the other answer choices. Every other answer choice must be compared to your benchmark. That choice is correct until proven otherwise by another answer choice beating it. If you find a better answer, then that one becomes your new benchmark. Once you've decided that no other choice answers the question as well as your benchmark, you have your final answer.

⊘ PREDICT THE ANSWER

Before you even start looking at the answer choices, it is often best to try to predict the answer. When you come up with the answer on your own, it is easier to avoid distractions and traps because you will know exactly what to look for. The right answer choice is unlikely to be word-for-word what you came up with, but it should be a close match. Even if you are confident that you have the right answer, you should still take the time to read each option before moving on.

General Strategies

⊘ TOUGH QUESTIONS

If you are stumped on a problem or it appears too hard or too difficult, don't waste time. Move on! Remember though, if you can quickly check for obviously incorrect answer choices, your chances of guessing correctly are greatly improved. Before you completely give up, at least try to knock out a couple of possible answers. Eliminate what you can and then guess at the remaining answer choices before moving on.

⊘ CHECK YOUR WORK

Since you will probably not know every term listed and the answer to every question, it is important that you get credit for the ones that you do know. Don't miss any questions through careless mistakes. If at all possible, try to take a second to look back over your answer selection and make sure you've selected the correct answer choice and haven't made a costly careless mistake (such as marking an answer choice that you didn't mean to mark). This quick double check should more than pay for itself in caught mistakes for the time it costs.

⊘ DON'T RUSH

It is very easy to make errors when you are in a hurry. Maintaining a fast pace in answering questions is pointless if it makes you miss questions that you would have gotten right otherwise. Test writers like to include distracting information and wrong answers that seem right. Taking a little extra time to avoid careless mistakes can make all the difference in your test score. Find a pace that allows you to be confident in the answers that you select.

⊘ KEEP MOVING

Panicking will not help you pass the test, so do your best to stay calm and keep moving. Taking deep breaths and going through the answer elimination steps you practiced can help to break through a stress barrier and keep your pace.

Final Notes

The combination of a solid foundation of content knowledge and the confidence that comes from practicing your plan for applying that knowledge is the key to maximizing your performance on test day. As your foundation of content knowledge is built up and strengthened, you'll find that the strategies included in this chapter become more and more effective in helping you quickly sift through the distractions and traps of the test to isolate the correct answer.

Now that you're preparing to move forward into the test content chapters of this book, be sure to keep your goal in mind. As you read, think about how you will be able to apply this information on the test. If you've already seen sample questions for the test and you have an idea of the question format and style, try to come up with questions of your own that you can answer based on what you're reading. This will give you valuable practice applying your knowledge in the same ways you can expect to on test day.

Good luck and good studying!

Mathematics

Fundamental Math Skills

NUMBER BASICS

CLASSIFICATIONS OF NUMBERS

Numbers are the basic building blocks of mathematics. Specific features of numbers are identified by the following terms:

Integer – any positive or negative whole number, including zero. Integers do not include fractions $\left(\frac{1}{3}\right)$, decimals (0.56), or mixed numbers $\left(7\frac{3}{4}\right)$.

Prime number – any whole number greater than 1 that has only two factors, itself and 1; that is, a number that can be divided evenly only by 1 and itself.

Composite number – any whole number greater than 1 that has more than two different factors; in other words, any whole number that is not a prime number. For example: The composite number 8 has the factors of 1, 2, 4, and 8.

Even number – any integer that can be divided by 2 without leaving a remainder. For example: 2, 4, 6, 8, and so on.

Odd number – any integer that cannot be divided evenly by 2. For example: 3, 5, 7, 9, and so on.

Decimal number – any number that uses a decimal point to show the part of the number that is less than one. Example: 1.234.

Decimal point – a symbol used to separate the ones place from the tenths place in decimals or dollars from cents in currency.

Decimal place – the position of a number to the right of the decimal point. In the decimal 0.123, the 1 is in the first place to the right of the decimal point, indicating tenths; the 2 is in the second place, indicating hundredths; and the 3 is in the third place, indicating thousandths.

The **decimal**, or base 10, system is a number system that uses ten different digits (0, 1, 2, 3, 4, 5, 6, 7, 8, 9). An example of a number system that uses something other than ten digits is the **binary**, or base 2, number system, used by computers, which uses only the numbers 0 and 1. It is thought that the decimal system originated because people had only their 10 fingers for counting.

Rational numbers include all integers, decimals, and fractions. Any terminating or repeating decimal number is a rational number.

Irrational numbers cannot be written as fractions or decimals because the number of decimal places is infinite and there is no recurring pattern of digits within the number. For example, pi (π) begins with 3.141592 and continues without terminating or repeating, so pi is an irrational number.

Real numbers are the set of all rational and irrational numbers.

NUMBERS IN WORD FORM AND PLACE VALUE

When writing numbers out in word form or translating word form to numbers, it is essential to understand how a place value system works. In the decimal or base-10 system, each digit of a number represents how many of the corresponding place value—a specific factor of 10—are contained in the number being represented. To make reading numbers easier, every three digits to the left of the decimal place is preceded by a comma. The following table demonstrates some of the place values:

Power of 10	10^3	10^2	10^1	10^0	10^{-1}	10^{-2}	10^{-3}
Value	1,000	100	10	1	0.1	0.01	0.001
Place	thousands	hundreds	tens	ones	tenths	hundredths	thousandths

For example, consider the number 4,546.09, which can be separated into each place value like this:

4: thousands
5: hundreds
4: tens
6: ones
0: tenths
9: hundredths

This number in word form would be *four thousand five hundred forty-six and nine hundredths*.

RATIONAL NUMBERS

The term **rational** means that the number can be expressed as a ratio or fraction. That is, a number, r, is rational if and only if it can be represented by a fraction $\frac{a}{b}$ where a and b are integers and b does not equal 0. The set of rational numbers includes integers and decimals. If there is no finite way to represent a value with a fraction of integers, then the number is **irrational**. Common examples of irrational numbers include: $\sqrt{5}$, $(1 + \sqrt{2})$, and π.

NUMBER LINES

A number line is a graph to see the distance between numbers. Basically, this graph shows the relationship between numbers. So a number line may have a point for zero and may show negative numbers on the left side of the line. Any positive numbers are placed on the right side of the line. For example, consider the points labeled on the following number line:

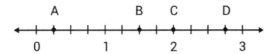

We can use the dashed lines on the number line to identify each point. Each dashed line between two whole numbers is $\frac{1}{4}$. The line halfway between two numbers is $\frac{1}{2}$.

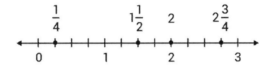

Review Video: **The Number Line**
Visit mometrix.com/academy and enter code: 816439

ABSOLUTE VALUE

A precursor to working with negative numbers is understanding what **absolute values** are. A number's absolute value is simply the distance away from zero a number is on the number line. The absolute value of a number is always positive and is written $|x|$. For example, the absolute value of 3, written as $|3|$, is 3 because the distance between 0 and 3 on a number line is three units. Likewise, the absolute value of –3, written as $|-3|$, is 3 because the distance between 0 and –3 on a number line is three units. So $|3| = |-3|$.

Review Video: **Absolute Value**
Visit mometrix.com/academy and enter code: 314669

OPERATIONS

An **operation** is simply a mathematical process that takes some value(s) as input(s) and produces an output. Elementary operations are often written in the following form: *value operation value*. For instance, in the expression $1 + 2$ the values are 1 and 2 and the operation is addition. Performing the operation gives the output of 3. In this way we can say that $1 + 2$ and 3 are equal, or $1 + 2 = 3$.

ADDITION

Addition increases the value of one quantity by the value of another quantity (both called **addends**). Example: $2 + 4 = 6$ or $8 + 9 = 17$. The result is called the **sum**. With addition, the order does not matter, $4 + 2 = 2 + 4$.

When adding signed numbers, if the signs are the same simply add the absolute values of the addends and apply the original sign to the sum. For example, $(+4) + (+8) = +12$ and $(-4) + (-8) = -12$. When the original signs are different, take the absolute values of the addends and subtract the smaller value from the larger value, then apply the original sign of the larger value to the difference. Example: $(+4) + (-8) = -4$ and $(-4) + (+8) = +4$.

SUBTRACTION

Subtraction is the opposite operation to addition; it decreases the value of one quantity (the **minuend**) by the value of another quantity (the **subtrahend**). For example, $6 - 4 = 2$ or $17 - 8 = 9$. The result is called the **difference**. Note that with subtraction, the order does matter, $6 - 4 \neq 4 - 6$.

For subtracting signed numbers, change the sign of the subtrahend and then follow the same rules used for addition. Example: $(+4) - (+8) = (+4) + (-8) = -4$

MULTIPLICATION

Multiplication can be thought of as repeated addition. One number (the **multiplier**) indicates how many times to add the other number (the **multiplicand**) to itself. Example: $3 \times 2 = 2 + 2 + 2 = 6$. With multiplication, the order does not matter, $2 \times 3 = 3 \times 2$ or $3 + 3 = 2 + 2 + 2$, either way the result (the **product**) is the same.

If the signs are the same, the product is positive when multiplying signed numbers. Example: $(+4) \times (+8) = +32$ and $(-4) \times (-8) = +32$. If the signs are opposite, the product is negative. Example: $(+4) \times (-8) = -32$ and $(-4) \times (+8) = -32$. When more than two factors are multiplied together, the sign of the product is determined by how many negative factors are present. If there are an odd number of negative factors then the product is negative, whereas an even number of negative factors indicates a positive product. Example: $(+4) \times (-8) \times (-2) = +64$ and $(-4) \times (-8) \times (-2) = -64$.

DIVISION

Division is the opposite operation to multiplication; one number (the **divisor**) tells us how many parts to divide the other number (the **dividend**) into. The result of division is called the **quotient**. Example: $20 \div 4 = 5$. If 20 is split into 4 equal parts, each part is 5. With division, the order of the numbers does matter, $20 \div 4 \neq 4 \div 20$.

The rules for dividing signed numbers are similar to multiplying signed numbers. If the dividend and divisor have the same sign, the quotient is positive. If the dividend and divisor have opposite signs, the quotient is negative. Example: $(-4) \div (+8) = -0.5$.

> **Review Video: Mathematical Operations**
> Visit mometrix.com/academy and enter code: 208095

PARENTHESES

Parentheses are used to designate which operations should be done first when there are multiple operations. Example: $4 - (2 + 1) = 1$; the parentheses tell us that we must add 2 and 1, and then subtract the sum from 4, rather than subtracting 2 from 4 and then adding 1 (this would give us an answer of 3).

> **Review Video: Mathematical Parentheses**
> Visit mometrix.com/academy and enter code: 978600

EXPONENTS

An **exponent** is a superscript number placed next to another number at the top right. It indicates how many times the base number is to be multiplied by itself. Exponents provide a shorthand way

to write what would be a longer mathematical expression, Example: $2^4 = 2 \times 2 \times 2 \times 2$. A number with an exponent of 2 is said to be "squared," while a number with an exponent of 3 is said to be "cubed." The value of a number raised to an exponent is called its power. So 8^4 is read as "8 to the 4th power," or "8 raised to the power of 4."

> **Review Video: Exponents**
> Visit mometrix.com/academy and enter code: 600998

ROOTS

A **root**, such as a square root, is another way of writing a fractional exponent. Instead of using a superscript, roots use the radical symbol ($\sqrt{}$) to indicate the operation. A radical will have a number underneath the bar, and may sometimes have a number in the upper left: $\sqrt[n]{a}$, read as "the nth root of a." The relationship between radical notation and exponent notation can be described by this equation:

$$\sqrt[n]{a} = a^{\frac{1}{n}}$$

The two special cases of $n = 2$ and $n = 3$ are called square roots and cube roots. If there is no number to the upper left, the radical is understood to be a square root ($n = 2$). Nearly all of the roots you encounter will be square roots. A square root is the same as a number raised to the one-half power. When we say that a is the square root of b ($a = \sqrt{b}$), we mean that a multiplied by itself equals b: ($a \times a = b$).

A **perfect square** is a number that has an integer for its square root. There are 10 perfect squares from 1 to 100: 1, 4, 9, 16, 25, 36, 49, 64, 81, 100 (the squares of integers 1 through 10).

> **Review Video: Roots**
> Visit mometrix.com/academy and enter code: 795655
>
> **Review Video: Perfect Squares and Square Roots**
> Visit mometrix.com/academy and enter code: 648063

WORD PROBLEMS AND MATHEMATICAL SYMBOLS

When working on word problems, you must be able to translate verbal expressions or "math words" into math symbols. This chart contains several "math words" and their appropriate symbols:

Phrase	Symbol
equal, is, was, will be, has, costs, gets to, is the same as, becomes	=
times, of, multiplied by, product of, twice, doubles, halves, triples	×
divided by, per, ratio of/to, out of	÷
plus, added to, sum, combined, and, more than, totals of	+
subtracted from, less than, decreased by, minus, difference between	−
what, how much, original value, how many, a number, a variable	x, n, etc.

EXAMPLES OF TRANSLATED MATHEMATICAL PHRASES

- The phrase four more than twice a number can be written algebraically as $2x + 4$.
- The phrase half a number decreased by six can be written algebraically as $\frac{1}{2}x - 6$.
- The phrase the sum of a number and the product of five and that number can be written algebraically as $x + 5x$.

17

- You may see a test question that says, "Olivia is constructing a bookcase from seven boards. Two of them are for vertical supports and five are for shelves. The height of the bookcase is twice the width of the bookcase. If the seven boards total 36 feet in length, what will be the height of Olivia's bookcase?" You would need to make a sketch and then create the equation to determine the width of the shelves. The height can be represented as double the width. (If x represents the width of the shelves in feet, then the height of the bookcase is $2x$. Since the seven boards total 36 feet, $2x + 2x + x + x + x + x + x = 36$ or $9x = 36$; $x = 4$. The height is twice the width, or 8 feet.)

SUBTRACTION WITH REGROUPING

A great way to make use of some of the features built into the decimal system would be regrouping when attempting longform subtraction operations. When subtracting within a place value, sometimes the minuend is smaller than the subtrahend, **regrouping** enables you to 'borrow' a unit from a place value to the left in order to get a positive difference. For example, consider subtracting 189 from 525 with regrouping.

First, set up the subtraction problem in vertical form:

$$
\begin{array}{r}
525 \\
-\ 189 \\
\hline
\end{array}
$$

Notice that the numbers in the ones and tens columns of 525 are smaller than the numbers in the ones and tens columns of 189. This means you will need to use regrouping to perform subtraction:

$$
\begin{array}{ccc}
5 & 2 & 5 \\
-\quad 1 & 8 & 9 \\
\hline
\end{array}
$$

To subtract 9 from 5 in the ones column you will need to borrow from the 2 in the tens columns:

$$
\begin{array}{ccc}
5 & 1 & 15 \\
-\quad 1 & 8 & 9 \\
\hline
 & & 6 \\
\end{array}
$$

Next, to subtract 8 from 1 in the tens column you will need to borrow from the 5 in the hundreds column:

$$
\begin{array}{ccc}
4 & 11 & 15 \\
-\quad 1 & 8 & 9 \\
\hline
 & 3 & 6 \\
\end{array}
$$

Last, subtract the 1 from the 4 in the hundreds column:

$$
\begin{array}{ccc}
4 & 11 & 15 \\
-\quad 1 & 8 & 9 \\
\hline
3 & 3 & 6 \\
\end{array}
$$

> **Review Video: Subtracting Large Numbers**
> Visit mometrix.com/academy and enter code: 603350

ORDER OF OPERATIONS

The **order of operations** is a set of rules that dictates the order in which we must perform each operation in an expression so that we will evaluate it accurately. If we have an expression that includes multiple different operations, the order of operations tells us which operations to do first. The most common mnemonic for the order of operations is **PEMDAS**, or "Please Excuse My Dear Aunt Sally." PEMDAS stands for parentheses, exponents, multiplication, division, addition, and subtraction. It is important to understand that multiplication and division have equal precedence, as do addition and subtraction, so those pairs of operations are simply worked from left to right in order.

For example, evaluating the expression $5 + 20 \div 4 \times (2 + 3)^2 - 6$ using the correct order of operations would be done like this:

- **P:** Perform the operations inside the parentheses: $(2 + 3) = 5$
- **E:** Simplify the exponents: $(5)^2 = 5 \times 5 = 25$
  - The expression now looks like this: $5 + 20 \div 4 \times 25 - 6$
- **MD:** Perform multiplication and division from left to right: $20 \div 4 = 5$; then $5 \times 25 = 125$
  - The expression now looks like this: $5 + 125 - 6$
- **AS:** Perform addition and subtraction from left to right: $5 + 125 = 130$; then $130 - 6 = 124$

> **Review Video: Order of Operations**
> Visit mometrix.com/academy and enter code: 259675

PROPERTIES OF EXPONENTS

The properties of exponents are as follows:

Property	Description
$a^1 = a$	Any number to the power of 1 is equal to itself
$1^n = 1$	The number 1 raised to any power is equal to 1
$a^0 = 1$	Any number raised to the power of 0 is equal to 1
$a^n \times a^m = a^{n+m}$	Add exponents to multiply powers of the same base number
$a^n \div a^m = a^{n-m}$	Subtract exponents to divide powers of the same base number
$(a^n)^m = a^{n \times m}$	When a power is raised to a power, the exponents are multiplied
$(a \times b)^n = a^n \times b^n$ $(a \div b)^n = a^n \div b^n$	Multiplication and division operations inside parentheses can be raised to a power. This is the same as each term being raised to that power.
$a^{-n} = \dfrac{1}{a^n}$	A negative exponent is the same as the reciprocal of a positive exponent

Note that exponents do not have to be integers. Fractional or decimal exponents follow all the rules above as well. Example: $5^{\frac{1}{4}} \times 5^{\frac{3}{4}} = 5^{\frac{1}{4}+\frac{3}{4}} = 5^1 = 5$.

> **Review Video: Properties of Exponents**
> Visit mometrix.com/academy and enter code: 532558

FACTORS AND MULTIPLES
FACTORS AND GREATEST COMMON FACTOR

Factors are numbers that are multiplied together to obtain a **product**. For example, in the equation $2 \times 3 = 6$, the numbers 2 and 3 are factors. A **prime number** has only two factors (1 and itself), but other numbers can have many factors.

A **common factor** is a number that divides exactly into two or more other numbers. For example, the factors of 12 are 1, 2, 3, 4, 6, and 12, while the factors of 15 are 1, 3, 5, and 15. The common factors of 12 and 15 are 1 and 3.

A **prime factor** is also a prime number. Therefore, the prime factors of 12 are 2 and 3. For 15, the prime factors are 3 and 5.

The **greatest common factor** (GCF) is the largest number that is a factor of two or more numbers. For example, the factors of 15 are 1, 3, 5, and 15; the factors of 35 are 1, 5, 7, and 35. Therefore, the greatest common factor of 15 and 35 is 5.

> **Review Video: Factors**
> Visit mometrix.com/academy and enter code: 920086
>
> **Review Video: Prime Numbers and Factorization**
> Visit mometrix.com/academy and enter code: 760669
>
> **Review Video: Greatest Common Factor and Least Common Multiple**
> Visit mometrix.com/academy and enter code: 838699

MULTIPLES AND LEAST COMMON MULTIPLE

Often listed out in multiplication tables, **multiples** are integer increments of a given factor. In other words, dividing a multiple by the factor will result in an integer. For example, the multiples of 7 include: $1 \times 7 = 7, 2 \times 7 = 14, 3 \times 7 = 21, 4 \times 7 = 28, 5 \times 7 = 35$. Dividing 7, 14, 21, 28, or 35 by 7 will result in the integers 1, 2, 3, 4, and 5, respectively.

The least common multiple (**LCM**) is the smallest number that is a multiple of two or more numbers. For example, the multiples of 3 include 3, 6, 9, 12, 15, etc.; the multiples of 5 include 5, 10, 15, 20, etc. Therefore, the least common multiple of 3 and 5 is 15.

> **Review Video: Multiples**
> Visit mometrix.com/academy and enter code: 626738

FRACTIONS, DECIMALS, AND PERCENTAGES
FRACTIONS

A **fraction** is a number that is expressed as one integer written above another integer, with a dividing line between them $\left(\frac{x}{y}\right)$. It represents the **quotient** of the two numbers "x divided by y." It can also be thought of as x out of y equal parts.

The top number of a fraction is called the **numerator**, and it represents the number of parts under consideration. The 1 in $\frac{1}{4}$ means that 1 part out of the whole is being considered in the calculation. The bottom number of a fraction is called the **denominator**, and it represents the total number of

equal parts. The 4 in $\frac{1}{4}$ means that the whole consists of 4 equal parts. A fraction cannot have a denominator of zero; this is referred to as *"undefined."*

Fractions can be manipulated, without changing the value of the fraction, by multiplying or dividing (but not adding or subtracting) both the numerator and denominator by the same number. If you divide both numbers by a common factor, you are **reducing** or simplifying the fraction. Two fractions that have the same value but are expressed differently are known as **equivalent fractions**. For example, $\frac{2}{10}, \frac{3}{15}, \frac{4}{20}$, and $\frac{5}{25}$ are all equivalent fractions. They can also all be reduced or simplified to $\frac{1}{5}$.

When two fractions are manipulated so that they have the same denominator, this is known as finding a **common denominator**. The number chosen to be that common denominator should be the least common multiple of the two original denominators. Example: $\frac{3}{4}$ and $\frac{5}{6}$; the least common multiple of 4 and 6 is 12. Manipulating to achieve the common denominator: $\frac{3}{4} = \frac{9}{12}; \frac{5}{6} = \frac{10}{12}$.

> **Review Video: Overview of Fractions**
> Visit mometrix.com/academy and enter code: 262335

PROPER FRACTIONS AND MIXED NUMBERS

A fraction whose denominator is greater than its numerator is known as a **proper fraction**, while a fraction whose numerator is greater than its denominator is known as an **improper fraction**. Proper fractions have values *less than one* and improper fractions have values *greater than one*.

A **mixed number** is a number that contains both an integer and a fraction. Any improper fraction can be rewritten as a mixed number. Example: $\frac{8}{3} = \frac{6}{3} + \frac{2}{3} = 2 + \frac{2}{3} = 2\frac{2}{3}$. Similarly, any mixed number can be rewritten as an improper fraction. Example: $1\frac{3}{5} = 1 + \frac{3}{5} = \frac{5}{5} + \frac{3}{5} = \frac{8}{5}$.

> **Review Video: Proper and Improper Fractions and Mixed Numbers**
> Visit mometrix.com/academy and enter code: 211077

ADDING AND SUBTRACTING FRACTIONS

If two fractions have a common denominator, they can be added or subtracted simply by adding or subtracting the two numerators and retaining the same denominator. If the two fractions do not already have the same denominator, one or both of them must be manipulated to achieve a common denominator before they can be added or subtracted. Example: $\frac{1}{2} + \frac{1}{4} = \frac{2}{4} + \frac{1}{4} = \frac{3}{4}$.

> **Review Video: Adding and Subtracting Fractions**
> Visit mometrix.com/academy and enter code: 378080

MULTIPLYING FRACTIONS

Two fractions can be multiplied by multiplying the two numerators to find the new numerator and the two denominators to find the new denominator. Example: $\frac{1}{3} \times \frac{2}{3} = \frac{1 \times 2}{3 \times 3} = \frac{2}{9}$.

DIVIDING FRACTIONS

Two fractions can be divided by flipping the numerator and denominator of the second fraction and then proceeding as though it were a multiplication problem. Example: $\frac{2}{3} \div \frac{3}{4} = \frac{2}{3} \times \frac{4}{3} = \frac{8}{9}$.

> **Review Video: Multiplying and Dividing Fractions**
> Visit mometrix.com/academy and enter code: 473632

MULTIPLYING A MIXED NUMBER BY A WHOLE NUMBER OR A DECIMAL

When multiplying a mixed number by something, it is usually best to convert it to an improper fraction first. Additionally, if the multiplicand is a decimal, it is most often simplest to convert it to a fraction. For instance, to multiply $4\frac{3}{8}$ by 3.5, begin by rewriting each quantity as a whole number plus a proper fraction. Remember, a mixed number is a fraction added to a whole number and a decimal is a representation of the sum of fractions, specifically tenths, hundredths, thousandths, and so on:

$$4\frac{3}{8} \times 3.5 = \left(4 + \frac{3}{8}\right) \times \left(3 + \frac{1}{2}\right)$$

Next, the quantities being added need to be expressed with the same denominator. This is achieved by multiplying and dividing the whole number by the denominator of the fraction. Recall that a whole number is equivalent to that number divided by 1:

$$= \left(\frac{4}{1} \times \frac{8}{8} + \frac{3}{8}\right) \times \left(\frac{3}{1} \times \frac{2}{2} + \frac{1}{2}\right)$$

When multiplying fractions, remember to multiply the numerators and denominators separately:

$$= \left(\frac{4 \times 8}{1 \times 8} + \frac{3}{8}\right) \times \left(\frac{3 \times 2}{1 \times 2} + \frac{1}{2}\right)$$
$$= \left(\frac{32}{8} + \frac{3}{8}\right) \times \left(\frac{6}{2} + \frac{1}{2}\right)$$

Now that the fractions have the same denominators, they can be added:

$$= \frac{35}{8} \times \frac{7}{2}$$

Finally, perform the last multiplication and then simplify:

$$= \frac{35 \times 7}{8 \times 2} = \frac{245}{16} = \frac{240}{16} + \frac{5}{16} = 15\frac{5}{16}$$

COMPARING FRACTIONS

It is important to master the ability to compare and order fractions. This skill is relevant to many real-world scenarios. For example, carpenters often compare fractional construction nail lengths when preparing for a project, and bakers often compare fractional measurements to have the correct ratio of ingredients. There are three commonly used strategies when comparing fractions.

These strategies are referred to as the common denominator approach, the decimal approach, and the cross-multiplication approach.

USING A COMMON DENOMINATOR TO COMPARE FRACTIONS

The fractions $\frac{2}{3}$ and $\frac{4}{7}$ have different denominators. $\frac{2}{3}$ has a denominator of 3, and $\frac{4}{7}$ has a denominator of 7. In order to precisely compare these two fractions, it is necessary to use a common denominator. A common denominator is a common multiple that is shared by both denominators. In this case, the denominators 3 and 7 share a multiple of 21. In general, it is most efficient to select the least common multiple for the two denominators.

Rewrite each fraction with the common denominator of 21. Then, calculate the new numerators as illustrated below.

$$\overset{\times 7}{\frac{2}{3}} = \frac{14}{21} \qquad \overset{\times 3}{\frac{4}{7}} = \frac{12}{21}$$
$$\underset{\times 7}{} \qquad \underset{\times 3}{}$$

For $\frac{2}{3}$, multiply the numerator and denominator by 7. The result is $\frac{14}{21}$.

For $\frac{4}{7}$, multiply the numerator and denominator by 3. The result is $\frac{12}{21}$.

Now that both fractions have a denominator of 21, the fractions can accurately be compared by comparing the numerators. Since 14 is greater than 12, the fraction $\frac{14}{21}$ is greater than $\frac{12}{21}$. This means that $\frac{2}{3}$ is greater than $\frac{4}{7}$.

USING DECIMALS TO COMPARE FRACTIONS

Sometimes decimal values are easier to compare than fraction values. For example, $\frac{5}{8}$ is equivalent to 0.625 and $\frac{3}{5}$ is equivalent to 0.6. This means that the comparison of $\frac{5}{8}$ and $\frac{3}{5}$ can be determined by comparing the decimals 0.625 and 0.6. When both decimal values are extended to the thousandths place, they become 0.625 and 0.600, respectively. It becomes clear that 0.625 is greater than 0.600 because 625 thousandths is greater than 600 thousandths. In other words, $\frac{5}{8}$ is greater than $\frac{3}{5}$ because 0.625 is greater than 0.6.

USING CROSS-MULTIPLICATION TO COMPARE FRACTIONS

Cross-multiplication is an efficient strategy for comparing fractions. This is a shortcut for the common denominator strategy. Start by writing each fraction next to one another. Multiply the numerator of the fraction on the left by the denominator of the fraction on the right. Write down the result next to the fraction on the left. Now multiply the numerator of the fraction on the right by the denominator of the fraction on the left. Write down the result next to the fraction on the right. Compare both products. The fraction with the larger result is the larger fraction.

Consider the fractions $\frac{4}{7}$ and $\frac{5}{9}$.

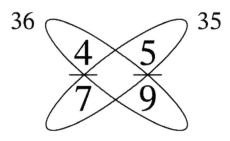

36 is greater than 35. Therefore, $\frac{4}{7}$ is greater than $\frac{5}{9}$.

Decimals

Decimals are one way to represent parts of a whole. Using the place value system, each digit to the right of a decimal point denotes the number of units of a corresponding *negative* power of ten. For example, consider the decimal 0.24. We can use a model to represent the decimal. Since a dime is worth one-tenth of a dollar and a penny is worth one-hundredth of a dollar, one possible model to represent this fraction is to have 2 dimes representing the 2 in the tenths place and 4 pennies representing the 4 in the hundredths place:

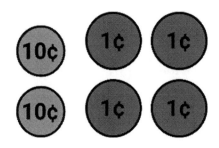

To write the decimal as a fraction, put the decimal in the numerator with 1 in the denominator. Multiply the numerator and denominator by tens until there are no more decimal places. Then simplify the fraction to lowest terms. For example, converting 0.24 to a fraction:

$$0.24 = \frac{0.24}{1} = \frac{0.24 \times 100}{1 \times 100} = \frac{24}{100} = \frac{6}{25}$$

Review Video: <u>Decimals</u>
Visit mometrix.com/academy and enter code: 837268

Operations with Decimals

Adding and Subtracting Decimals

When adding and subtracting decimals, the decimal points must always be aligned. Adding decimals is just like adding regular whole numbers. Example: $4.5 + 2.0 = 6.5$.

If the problem-solver does not properly align the decimal points, an incorrect answer of 4.7 may result. An easy way to add decimals is to align all of the decimal points in a vertical column visually. This will allow you to see exactly where the decimal should be placed in the final answer. Begin adding from right to left. Add each column in turn, making sure to carry the number to the left if a column adds up to more than 9. The same rules apply to the subtraction of decimals.

Review Video: <u>Adding and Subtracting Decimals</u>
Visit mometrix.com/academy and enter code: 381101

MULTIPLYING DECIMALS

A simple multiplication problem has two components: a **multiplicand** and a **multiplier**. When multiplying decimals, work as though the numbers were whole rather than decimals. Once the final product is calculated, count the number of places to the right of the decimal in both the multiplicand and the multiplier. Then, count that number of places from the right of the product and place the decimal in that position.

For example, 12.3 × 2.56 has a total of three places to the right of the respective decimals. Multiply 123 × 256 to get 31,488. Now, beginning on the right, count three places to the left and insert the decimal. The final product will be 31.488.

> **Review Video: How to Multiply Decimals**
> Visit mometrix.com/academy and enter code: 731574

DIVIDING DECIMALS

Every division problem has a **divisor** and a **dividend**. The dividend is the number that is being divided. In the problem 14 ÷ 7, 14 is the dividend and 7 is the divisor. In a division problem with decimals, the divisor must be converted into a whole number. Begin by moving the decimal in the divisor to the right until a whole number is created. Next, move the decimal in the dividend the same number of spaces to the right. For example, 4.9 into 24.5 would become 49 into 245. The decimal was moved one space to the right to create a whole number in the divisor, and then the same was done for the dividend. Once the whole numbers are created, the problem is carried out normally: 245 ÷ 49 = 5.

> **Review Video: Dividing Decimals**
> Visit mometrix.com/academy and enter code: 560690
>
> **Review Video: Dividing Decimals by Whole Numbers**
> Visit mometrix.com/academy and enter code: 535669

PERCENTAGES

Percentages can be thought of as fractions that are based on a whole of 100; that is, one whole is equal to 100%. The word **percent** means "per hundred." Percentage problems are often presented in three main ways:

- Find what percentage of some number another number is.
  - Example: What percentage of 40 is 8?
- Find what number is some percentage of a given number.
  - Example: What number is 20% of 40?
- Find what number another number is a given percentage of.
  - Example: What number is 8 20% of?

There are three components in each of these cases: a **whole** (W), a **part** (P), and a **percentage** (%). These are related by the equation: $P = W \times \%$. This can easily be rearranged into other forms that may suit different questions better: $\% = \frac{P}{W}$ and $W = \frac{P}{\%}$. Percentage problems are often also word problems. As such, a large part of solving them is figuring out which quantities are what. For example, consider the following word problem:

25

In a school cafeteria, 7 students choose pizza, 9 choose hamburgers, and 4 choose tacos. What percentage of student choose tacos?

To find the whole, you must first add all of the parts: $7 + 9 + 4 = 20$. The percentage can then be found by dividing the part by the whole $\left(\% = \frac{P}{W}\right)$: $\frac{4}{20} = \frac{20}{100} = 20\%$.

> **Review Video: Computation with Percentages**
> Visit mometrix.com/academy and enter code: 693099

CONVERTING BETWEEN PERCENTAGES, FRACTIONS, AND DECIMALS

Converting decimals to percentages and percentages to decimals is as simple as moving the decimal point. To *convert from a decimal to a percentage*, move the decimal point **two places to the right**. To *convert from a percentage to a decimal*, move it **two places to the left**. It may be helpful to remember that the percentage number will always be larger than the equivalent decimal number. Example:

$$0.23 = 23\% \quad 5.34 = 534\% \quad 0.007 = 0.7\%$$
$$700\% = 7.00 \quad 86\% = 0.86 \quad 0.15\% = 0.0015$$

To convert a fraction to a decimal, simply divide the numerator by the denominator in the fraction. To convert a decimal to a fraction, put the decimal in the numerator with 1 in the denominator. Multiply the numerator and denominator by tens until there are no more decimal places. Then simplify the fraction to lowest terms. For example, converting 0.24 to a fraction:

$$0.24 = \frac{0.24}{1} = \frac{0.24 \times 100}{1 \times 100} = \frac{24}{100} = \frac{6}{25}$$

Fractions can be converted to a percentage by finding equivalent fractions with a denominator of 100. Example:

$$\frac{7}{10} = \frac{70}{100} = 70\% \quad \frac{1}{4} = \frac{25}{100} = 25\%$$

To convert a percentage to a fraction, divide the percentage number by 100 and reduce the fraction to its simplest possible terms. Example:

$$60\% = \frac{60}{100} = \frac{3}{5} \quad 96\% = \frac{96}{100} = \frac{24}{25}$$

> **Review Video: Converting Fractions to Percentages and Decimals**
> Visit mometrix.com/academy and enter code: 306233
>
> **Review Video: Converting Percentages to Decimals and Fractions**
> Visit mometrix.com/academy and enter code: 287297
>
> **Review Video: Converting Decimals to Fractions and Percentages**
> Visit mometrix.com/academy and enter code: 986765
>
> **Review Video: Converting Decimals, Improper Fractions, and Mixed Numbers**
> Visit mometrix.com/academy and enter code: 696924

PROPORTIONS AND RATIOS

PROPORTIONS

A proportion is a relationship between two quantities that dictates how one changes when the other changes. A **direct proportion** describes a relationship in which a quantity increases by a set amount for every increase in the other quantity, or decreases by that same amount for every decrease in the other quantity. Example: Assuming a constant driving speed, the time required for a car trip increases as the distance of the trip increases. The distance to be traveled and the time required to travel are directly proportional.

An **inverse proportion** is a relationship in which an increase in one quantity is accompanied by a decrease in the other, or vice versa. Example: the time required for a car trip decreases as the speed increases and increases as the speed decreases, so the time required is inversely proportional to the speed of the car.

Review Video: Proportions
Visit mometrix.com/academy and enter code: 505355

RATIOS

A **ratio** is a comparison of two quantities in a particular order. Example: If there are 14 computers in a lab, and the class has 20 students, there is a student to computer ratio of 20 to 14, commonly written as 20: 14. Ratios are normally reduced to their smallest whole number representation, so 20: 14 would be reduced to 10: 7 by dividing both sides by 2.

Review Video: Ratios
Visit mometrix.com/academy and enter code: 996914

CONSTANT OF PROPORTIONALITY

When two quantities have a proportional relationship, there exists a **constant of proportionality** between the quantities. The product of this constant and one of the quantities is equal to the other quantity. For example, if one lemon costs $0.25, two lemons cost $0.50, and three lemons cost $0.75, there is a proportional relationship between the total cost of lemons and the number of lemons purchased. The constant of proportionality is the **unit price**, namely $0.25/lemon. Notice that the total price of lemons, t, can be found by multiplying the unit price of lemons, p, and the number of lemons, n: $t = pn$.

WORK/UNIT RATE

Unit rate expresses a quantity of one thing in terms of one unit of another. For example, if you travel 30 miles every two hours, a unit rate expresses this comparison in terms of one hour: in one hour you travel 15 miles, so your unit rate is 15 miles per hour. Other examples are how much one ounce of food costs (price per ounce) or figuring out how much one egg costs out of the dozen (price per 1 egg, instead of price per 12 eggs). The denominator of a unit rate is always 1. Unit rates are used to compare different situations to solve problems. For example, to make sure you get the best deal when deciding which kind of soda to buy, you can find the unit rate of each. If soda #1 costs $1.50 for a 1-liter bottle, and soda #2 costs $2.75 for a 2-liter bottle, it would be a better deal to buy soda #2, because its unit rate is only $1.375 per 1-liter, which is cheaper than soda #1. Unit rates can also help determine the length of time a given event will take. For example, if you can

27

paint 2 rooms in 4.5 hours, you can determine how long it will take you to paint 5 rooms by solving for the unit rate per room and then multiplying that by 5.

CROSS MULTIPLICATION
FINDING AN UNKNOWN IN EQUIVALENT EXPRESSIONS

It is often necessary to apply information given about a rate or proportion to a new scenario. For example, if you know that Jedha can run a marathon (26.2 miles) in 3 hours, how long would it take her to run 10 miles at the same pace? Start by setting up equivalent expressions:

$$\frac{26.2 \text{ mi}}{3 \text{ hr}} = \frac{10 \text{ mi}}{x \text{ hr}}$$

Now, cross multiply and solve for x:

$$26.2x = 30$$
$$x = \frac{30}{26.2} = \frac{15}{13.1}$$
$$x \approx 1.15 \text{ hrs } or \text{ 1 hr 9 min}$$

So, at this pace, Jedha could run 10 miles in about 1.15 hours or about 1 hour and 9 minutes.

Equations

SLOPE

On a graph with two points, (x_1, y_1) and (x_2, y_2), the **slope** is found with the formula $m = \frac{y_2 - y_1}{x_2 - x_1}$; where $x_1 \neq x_2$ and m stands for slope. If the value of the slope is **positive**, the line has an *upward direction* from left to right. If the value of the slope is **negative**, the line has a *downward direction* from left to right. Consider the following example:

A new book goes on sale in bookstores and online stores. In the first month, 5,000 copies of the book are sold. Over time, the book continues to grow in popularity. The data for the number of copies sold is in the table below.

# of Months on Sale	1	2	3	4	5
# of Copies Sold (In Thousands)	5	10	15	20	25

So, the number of copies that are sold and the time that the book is on sale is a proportional relationship. In this example, an equation can be used to show the data: $y = 5x$, where x is the number of months that the book is on sale. Also, y is the number of copies sold. So, the slope of the corresponding line is $\frac{\text{rise}}{\text{run}} = \frac{5}{1} = 5$.

LINEAR EQUATIONS

Equations that can be written as $ax + b = 0$, where $a \neq 0$, are referred to as **one variable linear equations**. A solution to such an equation is called a **root**. In the case where we have the equation $5x + 10 = 0$, if we solve for x we get a solution of $x = -2$. In other words, the root of the equation is –2. This is found by first subtracting 10 from both sides, which gives $5x = -10$. Next, simply divide both sides by the coefficient of the variable, in this case 5, to get $x = -2$. This can be checked by plugging –2 back into the original equation $(5)(-2) + 10 = -10 + 10 = 0$.

The **solution set** is the set of all solutions of an equation. In our example, the solution set would simply be –2. If there were more solutions (there usually are in multivariable equations) then they would also be included in the solution set. When an equation has no true solutions, it is referred to as an **empty set**. Equations with identical solution sets are **equivalent equations**. An **identity** is a term whose value or determinant is equal to 1.

Linear equations can be written many ways. Below is a list of some forms linear equations can take:

- **Standard Form**: $Ax + By = C$; the slope is $\frac{-A}{B}$ and the y-intercept is $\frac{C}{B}$
- **Slope Intercept Form**: $y = mx + b$, where m is the slope and b is the y-intercept
- **Point-Slope Form**: $y - y_1 = m(x - x_1)$, where m is the slope and (x_1, y_1) is a point on the line
- **Two-Point Form**: $\frac{y - y_1}{x - x_1} = \frac{y_2 - y_1}{x_2 - x_1}$, where (x_1, y_1) and (x_2, y_2) are two points on the given line
- **Intercept Form**: $\frac{x}{x_1} + \frac{y}{y_1} = 1$, where $(x_1, 0)$ is the point at which a line intersects the x-axis, and $(0, y_1)$ is the point at which the same line intersects the y-axis

> **Review Video: Slope-Intercept and Point-Slope Forms**
> Visit mometrix.com/academy and enter code: 113216
>
> **Review Video: Linear Equations Basics**
> Visit mometrix.com/academy and enter code: 793005

SOLVING EQUATIONS

SOLVING ONE-VARIABLE LINEAR EQUATIONS

Multiply all terms by the lowest common denominator to eliminate any fractions. Look for addition or subtraction to undo so you can isolate the variable on one side of the equal sign. Divide both sides by the coefficient of the variable. When you have a value for the variable, substitute this value into the original equation to make sure you have a true equation. Consider the following example:

Kim's savings are represented by the table below. Represent her savings, using an equation.

X (Months)	Y (Total Savings)
2	$1,300
5	$2,050
9	$3,050
11	$3,550
16	$4,800

29

The table shows a function with a constant rate of change, or slope, of 250. Given the points on the table, the slopes can be calculated as $\frac{(2{,}050-1300)}{(5-2)}$, $\frac{(3{,}050-2{,}050)}{(9-5)}$, $\frac{(3{,}550-3{,}050)}{(11-9)}$, and $\frac{(4{,}800-3{,}550)}{(16-11)}$, each of which equals 250. Thus, the table shows a constant rate of change, indicating a linear function. The slope-intercept form of a linear equation is written as $y = mx + b$, where m represents the slope and b represents the y-intercept. Substituting the slope into this form gives $y = 250x + b$. Substituting corresponding x- and y-values from any point into this equation will give the y-intercept, or b. Using the point, $(2, 1{,}300)$, gives $1{,}300 = 250(2) + b$, which simplifies as $b = 800$. Thus, her savings may be represented by the equation, $y = 250x + 800$.

RULES FOR MANIPULATING EQUATIONS
LIKE TERMS

Like terms are terms in an equation that have the same variable, regardless of whether or not they also have the same coefficient. This includes terms that *lack* a variable; all constants (i.e., numbers without variables) are considered like terms. If the equation involves terms with a variable raised to different powers, the like terms are those that have the variable raised to the same power.

For example, consider the equation $x^2 + 3x + 2 = 2x^2 + x - 7 + 2x$. In this equation, 2 and –7 are like terms; they are both constants. $3x$, x, and $2x$ are like terms, they all include the variable x raised to the first power. x^2 and $2x^2$ are like terms, they both include the variable x, raised to the second power. $2x$ and $2x^2$ are not like terms; although they both involve the variable x, the variable is not raised to the same power in both terms. The fact that they have the same coefficient, 2, is not relevant.

> **Review Video: Rules for Manipulating Equations**
> Visit mometrix.com/academy and enter code: 838871

CARRYING OUT THE SAME OPERATION ON BOTH SIDES OF AN EQUATION

When solving an equation, the general procedure is to carry out a series of operations on both sides of an equation, choosing operations that will tend to simplify the equation when doing so. The reason why the same operation must be carried out on both sides of the equation is because that leaves the meaning of the equation unchanged, and yields a result that is equivalent to the original equation. This would not be the case if we carried out an operation on one side of an equation and not the other. Consider what an equation means: it is a statement that two values or expressions are equal. If we carry out the same operation on both sides of the equation—add 3 to both sides, for example—then the two sides of the equation are changed in the same way, and so remain equal. If we do that to only one side of the equation—add 3 to one side but not the other—then that wouldn't be true; if we change one side of the equation but not the other then the two sides are no longer equal.

ADVANTAGE OF COMBINING LIKE TERMS

Combining like terms refers to adding or subtracting like terms—terms with the same variable—and therefore reducing sets of like terms to a single term. The main advantage of doing this is that it simplifies the equation. Often, combining like terms can be done as the first step in solving an equation, though it can also be done later, such as after distributing terms in a product.

For example, consider the equation $2(x + 3) + 3(2 + x + 3) = -4$. The 2 and the 3 in the second set of parentheses are like terms, and we can combine them, yielding $2(x + 3) + 3(x + 5) = -4$. Now we can carry out the multiplications implied by the parentheses, distributing the outer 2 and 3 accordingly: $2x + 6 + 3x + 15 = -4$. The $2x$ and the $3x$ are like terms, and we can add them together: $5x + 6 + 15 = -4$. Now, the constants 6, 15, and –4 are also like terms, and we can combine them as well: subtracting 6 and 15 from both sides of the equation, we get $5x = -4 - 6 - 15$, or $5x = -25$, which simplifies further to $x = -5$.

Review Video: Solving Equations by Combining Like Terms
Visit mometrix.com/academy and enter code: 668506

CANCELING TERMS ON OPPOSITE SIDES OF AN EQUATION

Two terms on opposite sides of an equation can be canceled if and only if they *exactly* match each other. They must have the same variable raised to the same power and the same coefficient. For example, in the equation $3x + 2x^2 + 6 = 2x^2 - 6$, $2x^2$ appears on both sides of the equation and can be canceled, leaving $3x + 6 = -6$. The 6 on each side of the equation *cannot* be canceled, because it is added on one side of the equation and subtracted on the other. While they cannot be canceled, however, the 6 and –6 are like terms and can be combined, yielding $3x = -12$, which simplifies further to $x = -4$.

It's also important to note that the terms to be canceled must be independent terms and cannot be part of a larger term. For example, consider the equation $2(x + 6) = 3(x + 4) + 1$. We cannot cancel the x's, because even though they match each other they are part of the larger terms $2(x + 6)$ and $3(x + 4)$. We must first distribute the 2 and 3, yielding $2x + 12 = 3x + 12 + 1$. Now we see that the terms with the x's do not match, but the 12s do, and can be canceled, leaving $2x = 3x + 1$, which simplifies to $x = -1$.

PROCESS FOR MANIPULATING EQUATIONS
ISOLATING VARIABLES

To **isolate a variable** means to manipulate the equation so that the variable appears by itself on one side of the equation, and does not appear at all on the other side. Generally, an equation or inequality is considered to be solved once the variable is isolated and the other side of the equation or inequality is simplified as much as possible. In the case of a two-variable equation or inequality, only one variable needs to be isolated; it will not usually be possible to simultaneously isolate both variables.

For a linear equation—an equation in which the variable only appears raised to the first power—isolating a variable can be done by first moving all the terms with the variable to one side of the equation and all other terms to the other side. (*Moving* a term really means adding the inverse of the term to both sides; when a term is *moved* to the other side of the equation its sign is flipped.) Then combine like terms on each side. Finally, divide both sides by the coefficient of the variable, if applicable. The steps need not necessarily be done in this order, but this order will always work.

Review Video: Solving One-Step Equations
Visit mometrix.com/academy and enter code: 777004

EQUATIONS WITH MORE THAN ONE SOLUTION

Some types of non-linear equations, such as equations involving squares of variables, may have more than one solution. For example, the equation $x^2 = 4$ has two solutions: 2 and –2. Equations with absolute values can also have multiple solutions: $|x| = 1$ has the solutions $x = 1$ and $x = -1$.

It is also possible for a linear equation to have more than one solution, but only if the equation is true regardless of the value of the variable. In this case, the equation is considered to have infinitely many solutions, because any possible value of the variable is a solution. We know a linear equation has infinitely many solutions if when we combine like terms the variables cancel, leaving a true statement. For example, consider the equation $2(3x + 5) = x + 5(x + 2)$. Distributing, we get $6x + 10 = x + 5x + 10$; combining like terms gives $6x + 10 = 6x + 10$, and the $6x$-terms cancel to leave $10 = 10$. This is clearly true, so the original equation is true for any value of x. We could also have canceled the 10s leaving $0 = 0$, but again this is clearly true—in general if both sides of the equation match exactly, it has infinitely many solutions.

EQUATIONS WITH NO SOLUTION

Some types of non-linear equations, such as equations involving squares of variables, may have no solution. For example, the equation $x^2 = -2$ has no solutions in the real numbers, because the square of any real number must be positive. Similarly, $|x| = -1$ has no solution, because the absolute value of a number is always positive.

It is also possible for an equation to have no solution even if does not involve any powers greater than one, absolute values, or other special functions. For example, the equation $2(x + 3) + x = 3x$ has no solution. We can see that if we try to solve it: first we distribute, leaving $2x + 6 + x = 3x$. But now if we try to combine all the terms with the variable, we find that they cancel: we have $3x$ on the left and $3x$ on the right, canceling to leave us with $6 = 0$. This is clearly false. In general, whenever the variable terms in an equation cancel leaving different constants on both sides, it means that the equation has no solution. (If we are left with the *same* constant on both sides, the equation has infinitely many solutions instead.)

FEATURES OF EQUATIONS THAT REQUIRE SPECIAL TREATMENT

LINEAR EQUATIONS

A linear equation is an equation in which variables only appear by themselves: not multiplied together, not with exponents other than one, and not inside absolute value signs or any other functions. For example, the equation $x + 1 - 3x = 5 - x$ is a linear equation; while x appears multiple times, it never appears with an exponent other than one, or inside any function. The two-variable equation $2x - 3y = 5 + 2x$ is also a linear equation. In contrast, the equation $x^2 - 5 = 3x$ is *not* a linear equation, because it involves the term x^2. $\sqrt{x} = 5$ is not a linear equation, because it involves a square root. $(x - 1)^2 = 4$ is not a linear equation because even though there's no exponent on the x directly, it appears as part of an expression that is squared. The two-variable equation $x + xy - y = 5$ is not a linear equation because it includes the term xy, where two variables are multiplied together.

Linear equations can always be solved (or shown to have no solution) by combining like terms and performing simple operations on both sides of the equation. Some non-linear equations can be solved by similar methods, but others may require more advanced methods of solution, if they can be solved analytically at all.

SOLVING EQUATIONS INVOLVING ROOTS

In an equation involving roots, the first step is to isolate the term with the root, if possible, and then raise both sides of the equation to the appropriate power to eliminate it. Consider an example equation, $2\sqrt{x + 1} - 1 = 3$. In this case, begin by adding 1 to both sides, yielding $2\sqrt{x + 1} = 4$, and then dividing both sides by 2, yielding $\sqrt{x + 1} = 2$. Now square both sides, yielding $x + 1 = 4$. Finally, subtracting 1 from both sides yields $x = 3$.

Squaring both sides of an equation may, however, yield a spurious solution—a solution to the squared equation that is *not* a solution of the original equation. It's therefore necessary to plug the solution back into the original equation to make sure it works. In this case, it does: $2\sqrt{3+1}-1 = 2\sqrt{4}-1 = 2(2)-1 = 4-1 = 3$.

The same procedure applies for other roots as well. For example, given the equation $3 + \sqrt[3]{2x} = 5$, we can first subtract 3 from both sides, yielding $\sqrt[3]{2x} = 2$ and isolating the root. Raising both sides to the third power yields $2x = 2^3$; i.e., $2x = 8$. We can now divide both sides by 2 to get $x = 4$.

> **Review Video: Solving Equations Involving Roots**
> Visit mometrix.com/academy and enter code: 297670

SOLVING EQUATIONS WITH EXPONENTS

To solve an equation involving an exponent, the first step is to isolate the variable with the exponent. We can then take the appropriate root of both sides to eliminate the exponent. For instance, for the equation $2x^3 + 17 = 5x^3 - 7$, we can subtract $5x^3$ from both sides to get $-3x^3 + 17 = -7$, and then subtract 17 from both sides to get $-3x^3 = -24$. Finally, we can divide both sides by –3 to get $x^3 = 8$. Finally, we can take the cube root of both sides to get $x = \sqrt[3]{8} = 2$.

One important but often overlooked point is that equations with an exponent greater than 1 may have more than one answer. The solution to $x^2 = 9$ isn't simply $x = 3$; it's $x = \pm3$ (that is, $x = 3$ or $x = -3$). For a slightly more complicated example, consider the equation $(x-1)^2 - 1 = 3$. Adding 1 to both sides yields $(x-1)^2 = 4$; taking the square root of both sides yields $x - 1 = 2$. We can then add 1 to both sides to get $x = 3$. However, there's a second solution. We also have the possibility that $x - 1 = -2$, in which case $x = -1$. Both $x = 3$ and $x = -1$ are valid solutions, as can be verified by substituting them both into the original equation.

> **Review Video: Solving Equations with Exponents**
> Visit mometrix.com/academy and enter code: 514557

SOLVING EQUATIONS WITH ABSOLUTE VALUES

When solving an equation with an absolute value, the first step is to isolate the absolute value term. We then consider two possibilities: when the expression inside the absolute value is positive or when it is negative. In the former case, the expression in the absolute value equals the expression on the other side of the equation; in the latter, it equals the additive inverse of that expression—the expression times negative one. We consider each case separately and finally check for spurious solutions.

For instance, consider solving $|2x-1| + x = 5$ for x. We can first isolate the absolute value by moving the x to the other side: $|2x-1| = -x + 5$. Now, we have two possibilities. First, that $2x - 1$ is positive, and hence $2x - 1 = -x + 5$. Rearranging and combining like terms yields $3x = 6$, and hence $x = 2$. The other possibility is that $2x - 1$ is negative, and hence $2x - 1 = -(-x + 5) = x - 5$. In this case, rearranging and combining like terms yields $x = -4$. Substituting $x = 2$ and $x = -4$ back into the original equation, we see that they are both valid solutions.

Note that the absolute value of a sum or difference applies to the sum or difference as a whole, not to the individual terms; in general, $|2x-1|$ is not equal to $|2x+1|$ or to $|2x|-1$.

SPURIOUS SOLUTIONS

A **spurious solution** may arise when we square both sides of an equation as a step in solving it or under certain other operations on the equation. It is a solution to the squared or otherwise modified equation that is *not* a solution of the original equation. To identify a spurious solution, it's

useful when you solve an equation involving roots or absolute values to plug the solution back into the original equation to make sure it's valid.

CHOOSING WHICH VARIABLE TO ISOLATE IN TWO-VARIABLE EQUATIONS

Similar to methods for a one-variable equation, solving a two-variable equation involves isolating a variable: manipulating the equation so that a variable appears by itself on one side of the equation, and not at all on the other side. However, in a two-variable equation, you will usually only be able to isolate one of the variables; the other variable may appear on the other side along with constant terms, or with exponents or other functions.

Often one variable will be much more easily isolated than the other, and therefore that's the variable you should choose. If one variable appears with various exponents, and the other is only raised to the first power, the latter variable is the one to isolate: given the equation $a^2 + 2b = a^3 + b + 3$, the b only appears to the first power, whereas a appears squared and cubed, so b is the variable that can be solved for: combining like terms and isolating the b on the left side of the equation, we get $b = a^3 - a^2 + 3$. If both variables are equally easy to isolate, then it's best to isolate the dependent variable, if one is defined; if the two variables are x and y, the convention is that y is the dependent variable.

> **Review Video: Solving Equations with Variables on Both Sides**
> Visit mometrix.com/academy and enter code: 402497

INEQUALITIES
WORKING WITH INEQUALITIES

Commonly in algebra and other upper-level fields of math you find yourself working with mathematical expressions that do not equal each other. The statement comparing such expressions with symbols such as < (less than) or > (greater than) is called an *inequality*. An example of an inequality is $7x > 5$. To solve for x, simply divide both sides by 7 and the solution is shown to be $x > \frac{5}{7}$. Graphs of the solution set of inequalities are represented on a number line. Open circles are used to show that an expression approaches a number but is never quite equal to that number.

> **Review Video: Solving Multi-Step Inequalities**
> Visit mometrix.com/academy and enter code: 347842
>
> **Review Video: Solving Inequalities Using All 4 Basic Operations**
> Visit mometrix.com/academy and enter code: 401111

Conditional inequalities are those with certain values for the variable that will make the condition true and other values for the variable where the condition will be false. **Absolute inequalities** can have any real number as the value for the variable to make the condition true, while there is no real number value for the variable that will make the condition false. Solving inequalities is done by following the same rules for solving equations with the exception that when multiplying or dividing by a negative number the direction of the inequality sign must be flipped or reversed. **Double inequalities** are situations where two inequality statements apply to the same variable expression. Example: $-c < ax + b < c$.

> **Review Video: Conditional and Absolute Inequalities**
> Visit mometrix.com/academy and enter code: 980164

34

DETERMINING SOLUTIONS TO INEQUALITIES

To determine whether a coordinate is a solution of an inequality, you can substitute the values of the coordinate into the inequality, simplify, and check whether the resulting statement holds true. For instance, to determine whether $(-2,4)$ is a solution of the inequality $y \geq -2x + 3$, substitute the values into the inequality, $4 \geq -2(-2) + 3$. Simplify the right side of the inequality and the result is $4 \geq 7$, which is a false statement. Therefore, the coordinate is not a solution of the inequality. You can also use this method to determine which part of the graph of an inequality is shaded. The graph of $y \geq -2x + 3$ includes the solid line $y = -2x + 3$ and, since it excludes the point $(-2,4)$ to the left of the line, it is shaded to the right of the line.

> **Review Video: Graphing Linear Inequalities**
> Visit mometrix.com/academy and enter code: 439421

FLIPPING INEQUALITY SIGNS

When given an inequality, we can always turn the entire inequality around, swapping the two sides of the inequality and changing the inequality sign. For instance, $x + 2 > 2x - 3$ is equivalent to $2x - 3 < x + 2$. Aside from that, normally the inequality does not change if we carry out the same operation on both sides of the inequality. There is, however, one principal exception: if we *multiply* or *divide* both sides of the inequality by a *negative number*, the inequality is flipped. For example, if we take the inequality $-2x < 6$ and divide both sides by -2, the inequality flips and we are left with $x > -3$. This *only* applies to multiplication and division, and only with negative numbers. Multiplying or dividing both sides by a positive number, or adding or subtracting any number regardless of sign, does not flip the inequality. Another special case that flips the inequality sign is when reciprocals are used. For instance, $3 > 2$ but the relation of the reciprocals is $\frac{1}{2} < \frac{1}{3}$.

COMPOUND INEQUALITIES

A **compound inequality** is an equality that consists of two inequalities combined with *and* or *or*. The two components of a proper compound inequality must be of opposite type: that is, one must be greater than (or greater than or equal to), the other less than (or less than or equal to). For instance, "$x + 1 < 2$ or $x + 1 > 3$" is a compound inequality, as is "$2x \geq 4$ and $2x \leq 6$." An *and* inequality can be written more compactly by having one inequality on each side of the common part: "$2x \geq 1$ and $2x \leq 6$," can also be written as $1 \leq 2x \leq 6$.

In order for the compound inequality to be meaningful, the two parts of an *and* inequality must overlap; otherwise, no numbers satisfy the inequality. On the other hand, if the two parts of an *or* inequality overlap, then *all* numbers satisfy the inequality and as such the inequality is usually not meaningful.

Solving a compound inequality requires solving each part separately. For example, given the compound inequality "$x + 1 < 2$ or $x + 1 > 3$," the first inequality, $x + 1 < 2$, reduces to $x < 1$, and the second part, $x + 1 > 3$, reduces to $x > 2$, so the whole compound inequality can be written as "$x < 1$ or $x > 2$." Similarly, $1 \leq 2x \leq 6$ can be solved by dividing each term by 2, yielding $\frac{1}{2} \leq x \leq 3$.

> **Review Video: Compound Inequalities**
> Visit mometrix.com/academy and enter code: 786318

SOLVING INEQUALITIES INVOLVING ABSOLUTE VALUES

To solve an inequality involving an absolute value, first isolate the term with the absolute value. Then proceed to treat the two cases separately as with an absolute value equation, but flipping the inequality in the case where the expression in the absolute value is negative (since that essentially involves multiplying both sides by –1.) The two cases are then combined into a compound inequality; if the absolute value is on the greater side of the inequality, then it is an *or* compound inequality, if on the lesser side, then it's an *and*.

Consider the inequality $2 + |x - 1| \geq 3$. We can isolate the absolute value term by subtracting 2 from both sides: $|x - 1| \geq 1$. Now, we're left with the two cases $x - 1 \geq 1$ or $x - 1 \leq -1$: note that in the latter, negative case, the inequality is flipped. $x - 1 \geq 1$ reduces to $x \geq 2$, and $x - 1 \leq -1$ reduces to $x \leq 0$. Since in the inequality $|x - 1| \geq 1$ the absolute value is on the greater side, the two cases combine into an *or* compound inequality, so the final, solved inequality is "$x \leq 0$ or $x \geq 2$."

> **Review Video: <u>Solving Absolute Value Inequalities</u>**
> Visit mometrix.com/academy and enter code: 997008

SOLVING INEQUALITIES INVOLVING SQUARE ROOTS

Solving an inequality with a square root involves two parts. First, we solve the inequality as if it were an equation, isolating the square root and then squaring both sides of the equation. Second, we restrict the solution to the set of values of x for which the value inside the square root sign is non-negative.

For example, in the inequality, $\sqrt{x - 2} + 1 < 5$, we can isolate the square root by subtracting 1 from both sides, yielding $\sqrt{x - 2} < 4$. Squaring both sides of the inequality yields $x - 2 < 16$, so $x < 18$. Since we can't take the square root of a negative number, we also require the part inside the square root to be non-negative. In this case, that means $x - 2 \geq 0$. Adding 2 to both sides of the inequality yields $x \geq 2$. Our final answer is a compound inequality combining the two simple inequalities: $x \geq 2$ and $x < 18$, or $2 \leq x < 18$.

Note that we only get a compound inequality if the two simple inequalities are in opposite directions; otherwise, we take the one that is more restrictive.

The same technique can be used for other even roots, such as fourth roots. It is *not*, however, used for cube roots or other odd roots—negative numbers *do* have cube roots, so the condition that the quantity inside the root sign cannot be negative does not apply.

> **Review Video: <u>Solving Inequalities Involving Square Roots</u>**
> Visit mometrix.com/academy and enter code: 800288

SPECIAL CIRCUMSTANCES

Sometimes an inequality involving an absolute value or an even exponent is true for all values of x, and we don't need to do any further work to solve it. This is true if the inequality, once the absolute value or exponent term is isolated, says that term is greater than a negative number (or greater than or equal to zero). Since an absolute value or a number raised to an even exponent is *always* non-negative, this inequality is always true.

GRAPHICAL SOLUTIONS TO INEQUALITIES
GRAPHING SIMPLE INEQUALITIES

To graph a simple inequality, we first mark on the number line the value that signifies the end point of the inequality. If the inequality is strict (involves a less than or greater than), we use a hollow circle; if it is not strict (less than or equal to or greater than or equal to), we use a solid circle. We then fill in the part of the number line that satisfies the inequality: to the left of the marked point for less than (or less than or equal to), to the right for greater than (or greater than or equal to).

For example, we would graph the inequality $x < 5$ by putting a hollow circle at 5 and filling in the part of the line to the left:

GRAPHING COMPOUND INEQUALITIES

To graph a compound inequality, we fill in both parts of the inequality for an *or* inequality, or the overlap between them for an *and* inequality. More specifically, we start by plotting the endpoints of each inequality on the number line. For an *or* inequality, we then fill in the appropriate side of the line for each inequality. Typically, the two component inequalities do not overlap, which means the shaded part is *outside* the two points. For an *and* inequality, we instead fill in the part of the line that meets both inequalities.

For the inequality "$x \leq -3$ or $x > 4$," we first put a solid circle at –3 and a hollow circle at 4. We then fill the parts of the line *outside* these circles:

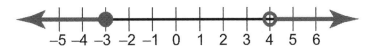

GRAPHING INEQUALITIES INCLUDING ABSOLUTE VALUES

An inequality with an absolute value can be converted to a compound inequality. To graph the inequality, first convert it to a compound inequality, and then graph that normally. If the absolute value is on the greater side of the inequality, we end up with an *or* inequality; we plot the endpoints of the inequality on the number line and fill in the part of the line *outside* those points. If the absolute value is on the smaller side of the inequality, we end up with an *and* inequality; we plot the endpoints of the inequality on the number line and fill in the part of the line *between* those points.

For example, the inequality $|x + 1| \geq 4$ can be rewritten as $x \geq 3$ or $x \leq -5$. We place solid circles at the points 3 and –5 and fill in the part of the line *outside* them:

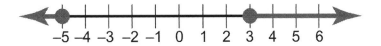

GRAPHING INEQUALITIES IN TWO VARIABLES

To graph an inequality in two variables, we first graph the border of the inequality. This means graphing the equation that we get if we replace the inequality sign with an equals sign. If the inequality is strict ($>$ or $<$), we graph the border with a dashed or dotted line; if it is not strict ($\geq$ or $\leq$), we use a solid line. We can then test any point not on the border to see if it satisfies the inequality. If it does, we shade in that side of the border; if not, we shade in the other side. As an example, consider $y > 2x + 2$. To graph this inequality, we first graph the border, $y = 2x + 2$. Since it is a strict inequality, we use a dashed line. Then, we choose a test point. This can be any point not on the border; in this case, we will choose the origin, (0,0). (This makes the calculation easy and is generally a good choice unless the border passes through the origin.) Putting this into the original inequality, we get $0 > 2(0) + 2$, i.e., $0 > 2$. This is *not* true, so we shade in the side of the border that does *not* include the point (0,0):

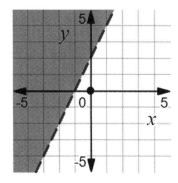

GRAPHING COMPOUND INEQUALITIES IN TWO VARIABLES

One way to graph a compound inequality in two variables is to first graph each of the component inequalities. For an *and* inequality, we then shade in only the parts where the two graphs overlap; for an *or* inequality, we shade in any region that pertains to either of the individual inequalities.

Consider the graph of "$y \geq x - 1$ and $y \leq -x$":

We first shade in the individual inequalities:

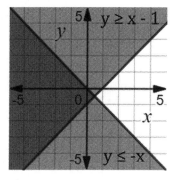

Now, since the compound inequality has an *and*, we only leave shaded the overlap—the part that pertains to *both* inequalities:

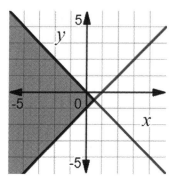

38

If instead the inequality had been "$y \geq x - 1$ or $y \leq -x$," our final graph would involve the *total* shaded area:

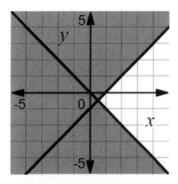

SYSTEMS OF EQUATIONS
SOLVING SYSTEMS OF EQUATIONS

A **system of equations** is a set of simultaneous equations that all use the same variables. A solution to a system of equations must be true for each equation in the system. **Consistent systems** are those with at least one solution. **Inconsistent systems** are systems of equations that have no solution.

SUBSTITUTION

To solve a system of linear equations by **substitution**, start with the easier equation and solve for one of the variables. Express this variable in terms of the other variable. Substitute this expression in the other equation and solve for the other variable. The solution should be expressed in the form (x, y). Substitute the values into both of the original equations to check your answer. Consider the following system of equations:

$$x + 6y = 15$$
$$3x - 12y = 18$$

Solving the first equation for x: $x = 15 - 6y$

Substitute this value in place of x in the second equation, and solve for y:

$$3(15 - 6y) - 12y = 18$$
$$45 - 18y - 12y = 18$$
$$30y = 27$$
$$y = \frac{27}{30} = \frac{9}{10} = 0.9$$

Plug this value for y back into the first equation to solve for x:

$$x = 15 - 6(0.9) = 15 - 5.4 = 9.6$$

Check both equations if you have time:

$$9.6 + 6(0.9) = 15 \qquad\qquad 3(9.6) - 12(0.9) = 18$$
$$9.6 + 5.4 = 15 \qquad\qquad 28.8 - 10.8 = 18$$
$$15 = 15 \qquad\qquad 18 = 18$$

Therefore, the solution is (9.6,0.9).

Review Video: <u>The Substitution Method</u>
Visit mometrix.com/academy and enter code: 565151
Review Video: <u>Substitution and Elimination</u>
Visit mometrix.com/academy and enter code: 958611

ELIMINATION

To solve a system of equations using **elimination**, begin by rewriting both equations in standard form $Ax + By = C$. Check to see if the coefficients of one pair of like variables add to zero. If not, multiply one or both of the equations by a non-zero number to make one set of like variables add to zero. Add the two equations to solve for one of the variables. Substitute this value into one of the original equations to solve for the other variable. Check your work by substituting into the other equation. Now, let's look at solving the following system using the elimination method:

$$5x + 6y = 4$$
$$x + 2y = 4$$

If we multiply the second equation by -3, we can eliminate the y-terms:

$$5x + 6y = 4$$
$$-3x - 6y = -12$$

Add the equations together and solve for x:

$$2x = -8$$
$$x = \frac{-8}{2} = -4$$

Plug the value for x back in to either of the original equations and solve for y:

$$-4 + 2y = 4$$
$$y = \frac{4 + 4}{2} = 4$$

Check both equations if you have time:

$$5(-4) + 6(4) = 4 \qquad\qquad -4 + 2(4) = 4$$
$$-20 + 24 = 4 \qquad\qquad -4 + 8 = 4$$
$$4 = 4 \qquad\qquad 4 = 4$$

Therefore, the solution is $(-4,4)$.

Review Video: The Elimination Method
Visit mometrix.com/academy and enter code: 449121

GRAPHICALLY

To solve a system of linear equations **graphically**, plot both equations on the same graph. The solution of the equations is the point where both lines cross. If the lines do not cross (are parallel), then there is **no solution**.

For example, consider the following system of equations:

$$y = 2x + 7$$
$$y = -x + 1$$

Since these equations are given in slope-intercept form, they are easy to graph; the y-intercepts of the lines are $(0,7)$ and $(0,1)$. The respective slopes are 2 and –1, thus the graphs look like this:

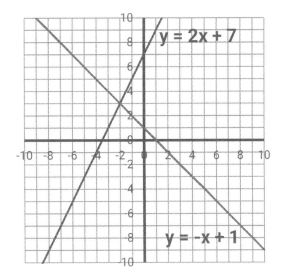

The two lines intersect at the point $(-2,3)$, thus this is the solution to the system of equations.

Solving a system graphically is generally only practical if both coordinates of the solution are integers; otherwise the intersection will lie between gridlines on the graph and the coordinates will be difficult or impossible to determine exactly. It also helps if, as in this example, the equations are in slope-intercept form or some other form that makes them easy to graph. Otherwise, another method of solution (by substitution or elimination) is likely to be more useful.

Review Video: Solving Systems by Graphing
Visit mometrix.com/academy and enter code: 634812

SOLVING SYSTEMS OF EQUATIONS USING THE TRACE FEATURE

Using the trace feature on a calculator requires that you rewrite each equation, isolating the y-variable on one side of the equal sign. Enter both equations in the graphing calculator and plot the graphs simultaneously. Use the trace cursor to find where the two lines cross. Use the zoom feature if necessary to obtain more accurate results. Always check your answer by substituting into the original equations. The trace method is likely to be less accurate than other methods due to the resolution of graphing calculators but is a useful tool to provide an approximate answer.

ADVANCED SYSTEMS OF EQUATIONS

SOLVING A SYSTEM OF EQUATIONS CONSISTING OF A LINEAR EQUATION AND A QUADRATIC EQUATION

ALGEBRAICALLY

Generally, the simplest way to solve a system of equations consisting of a linear equation and a quadratic equation algebraically is through the method of substitution. One possible strategy is to solve the linear equation for y and then substitute that expression into the quadratic equation. After expansion and combining like terms, this will result in a new quadratic equation for x, which, like all quadratic equations, may have zero, one, or two solutions. Plugging each solution for x back into one of the original equations will then produce the corresponding value of y.

For example, consider the following system of equations:

$$x + y = 1$$
$$y = (x + 3)^2 - 2$$

We can solve the linear equation for y to yield $y = -x + 1$. Substituting this expression into the quadratic equation produces $-x + 1 = (x + 3)^2 - 2$. We can simplify this equation:

$$-x + 1 = (x + 3)^2 - 2$$
$$-x + 1 = x^2 + 6x + 9 - 2$$
$$-x + 1 = x^2 + 6x + 7$$
$$0 = x^2 + 7x + 6$$

This quadratic equation can be factored as $(x + 1)(x + 6) = 0$. It therefore has two solutions: $x_1 = -1$ and $x_2 = -6$. Plugging each of these back into the original linear equation yields $y_1 = -x_1 + 1 = -(-1) + 1 = 2$ and $y_2 = -x_2 + 1 = -(-6) + 1 = 7$. Thus, this system of equations has two solutions, $(-1, 2)$ and $(-6, 7)$.

It may help to check your work by putting each x- and y-value back into the original equations and verifying that they do provide a solution.

GRAPHICALLY

To solve a system of equations consisting of a linear equation and a quadratic equation graphically, plot both equations on the same graph. The linear equation will, of course, produce a straight line, while the quadratic equation will produce a parabola. These two graphs will intersect at zero, one, or two points; each point of intersection is a solution of the system.

For example, consider the following system of equations:

$$y = -2x + 2$$
$$y = -2x^2 + 4x + 2$$

The linear equation describes a line with a y-intercept of $(0,2)$ and a slope of -2.

To graph the quadratic equation, we can first find the vertex of the parabola: the x-coordinate of the vertex is $h = -\dfrac{b}{2a} = -\dfrac{4}{2(-2)} = 1$, and the y-coordinate is $k = -2(1)^2 + 4(1) + 2 = 4$. Thus, the vertex lies at $(1,4)$. To get a feel for the rest of the parabola, we can plug in a few more values of x to

find more points; by putting in $x = 2$ and $x = 3$ in the quadratic equation, we find that the points $(2,2)$ and $(3,-4)$ lie on the parabola; by symmetry, so must $(0,2)$ and $(-1,-4)$. We can now plot both equations:

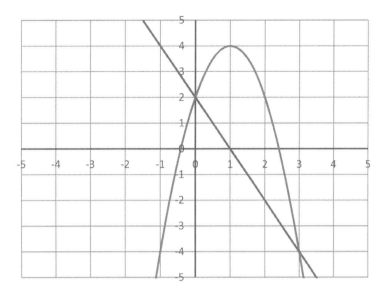

These two curves intersect at the points $(0,2)$ and $(3,-4)$, thus these are the solutions of the equation.

> **Review Video: <u>Solving a System of Linear and Quadratic Equations</u>**
> Visit mometrix.com/academy and enter code: 194870

QUADRATICS
SOLVING QUADRATIC EQUATIONS

Quadratic equations are a special set of trinomials of the form $y = ax^2 + bx + c$ that occur commonly in math and real-world applications. The **roots** of a quadratic equation are the solutions that satisfy the equation when $y = 0$; in other words, where the graph touches the x-axis. There are several ways to determine these solutions including using the quadratic formula, factoring, completing the square, and graphing the function.

> **Review Video: <u>Quadratic Equations Overview</u>**
> Visit mometrix.com/academy and enter code: 476276
>
> **Review Video: <u>Solutions of a Quadratic Equation on a Graph</u>**
> Visit mometrix.com/academy and enter code: 328231

QUADRATIC FORMULA

The **quadratic formula** is used to solve quadratic equations when other methods are more difficult. To use the quadratic formula to solve a quadratic equation, begin by rewriting the equation in standard form $ax^2 + bx + c = 0$, where a, b, and c are coefficients. Once you have identified the values of the coefficients, substitute those values into the quadratic formula

$$x = \frac{-b \pm \sqrt{b^2 - 4ac}}{2a}$$

43

Evaluate the equation and simplify the expression. Again, check each root by substituting into the original equation. In the quadratic formula, the portion of the formula under the radical ($b^2 - 4ac$) is called the **discriminant**. If the discriminant is zero, there is only one root: $-\frac{b}{2a}$. If the discriminant is positive, there are two different real roots. If the discriminant is negative, there are no real roots; you will instead find complex roots. Often these solutions don't make sense in context and are ignored.

> **Review Video: Using the Quadratic Formula**
> Visit mometrix.com/academy and enter code: 163102

FACTORING

To solve a quadratic equation by factoring, begin by rewriting the equation in standard form, $x^2 + bx + c = 0$. Remember that the goal of factoring is to find numbers f and g such that $(x + f)(x + g) = x^2 + (f + g)x + fg$, in other words $(f + g) = b$ and $fg = c$. This can be a really useful method when b and c are integers. Determine the factors of c and look for pairs that could sum to b.

For example, consider finding the roots of $x^2 + 6x - 16 = 0$. The factors of -16 include, -4 and 4, -8 and 2, -2 and 8, -1 and 16, and 1 and -16. The factors that sum to 6 are -2 and 8. Write these factors as the product of two binomials, $0 = (x - 2)(x + 8)$. Finally, since these binomials multiply together to equal zero, set them each equal to zero and solve each for x. This results in $x - 2 = 0$, which simplifies to $x = 2$ and $x + 8 = 0$, which simplifies to $x = -8$. Therefore, the roots of the equation are 2 and -8.

> **Review Video: Factoring Quadratic Equations**
> Visit mometrix.com/academy and enter code: 336566

COMPLETING THE SQUARE

One way to find the roots of a quadratic equation is to find a way to manipulate it such that it follows the form of a perfect square ($x^2 + 2px + p^2$) by adding and subtracting a constant. This process is called **completing the square**. In other words, if you are given a quadratic that is not a perfect square, $x^2 + bx + c = 0$, you can find a constant d that could be added in to make it a perfect square:

$$x^2 + bx + c + (d - d) = 0; \{\text{Let } b = 2p \text{ and } c + d = p^2\}$$

then:

$$x^2 + 2px + p^2 - d = 0 \text{ and } d = \frac{b^2}{4} - c$$

Once you have completed the square you can find the roots of the resulting equation:

$$x^2 + 2px + p^2 - d = 0$$
$$(x + p)^2 = d$$
$$x + p = \pm\sqrt{d}$$
$$x = -p \pm \sqrt{d}$$

It is worth noting that substituting the original expressions into this solution gives the same result as the quadratic formula where $a = 1$:

$$x = -p \pm \sqrt{d} = -\frac{b}{2} \pm \sqrt{\frac{b^2}{4} - c} = -\frac{b}{2} \pm \frac{\sqrt{b^2 - 4c}}{2} = \frac{-b \pm \sqrt{b^2 - 4c}}{2}$$

Completing the square can be seen as arranging block representations of each of the terms to be as close to a square as possible and then filling in the gaps. For example, consider the quadratic expression $x^2 + 6x + 2$:

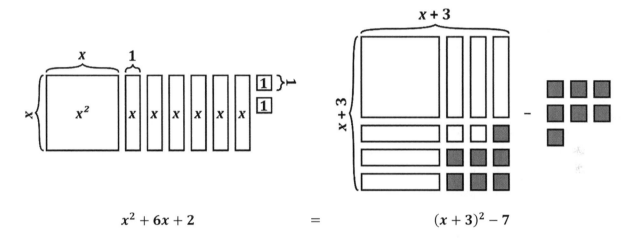

$$x^2 + 6x + 2 \qquad = \qquad (x + 3)^2 - 7$$

> **Review Video: Completing the Square**
> Visit mometrix.com/academy and enter code: 982479

USING GIVEN ROOTS TO FIND QUADRATIC EQUATION

One way to find the roots of a quadratic equation is to factor the equation and use the **zero product property**, setting each factor of the equation equal to zero to find the corresponding root. We can use this technique in reverse to find an equation given its roots. Each root corresponds to a linear equation which in turn corresponds to a factor of the quadratic equation.

For example, we can find a quadratic equation whose roots are $x = 2$ and $x = -1$. The root $x = 2$ corresponds to the equation $x - 2 = 0$, and the root $x = -1$ corresponds to the equation $x + 1 = 0$.

These two equations correspond to the factors $(x - 2)$ and $(x + 1)$, from which we can derive the equation $(x - 2)(x + 1) = 0$, or $x^2 - x - 2 = 0$.

Any integer multiple of this entire equation will also yield the same roots, as the integer will simply cancel out when the equation is factored. For example, $2x^2 - 2x - 4 = 0$ factors as $2(x - 2)(x + 1) = 0$.

Expressions

LINEAR EXPRESSIONS

TERMS AND COEFFICIENTS

Mathematical expressions consist of a combination of one or more values arranged in terms that are added together. As such, an expression could be just a single number, including zero. A **variable**

term is the product of a real number, also called a **coefficient**, and one or more variables, each of which may be raised to an exponent. Expressions may also include numbers without a variable, called **constants** or **constant terms**. The expression $6s^2$, for example, is a single term where the coefficient is the real number 6 and the variable term is s^2. Note that if a term is written as simply a variable to some exponent, like t^2, then the coefficient is 1, because $t^2 = 1t^2$.

LINEAR EXPRESSIONS

A **single variable linear expression** is the sum of a single variable term, where the variable has no exponent, and a constant, which may be zero. For instance, the expression $2w + 7$ has $2w$ as the variable term and 7 as the constant term. It is important to realize that terms are separated by addition or subtraction. Since an expression is a sum of terms, expressions such as $5x - 3$ can be written as $5x + (-3)$ to emphasize that the constant term is negative. A real-world example of a single variable linear expression is the perimeter of a square, four times the side length, often expressed: $4s$.

In general, a **linear expression** is the sum of any number of variable terms so long as none of the variables have an exponent. For example, $3m + 8n - \frac{1}{4}p + 5.5q - 1$ is a linear expression, but $3y^3$ is not. In the same way, the expression for the perimeter of a general triangle, the sum of the side lengths $(a + b + c)$ is considered to be linear, but the expression for the area of a square, the side length squared (s^2) is not.

RATIONAL EXPRESSIONS

Rational expressions are fractions with polynomials in both the numerator and the denominator; the value of the polynomial in the denominator cannot be equal to zero. Be sure to keep track of values that make the denominator of the original expression zero as the final result inherits the same restrictions. For example, a denominator of $x - 3$ indicates that the expression is not defined when $x = 3$ and, as such, regardless of any operations done to the expression, it remains undefined there.

To **add or subtract** rational expressions, first find the common denominator, then rewrite each fraction as an equivalent fraction with the common denominator. Finally, add or subtract the numerators to get the numerator of the answer, and keep the common denominator as the denominator of the answer.

When **multiplying** rational expressions, factor each polynomial and cancel like factors (a factor which appears in both the numerator and the denominator). Then, multiply all remaining factors in the numerator to get the numerator of the product, and multiply the remaining factors in the denominator to get the denominator of the product. Remember: cancel entire factors, not individual terms.

To **divide** rational expressions, take the reciprocal of the divisor (the rational expression you are dividing by) and multiply by the dividend.

> **Review Video: Rational Expressions**
> Visit mometrix.com/academy and enter code: 415183

SIMPLIFYING RATIONAL EXPRESSIONS

To simplify a rational expression, factor the numerator and denominator completely. Factors that are the same and appear in the numerator and denominator have a ratio of 1. For example, look at the following expression:

$$\frac{x-1}{1-x^2}$$

The denominator, $(1-x^2)$, is a difference of squares. It can be factored as $(1-x)(1+x)$. The factor $1-x$ and the numerator $x-1$ are opposites and have a ratio of –1. Rewrite the numerator as $-1(1-x)$. So, the rational expression can be simplified as follows:

$$\frac{x-1}{1-x^2} = \frac{-1(1-x)}{(1-x)(1+x)} = \frac{-1}{1+x}$$

Note that since the original expression is only defined for $x \neq \{-1, 1\}$, the simplified expression has the same restrictions.

> **Review Video: Reducing Rational Expressions**
> Visit mometrix.com/academy and enter code: 788868

Polynomials

POLYNOMIALS

MONOMIALS AND POLYNOMIALS

A **monomial** is a single constant, variable, or product of constants and variables, such as 7, x, $2x$, or x^3y. There will never be addition or subtraction symbols in a monomial. Like monomials have like variables, but they may have different coefficients. **Polynomials** are algebraic expressions that use addition and subtraction to combine two or more monomials. Two terms make a **binomial**, three terms make a **trinomial**, etc. The **degree of a monomial** is the sum of the exponents of the variables. The **degree of a polynomial** is the highest degree of any individual term.

> **Review Video: Polynomials**
> Visit mometrix.com/academy and enter code: 305005

SIMPLIFYING POLYNOMIALS

Simplifying polynomials requires combining like terms. The like terms in a polynomial expression are those that have the same variable raised to the same power. It is often helpful to connect the like terms with arrows or lines in order to separate them from the other monomials. Once you have determined the like terms, you can rearrange the polynomial by placing them together. Remember to include the sign that is in front of each term. Once the like terms are placed together, you can apply each operation and simplify. When adding and subtracting polynomials, only add and subtract the **coefficient**, or the number part; the variable and exponent stay the same.

ADD POLYNOMIALS

To add polynomials, you need to add like terms. These terms have the same variable part. An example is $4x^2$ and $3x^2$ have x^2 terms. To find the sum of like terms, find the sum of the coefficients.

47

Then, keep the same variable part. You can use the distributive property to distribute the plus sign to each term of the polynomial. For example:

$(4x^2 - 5x + 7) + (3x^2 + 2x + 1) =$
$(4x^2 - 5x + 7) + 3x^2 + 2x + 1 =$
$(4x^2 + 3x^2) + (-5x + 2x) + (7 + 1) =$
$7x^2 - 3x + 8$

SUBTRACT POLYNOMIALS

To subtract polynomials, you need to subtract like terms. To find the difference of like terms, find the difference of the coefficients. Then, keep the same variable part. You can use the distributive property to distribute the minus sign to each term of the polynomial. For example:

$(-2x^2 - x + 5) - (3x^2 - 4x + 1) =$
$(-2x^2 - x + 5) - 3x^2 + 4x - 1 =$
$(-2x^2 - 3x^2) + (-x + 4x) + (5 - 1) =$
$-5x^2 + 3x + 4$

> **Review Video: Adding and Subtracting Polynomials**
> Visit mometrix.com/academy and enter code: 124088

MULTIPLYING POLYNOMIALS

In general, multiplying polynomials is done by multiplying each term in one polynomial by each term in the other and adding the results. In the specific case for multiplying binomials, there is a useful acronym, FOIL, that can help you make sure to cover each combination of terms. The **FOIL method** for $(Ax + By)(Cx + Dy)$ would be:

F	Multiply the *first* terms of each binomial	$(\overset{first}{\overbrace{Ax}} + By)(\overset{first}{\overbrace{Cx}} + Dy)$	ACx^2
O	Multiply the *outer* terms	$(\overset{outer}{\overbrace{Ax}} + By)(Cx + \overset{outer}{\overbrace{Dy}})$	$ADxy$
I	Multiply the *inner* terms	$(Ax + \overset{inner}{\overbrace{By}})(\overset{inner}{\overbrace{Cx}} + Dy)$	$BCxy$
L	Multiply the *last* terms of each binomial	$(Ax + \overset{last}{\overbrace{By}})(Cx + \overset{last}{\overbrace{Dy}})$	BDy^2

Then, add up the result of each and combine like terms: $ACx^2 + (AD + BC)xy + BDy^2$.

For example, using the FOIL method on binomials $(x + 2)$ and $(x - 3)$:

First: $(\boxed{x} + 2)(\boxed{x} + (-3)) \rightarrow (x)(x) = x^2$
Outer: $(\boxed{x} + 2)(x + \boxed{(-3)}) \rightarrow (x)(-3) = -3x$
Inner: $(x + \boxed{2})(\boxed{x} + (-3)) \rightarrow (2)(x) = 2x$
Last: $(x + \boxed{2})(x + \boxed{(-3)}) \rightarrow (2)(-3) = -6$

This results in: $(x^2) + (-3x) + (2x) + (-6)$

Combine like terms: $x^2 + (-3 + 2)x + (-6) = x^2 - x - 6$

> **Review Video: Multiplying Terms Using the FOIL Method**
> Visit mometrix.com/academy and enter code: 854792

DIVIDING POLYNOMIALS

Use long division to divide a polynomial by either a monomial or another polynomial of equal or lesser degree.

When **dividing by a monomial**, divide each term of the polynomial by the monomial.

When **dividing by a polynomial**, begin by arranging the terms of each polynomial in order of one variable. You may arrange in ascending or descending order, but be consistent with both polynomials. To get the first term of the quotient, divide the first term of the dividend by the first term of the divisor. Multiply the first term of the quotient by the entire divisor and subtract that product from the dividend. Repeat for the second and successive terms until you either get a remainder of zero or a remainder whose degree is less than the degree of the divisor. If the quotient has a remainder, write the answer as a mixed expression in the form:

$$\text{quotient} + \frac{\text{remainder}}{\text{divisor}}$$

For example, we can evaluate the following expression in the same way as long division:

$$\frac{x^3 - 3x^2 - 2x + 5}{x - 5}$$

$$
\begin{array}{r}
x^2 + 2x + 8 \\
x - 5 \overline{\smash{)}\ x^3 - 3x^2 - 2x + 5} \\
\underline{-(x^3 - 5x^2)} \\
2x^2 - 2x \\
\underline{-(2x^2 - 10x)} \\
8x + 5 \\
\underline{-(8x - 40)} \\
45
\end{array}
$$

$$\frac{x^3 - 3x^2 - 2x + 5}{x - 5} = x^2 + 2x + 8 + \frac{45}{x - 5}$$

When **factoring** a polynomial, first check for a common monomial factor, that is, look to see if each coefficient has a common factor or if each term has an x in it. If the factor is a trinomial but not a perfect trinomial square, look for a factorable form, such as one of these:

$$x^2 + (a + b)x + ab = (x + a)(x + b)$$
$$(ac)x^2 + (ad + bc)x + bd = (ax + b)(cx + d)$$

For factors with four terms, look for groups to factor. Once you have found the factors, write the original polynomial as the product of all the factors. Make sure all of the polynomial factors are prime. Monomial factors may be *prime* or *composite*. Check your work by multiplying the factors to make sure you get the original polynomial.

Below are patterns of some special products to remember to help make factoring easier:

- Perfect trinomial squares: $x^2 + 2xy + y^2 = (x + y)^2$ or $x^2 - 2xy + y^2 = (x - y)^2$
- Difference between two squares: $x^2 - y^2 = (x + y)(x - y)$
- Sum of two cubes: $x^3 + y^3 = (x + y)(x^2 - xy + y^2)$

49

- o Note: the second factor is *not* the same as a perfect trinomial square, so do not try to factor it further.
- Difference between two cubes: $x^3 - y^3 = (x - y)(x^2 + xy + y^2)$
  - o Again, the second factor is *not* the same as a perfect trinomial square.
- Perfect cubes: $x^3 + 3x^2y + 3xy^2 + y^3 = (x + y)^3$ and $x^3 - 3x^2y + 3xy^2 - y^3 = (x - y)^3$

Coordinate Plane

GRAPHING EQUATIONS
GRAPHICAL SOLUTIONS TO EQUATIONS

When equations are shown graphically, they are usually shown on a **Cartesian coordinate plane**. The Cartesian coordinate plane consists of two number lines placed perpendicular to each other and intersecting at the zero point, also known as the origin. The horizontal number line is known as the x-axis, with positive values to the right of the origin, and negative values to the left of the origin. The vertical number line is known as the y-axis, with positive values above the origin, and negative values below the origin. Any point on the plane can be identified by an ordered pair in the form (x, y), called coordinates. The x-value of the coordinate is called the abscissa, and the y-value of the coordinate is called the ordinate. The two number lines divide the plane into **four quadrants**: I, II, III, and IV.

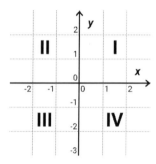

Note that in quadrant I $x > 0$ and $y > 0$, in quadrant II $x < 0$ and $y > 0$, in quadrant III $x < 0$ and $y < 0$, and in quadrant IV $x > 0$ and $y < 0$.

Recall that if the value of the slope of a line is positive, the line slopes upward from left to right. If the value of the slope is negative, the line slopes downward from left to right. If the y-coordinates are the same for two points on a line, the slope is 0 and the line is a **horizontal line**. If the x-coordinates are the same for two points on a line, there is no slope and the line is a **vertical line**. Two or more lines that have equivalent slopes are **parallel lines**. **Perpendicular lines** have slopes that are negative reciprocals of each other, such as $\frac{a}{b}$ and $\frac{-b}{a}$.

> **Review Video: Cartesian Coordinate Plane and Graphing**
> Visit mometrix.com/academy and enter code: 115173

GRAPHING EQUATIONS IN TWO VARIABLES

One way of graphing an equation in two variables is to plot enough points to get an idea for its shape and then draw the appropriate curve through those points. A point can be plotted by substituting in a value for one variable and solving for the other. If the equation is linear, we only need two points and can then draw a straight line between them.

For example, consider the equation $y = 2x - 1$. This is a linear equation—both variables only appear raised to the first power—so we only need two points. When $x = 0$, $y = 2(0) - 1 = -1$. When $x = 2$, $y = 2(2) - 1 = 3$. We can therefore choose the points $(0, -1)$ and $(2, 3)$, and draw a line between them:

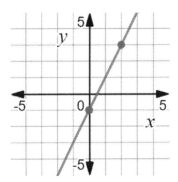

CALCULATIONS USING POINTS

Sometimes you need to perform calculations using only points on a graph as input data. Using points, you can determine what the **midpoint** and **distance** are. If you know the equation for a line, you can calculate the distance between the line and the point.

To find the **midpoint** of two points (x_1, y_1) and (x_2, y_2), average the x-coordinates to get the x-coordinate of the midpoint, and average the y-coordinates to get the y-coordinate of the midpoint. The formula is: $\left(\frac{x_1+x_2}{2}, \frac{y_1+y_2}{2}\right)$.

The **distance** between two points is the same as the length of the hypotenuse of a right triangle with the two given points as endpoints, and the two sides of the right triangle parallel to the x-axis and y-axis, respectively. The length of the segment parallel to the x-axis is the difference between the x-coordinates of the two points. The length of the segment parallel to the y-axis is the difference between the y-coordinates of the two points. Use the Pythagorean theorem $a^2 + b^2 = c^2$ or $c = \sqrt{a^2 + b^2}$ to find the distance. The formula is $d = \sqrt{(x_2 - x_1)^2 + (y_2 - y_1)^2}$.

When a line is in the format $Ax + By + C = 0$, where A, B, and C are coefficients, you can use a point (x_1, y_1) not on the line and apply the formula $d = \frac{|Ax_1 + By_1 + C|}{\sqrt{A^2 + B^2}}$ to find the distance between the line and the point (x_1, y_1).

> **Review Video: Calculations Using Points on a Graph**
> Visit mometrix.com/academy and enter code: 883228

BASIC FUNCTIONS

FUNCTION AND RELATION

When expressing functional relationships, the **variables** x and y are typically used. These values are often written as the **coordinates** (x, y). The x-value is the independent variable and the y-value is the dependent variable. A **relation** is a set of data in which there is not a unique y-value for each x-value in the dataset. This means that there can be two of the same x-values assigned to different y-values. A relation is simply a relationship between the x- and y-values in each coordinate but does not apply to the relationship between the values of x and y in the data set. A **function** is a

51

relation where one quantity depends on the other. For example, the amount of money that you make depends on the number of hours that you work. In a function, each x-value in the data set has one unique y-value because the y-value depends on the x-value.

FUNCTIONS

A function has exactly one value of **output variable** (dependent variable) for each value of the **input variable** (independent variable). The set of all values for the input variable (here assumed to be x) is the domain of the function, and the set of all corresponding values of the output variable (here assumed to be y) is the range of the function. When looking at a graph of an equation, the easiest way to determine if the equation is a function or not is to conduct the vertical line test. If a vertical line drawn through any value of x crosses the graph in more than one place, the equation is not a function.

DETERMINING A FUNCTION

You can determine whether an equation is a **function** by substituting different values into the equation for x. You can display and organize these numbers in a data table. A **data table** contains the values for x and y, which you can also list as coordinates. In order for a function to exist, the table cannot contain any repeating x-values that correspond with different y-values. If each x-coordinate has a unique y-coordinate, the table contains a function. However, there can be repeating y-values that correspond with different x-values. An example of this is when the function contains an exponent. Example: if $x^2 = y$, $2^2 = 4$, and $(-2)^2 = 4$.

> **Review Video: Definition of a Function**
> Visit mometrix.com/academy and enter code: 784611

FINDING THE DOMAIN AND RANGE OF A FUNCTION

The **domain** of a function $f(x)$ is the set of all input values for which the function is defined. The **range** of a function $f(x)$ is the set of all possible output values of the function—that is, of every possible value of $f(x)$, for any value of x in the function's domain. For a function expressed in a table, every input-output pair is given explicitly. To find the domain, we just list all the x-values and to find the range, we just list all the values of $f(x)$. Consider the following example:

x	−1	4	2	1	0	3	8	6
$f(x)$	3	0	3	−1	−1	2	4	6

In this case, the domain would be $\{-1, 4, 2, 1, 0, 3, 8, 6\}$ or, putting them in ascending order, $\{-1, 0, 1, 2, 3, 4, 6, 8\}$. (Putting the values in ascending order isn't strictly necessary, but generally makes the set easier to read.) The range would be $\{3, 0, 3, -1, -1, 2, 4, 6\}$. Note that some of these values appear more than once. This is entirely permissible for a function; while each value of x must be matched to a unique value of $f(x)$, the converse is not true. We don't need to list each value more than once, so eliminating duplicates, the range is $\{3, 0, -1, 2, 4, 6\}$, or, putting them in ascending order, $\{-1, 0, 2, 3, 4, 6\}$.

Note that by definition of a function, no input value can be matched to more than one output value. It is good to double-check to make sure that the data given follows this and is therefore actually a function.

> **Review Video: Domain and Range**
> Visit mometrix.com/academy and enter code: 778133

Mathematics

WRITING A FUNCTION RULE USING A TABLE

If given a set of data, place the corresponding x- and y-values into a table and analyze the relationship between them. Consider what you can do to each x-value to obtain the corresponding y-value. Try adding or subtracting different numbers to and from x and then try multiplying or dividing different numbers to and from x. If none of these **operations** give you the y-value, try combining the operations. Once you find a rule that works for one pair, make sure to try it with each additional set of ordered pairs in the table. If the same operation or combination of operations satisfies each set of coordinates, then the table contains a function. The rule is then used to write the equation of the function in "$y = f(x)$" form.

DIRECT AND INVERSE VARIATIONS OF VARIABLES

Variables that vary directly are those that either both increase at the same rate or both decrease at the same rate. For example, in the functions $y = kx$ or $y = kx^n$, where k and n are positive, the value of y increases as the value of x increases and decreases as the value of x decreases.

Variables that vary inversely are those where one increases while the other decreases. For example, in the functions $y = \frac{k}{x}$ or $y = \frac{k}{x^n}$ where k and n are positive, the value of y increases as the value of x decreases and decreases as the value of x increases.

In both cases, k is the constant of variation.

PROPERTIES OF FUNCTIONS

There are many different ways to classify functions based on their structure or behavior. Important features of functions include:

- **End behavior**: the behavior of the function at extreme values ($f(x)$ as $x \to \pm\infty$)
- **y-intercept**: the value of the function at $f(0)$
- **Roots**: the values of x where the function equals zero ($f(x) = 0$)
- **Extrema**: minimum or maximum values of the function or where the function changes direction ($f(x) \geq k$ or $f(x) \leq k$)

CLASSIFICATION OF FUNCTIONS

An **invertible function** is defined as a function, $f(x)$, for which there is another function, $f^{-1}(x)$, such that $f^{-1}(f(x)) = x$. For example, if $f(x) = 3x - 2$ the inverse function, $f^{-1}(x)$, can be found:

$$x = 3(f^{-1}(x)) - 2$$
$$\frac{x + 2}{3} = f^{-1}(x)$$

$$f^{-1}(f(x)) = \frac{3x - 2 + 2}{3}$$
$$= \frac{3x}{3}$$
$$= x$$

Note that $f^{-1}(x)$ is a valid function over all values of x.

In a **one-to-one function**, each value of x has exactly one value for y on the coordinate plane (this is the definition of a function) and each value of y has exactly one value for x. While the vertical line test will determine if a graph is that of a function, the horizontal line test will determine if a function is a one-to-one function. If a horizontal line drawn at any value of y intersects the graph in more

53

than one place, the graph is not that of a one-to-one function. Do not make the mistake of using the horizontal line test exclusively in determining if a graph is that of a one-to-one function. A one-to-one function must pass both the vertical line test and the horizontal line test. As such, one-to-one functions are invertible functions.

A **many-to-one function** is a function whereby the relation is a function, but the inverse of the function is not a function. In other words, each element in the domain is mapped to one and only one element in the range. However, one or more elements in the range may be mapped to the same element in the domain. A graph of a many-to-one function would pass the vertical line test, but not the horizontal line test. This is why many-to-one functions are not invertible.

A **monotone function** is a function whose graph either constantly increases or constantly decreases. Examples include the functions $f(x) = x$, $f(x) = -x$, or $f(x) = x^3$.

An **even function** has a graph that is symmetric with respect to the y-axis and satisfies the equation $f(x) = f(-x)$. Examples include the functions $f(x) = x^2$ and $f(x) = ax^n$, where a is any real number and n is a positive even integer.

An **odd function** has a graph that is symmetric with respect to the origin and satisfies the equation $f(x) = -f(-x)$. Examples include the functions $f(x) = x^3$ and $f(x) = ax^n$, where a is any real number and n is a positive odd integer.

> **Review Video: Even and Odd Functions**
> Visit mometrix.com/academy and enter code: 278985

Constant functions are given by the equation $f(x) = b$, where b is a real number. There is no independent variable present in the equation, so the function has a constant value for all x. The graph of a constant function is a horizontal line of slope 0 that is positioned b units from the x-axis. If b is positive, the line is above the x-axis; if b is negative, the line is below the x-axis.

Identity functions are identified by the equation $f(x) = x$, where every value of the function is equal to its corresponding value of x. The only zero is the point (0,0). The graph is a line with a slope of 1.

In **linear functions**, the value of the function changes in direct proportion to x. The rate of change, represented by the slope on its graph, is constant throughout. The standard form of a linear equation is $ax + cy = d$, where a, c, and d are real numbers. As a function, this equation is commonly in the form $y = mx + b$ or $f(x) = mx + b$ where $m = -\frac{a}{c}$ and $b = \frac{d}{c}$. This is known as the slope-intercept form, because the coefficients give the slope of the graphed function (m) and its y-intercept (b). Solve the equation $mx + b = 0$ for x to get $x = -\frac{b}{m}$, which is the only zero of the function. The domain and range are both the set of all real numbers.

> **Review Video: Graphing Linear Functions**
> Visit mometrix.com/academy and enter code: 699478

Algebraic functions are those that exclusively use polynomials and roots. These would include polynomial functions, rational functions, square root functions, and all combinations of these

functions, such as polynomials as the radicand. These combinations may be joined by addition, subtraction, multiplication, or division, but may not include variables as exponents.

> **Review Video: Common Functions**
> Visit mometrix.com/academy and enter code: 629798

ABSOLUTE VALUE FUNCTIONS

An **absolute value function** is in the format $f(x) = |ax + b|$. Like other functions, the domain is the set of all real numbers. However, because absolute value indicates positive numbers, the range is limited to positive real numbers. To find the zero of an absolute value function, set the portion inside the absolute value sign equal to zero and solve for x. An absolute value function is also known as a piecewise function because it must be solved in pieces—one for if the value inside the absolute value sign is positive, and one for if the value is negative. The function can be expressed as:

$$f(x) = \begin{cases} ax + b & \text{if } ax + b \geq 0 \\ -(ax + b) & \text{if } ax + b < 0 \end{cases}$$

This will allow for an accurate statement of the range. The graph of an example absolute value function, $f(x) = |2x - 1|$, is below:

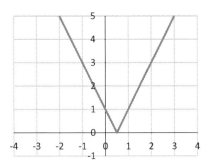

PIECEWISE FUNCTIONS

A **piecewise function** is a function that has different definitions on two or more different intervals. The following, for instance, is one example of a piecewise-defined function:

$$f(x) = \begin{cases} x^2, & x < 0 \\ x, & 0 \leq x \leq 2 \\ (x - 2)^2, & x > 2 \end{cases}$$

To graph this function, you would simply graph each part separately in the appropriate domain. The final graph would look like this:

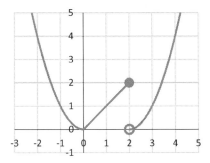

55

Note the filled and hollow dots at the discontinuity at $x = 2$. This is important to show which side of the graph that point corresponds to. Because $f(x) = x$ on the closed interval $0 \le x \le 2$, $f(2) = 2$. The point $(2, 2)$ is therefore marked with a filled circle, and the point $(2,0)$, which is the endpoint of the rightmost $(x - 2)^2$ part of the graph but *not actually part of the function*, is marked with a hollow dot to indicate this.

> **Review Video: Piecewise Functions**
> Visit mometrix.com/academy and enter code: 707921

QUADRATIC FUNCTIONS

A **quadratic function** is a function in the form $y = ax^2 + bx + c$, where a does not equal 0. While a linear function forms a line, a quadratic function forms a **parabola**, which is a u-shaped figure that either opens upward or downward. A parabola that opens upward is said to be a **positive quadratic function,** and a parabola that opens downward is said to be a **negative quadratic function**. The shape of a parabola can differ, depending on the values of a, b, and c. All parabolas contain a **vertex**, which is the highest possible point, the **maximum**, or the lowest possible point, the **minimum**. This is the point where the graph begins moving in the opposite direction. A quadratic function can have zero, one, or two solutions, and therefore zero, one, or two x-intercepts. Recall that the x-intercepts are referred to as the zeros, or roots, of a function. A quadratic function will have only one y-intercept. Understanding the basic components of a quadratic function can give you an idea of the shape of its graph.

Example graph of a positive quadratic function, $x^2 + 2x - 3$:

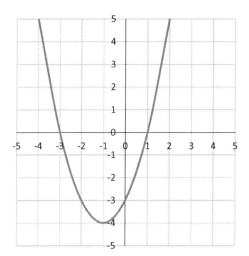

POLYNOMIAL FUNCTIONS

A **polynomial function** is a function with multiple terms and multiple powers of x, such as:

$$f(x) = a_n x^n + a_{n-1} x^{n-1} + a_{n-2} x^{n-2} + \cdots + a_1 x + a_0$$

where n is a non-negative integer that is the highest exponent in the polynomial and $a_n \ne 0$. The domain of a polynomial function is the set of all real numbers. If the greatest exponent in the polynomial is even, the polynomial is said to be of even degree and the range is the set of real numbers that satisfy the function. If the greatest exponent in the polynomial is odd, the polynomial is said to be odd and the range, like the domain, is the set of all real numbers.

RATIONAL FUNCTIONS

A **rational function** is a function that can be constructed as a ratio of two polynomial expressions: $f(x) = \frac{p(x)}{q(x)}$, where $p(x)$ and $q(x)$ are both polynomial expressions and $q(x) \neq 0$. The domain is the set of all real numbers, except any values for which $q(x) = 0$. The range is the set of real numbers that satisfies the function when the domain is applied. When you graph a rational function, you will have vertical asymptotes wherever $q(x) = 0$. If the polynomial in the numerator is of lesser degree than the polynomial in the denominator, the x-axis will also be a horizontal asymptote. If the numerator and denominator have equal degrees, there will be a horizontal asymptote not on the x-axis. If the degree of the numerator is exactly one greater than the degree of the denominator, the graph will have an oblique, or diagonal, asymptote. The asymptote will be along the line $y = \frac{p_n}{q_{n-1}} x + \frac{p_{n-1}}{q_{n-1}}$, where p_n and q_{n-1} are the coefficients of the highest degree terms in their respective polynomials.

SQUARE ROOT FUNCTIONS

A **square root function** is a function that contains a radical and is in the format $f(x) = \sqrt{ax + b}$. The domain is the set of all real numbers that yields a positive radicand or a radicand equal to zero. Because square root values are assumed to be positive unless otherwise identified, the range is all real numbers from zero to infinity. To find the zero of a square root function, set the radicand equal to zero and solve for x. The graph of a square root function is always to the right of the zero and always above the x-axis.

Example graph of a square root function, $f(x) = \sqrt{2x + 1}$:

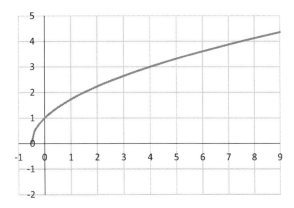

Reading

Transform passive reading into active learning! After immersing yourself in this chapter, put your comprehension to the test by taking a quiz. The insights you gained will stay with you longer this way. Scan the QR code to go directly to the chapter quiz interface for this study guide. If you're using a computer, simply visit the bonus page at **mometrix.com/bonus948/pert** and click the Chapter Quizzes link.

Vocabulary

WORD ROOTS AND PREFIXES AND SUFFIXES

AFFIXES

Affixes in the English language are morphemes that are added to words to create related but different words. Derivational affixes form new words based on and related to the original words. For example, the affix *–ness* added to the end of the adjective *happy* forms the noun *happiness*. Inflectional affixes form different grammatical versions of words. For example, the plural affix *–s* changes the singular noun *book* to the plural noun *books*, and the past tense affix *–ed* changes the present tense verb *look* to the past tense *looked*. Prefixes are affixes placed in front of words. For example, *heat* means to make hot; *preheat* means to heat in advance. Suffixes are affixes placed at the ends of words. The *happiness* example above contains the suffix *–ness*. Circumfixes add parts both before and after words, such as how *light* becomes *enlighten* with the prefix *en-* and the suffix *–en*. Interfixes create compound words via central affixes: *speed* and *meter* become *speedometer* via the interfix *–o–*.

> **Review Video: Affixes**
> Visit mometrix.com/academy and enter code: 782422

WORD ROOTS, PREFIXES, AND SUFFIXES TO HELP DETERMINE MEANINGS OF WORDS

Many English words were formed from combining multiple sources. For example, the Latin *habēre* means "to have," and the prefixes *in-* and *im-* mean a lack or prevention of something, as in *insufficient* and *imperfect*. Latin combined *in-* with *habēre* to form *inhibēre*, whose past participle was *inhibitus*. This is the origin of the English word *inhibit*, meaning to prevent from having. Hence by knowing the meanings of both the prefix and the root, one can decipher the word meaning. In Greek, the root *enkephalo-* refers to the brain. Many medical terms are based on this root, such as encephalitis and hydrocephalus. Understanding the prefix and suffix meanings (*-itis* means inflammation; *hydro-* means water) allows a person to deduce that encephalitis refers to brain inflammation and hydrocephalus refers to water (or other fluid) in the brain.

> **Review Video: Determining Word Meanings**
> Visit mometrix.com/academy and enter code: 894894

PREFIXES

Knowing common prefixes is helpful for all readers as they try to determining meanings or definitions of unfamiliar words. For example, a common word used when cooking is *preheat*. Knowing that *pre-* means in advance can also inform them that *presume* means to assume in advance, that *prejudice* means advance judgment, and that this understanding can be applied to

many other words beginning with *pre-.* Knowing that the prefix *dis-* indicates opposition informs the meanings of words like *disbar, disagree, disestablish,* and many more. Knowing *dys-* means bad, impaired, abnormal, or difficult informs *dyslogistic, dysfunctional, dysphagia,* and *dysplasia.*

<u>SUFFIXES</u>

In English, certain suffixes generally indicate both that a word is a noun, and that the noun represents a state of being or quality. For example, *-ness* is commonly used to change an adjective into its noun form, as with *happy* and *happiness, nice* and *niceness,* and so on. The suffix *–tion* is commonly used to transform a verb into its noun form, as with *converse* and *conversation or move* and *motion*. Thus, if readers are unfamiliar with the second form of a word, knowing the meaning of the transforming suffix can help them determine meaning.

<u>PREFIXES FOR NUMBERS</u>

Prefix	Definition	Examples
bi-	two	bisect, biennial
mono-	one, single	monogamy, monologue
poly-	many	polymorphous, polygamous
semi-	half, partly	semicircle, semicolon
uni-	one	uniform, unity

Mometrix

PREFIXES FOR TIME, DIRECTION, AND SPACE

Prefix	Definition	Examples
a-	in, on, of, up, to	abed, afoot
ab-	from, away, off	abdicate, abjure
ad-	to, toward	advance, adventure
ante-	before, previous	antecedent, antedate
anti-	against, opposing	antipathy, antidote
cata-	down, away, thoroughly	catastrophe, cataclysm
circum-	around	circumspect, circumference
com-	with, together, very	commotion, complicate
contra-	against, opposing	contradict, contravene
de-	from	depart
dia-	through, across, apart	diameter, diagnose
dis-	away, off, down, not	dissent, disappear
epi-	upon	epilogue
ex-	out	extract, excerpt
hypo-	under, beneath	hypodermic, hypothesis
inter-	among, between	intercede, interrupt
intra-	within	intramural, intrastate
ob-	against, opposing	objection
per-	through	perceive, permit
peri-	around	periscope, perimeter
post-	after, following	postpone, postscript
pre-	before, previous	prevent, preclude
pro-	forward, in place of	propel, pronoun
retro-	back, backward	retrospect, retrograde
sub-	under, beneath	subjugate, substitute
super-	above, extra	supersede, supernumerary
trans-	across, beyond, over	transact, transport
ultra-	beyond, excessively	ultramodern, ultrasonic

NEGATIVE PREFIXES

Prefix	Definition	Examples
a-	without, lacking	atheist, agnostic
in-	not, opposing	incapable, ineligible
non-	not	nonentity, nonsense
un-	not, reverse of	unhappy, unlock

60

EXTRA PREFIXES

Prefix	Definition	Examples
for-	away, off, from	forget, forswear
fore-	previous	foretell, forefathers
homo-	same, equal	homogenized, homonym
hyper-	excessive, over	hypercritical, hypertension
in-	in, into	intrude, invade
mal-	bad, poorly, not	malfunction, malpractice
mis-	bad, poorly, not	misspell, misfire
neo-	new	Neolithic, neoconservative
omni-	all, everywhere	omniscient, omnivore
ortho-	right, straight	orthogonal, orthodox
over-	above	overbearing, oversight
pan-	all, entire	panorama, pandemonium
para-	beside, beyond	parallel, paradox
re-	backward, again	revoke, recur
sym-	with, together	sympathy, symphony

Below is a list of common suffixes and their meanings:

ADJECTIVE SUFFIXES

Suffix	Definition	Examples
-able (-ible)	capable of being	toler*able*, ed*ible*
-esque	in the style of, like	picturesque, grotesque
-ful	filled with, marked by	thankful, zestful
-ific	make, cause	terrific, beatific
-ish	suggesting, like	churlish, childish
-less	lacking, without	hopeless, countless
-ous	marked by, given to	religious, riotous

Reading

61

NOUN SUFFIXES

Suffix	Definition	Examples
-acy	state, condition	accuracy, privacy
-ance	act, condition, fact	acceptance, vigilance
-ard	one that does excessively	drunkard, sluggard
-ation	action, state, result	occupation, starvation
-dom	state, rank, condition	serfdom, wisdom
-er (-or)	office, action	teacher, elevator, honor
-ess	feminine	waitress, duchess
-hood	state, condition	manhood, statehood
-ion	action, result, state	union, fusion
-ism	act, manner, doctrine	barbarism, socialism
-ist	worker, follower	monopolist, socialist
-ity (-ty)	state, quality, condition	acidity, civility, twenty
-ment	result, action	Refreshment
-ness	quality, state	greatness, tallness
-ship	position	internship, statesmanship
-sion (-tion)	state, result	revision, expedition
-th	act, state, quality	warmth, width
-tude	quality, state, result	magnitude, fortitude

VERB SUFFIXES

Suffix	Definition	Examples
-ate	having, showing	separate, desolate
-en	cause to be, become	deepen, strengthen
-fy	make, cause to have	glorify, fortify
-ize	cause to be, treat with	sterilize, mechanize

NUANCE AND WORD MEANINGS

SYNONYMS AND ANTONYMS

When you understand how words relate to each other, you will discover more in a passage. This is explained by understanding **synonyms** (e.g., words that mean the same thing) and **antonyms** (e.g., words that mean the opposite of one another). As an example, *dry* and *arid* are synonyms, and *dry* and *wet* are antonyms.

There are many pairs of words in English that can be considered synonyms, despite having slightly different definitions. For instance, the words *friendly* and *collegial* can both be used to describe a warm interpersonal relationship, and one would be correct to call them synonyms. However, *collegial* (kin to *colleague*) is often used in reference to professional or academic relationships, and *friendly* has no such connotation.

If the difference between the two words is too great, then they should not be called synonyms. *Hot* and *warm* are not synonyms because their meanings are too distinct. A good way to determine whether two words are synonyms is to substitute one word for the other word and verify that the meaning of the sentence has not changed. Substituting *warm* for *hot* in a sentence would convey a different meaning. Although warm and hot may seem close in meaning, warm generally means that the temperature is moderate, and hot generally means that the temperature is excessively high.

Antonyms are words with opposite meanings. *Light* and *dark*, *up* and *down*, *right* and *left*, *good* and *bad*: these are all sets of antonyms. Be careful to distinguish between antonyms and pairs of words that are simply different. *Black* and *gray*, for instance, are not antonyms because gray is not the opposite of black. *Black* and *white*, on the other hand, are antonyms.

Not every word has an antonym. For instance, many nouns do not. What would be the antonym of *chair*? During your exam, the questions related to antonyms are more likely to concern adjectives. You will recall that adjectives are words that describe a noun. Some common adjectives include *purple*, *fast*, *skinny*, and *sweet*. From those four adjectives, *purple* is the item that lacks a group of obvious antonyms.

> **Review Video: <u>Synonyms and Antonyms</u>**
> Visit mometrix.com/academy and enter code: 105612

DENOTATIVE VS. CONNOTATIVE MEANING

The **denotative** meaning of a word is the literal meaning. The **connotative** meaning goes beyond the denotative meaning to include the emotional reaction that a word may invoke. The connotative meaning often takes the denotative meaning a step further due to associations the reader makes with the denotative meaning. Readers can differentiate between the denotative and connotative meanings by first recognizing how authors use each meaning. Most non-fiction, for example, is fact-based and authors do not use flowery, figurative language. The reader can assume that the writer is using the denotative meaning of words. In fiction, the author may use the connotative meaning. Readers can determine whether the author is using the denotative or connotative meaning of a word by implementing context clues.

> **Review Video: <u>Connotation and Denotation</u>**
> Visit mometrix.com/academy and enter code: 310092

NUANCES OF WORD MEANING RELATIVE TO CONNOTATION, DENOTATION, DICTION, AND USAGE

A word's denotation is simply its objective dictionary definition. However, its connotation refers to the subjective associations, often emotional, that specific words evoke in listeners and readers. Two or more words can have the same dictionary meaning, but very different connotations. Writers use diction (word choice) to convey various nuances of thought and emotion by selecting synonyms for other words that best communicate the associations they want to trigger for readers. For example, a car engine is naturally greasy; in this sense, "greasy" is a neutral term. But when a person's smile, appearance, or clothing is described as "greasy," it has a negative connotation. Some words have even gained additional or different meanings over time. For example, *awful* used to be used to describe things that evoked a sense of awe. When *awful* is separated into its root word, awe, and suffix, -ful, it can be understood to mean "full of awe." However, the word is now commonly used to describe things that evoke repulsion, terror, or another intense, negative reaction.

> **Review Video: <u>Word Usage in Sentences</u>**
> Visit mometrix.com/academy and enter code: 197863

USING CONTEXT TO DETERMINE MEANING
CONTEXT CLUES

Readers of all levels will encounter words that they have either never seen or have encountered only on a limited basis. The best way to define a word in **context** is to look for nearby words that can assist in revealing the meaning of the word. For instance, unfamiliar nouns are often accompanied by examples that provide a definition. Consider the following sentence: *Dave arrived*

63

at the party in hilarious garb: a leopard-print shirt, buckskin trousers, and bright green sneakers. If a reader was unfamiliar with the meaning of garb, he or she could read the examples (i.e., a leopard-print shirt, buckskin trousers, and bright green sneakers) and quickly determine that the word means *clothing*. Examples will not always be this obvious. Consider this sentence: *Parsley, lemon, and flowers were just a few of the items he used as garnishes.* Here, the word *garnishes* is exemplified by parsley, lemon, and flowers. Readers who have eaten in a variety of restaurants will probably be able to identify a garnish as something used to decorate a plate.

> **Review Video: <u>Reading Comprehension: Using Context Clues</u>**
> Visit mometrix.com/academy and enter code: 613660

USING CONTRAST IN CONTEXT CLUES

In addition to looking at the context of a passage, readers can use contrast to define an unfamiliar word in context. In many sentences, the author will not describe the unfamiliar word directly; instead, he or she will describe the opposite of the unfamiliar word. Thus, you are provided with some information that will bring you closer to defining the word. Consider the following example: *Despite his intelligence, Hector's low brow and bad posture made him look obtuse.* The author writes that Hector's appearance does not convey intelligence. Therefore, *obtuse* must mean unintelligent. Here is another example: *Despite the horrible weather, we were beatific about our trip to Alaska.* The word *despite* indicates that the speaker's feelings were at odds with the weather. Since the weather is described as *horrible*, then *beatific* must mean something positive.

SUBSTITUTION TO FIND MEANING

In some cases, there will be very few contextual clues to help a reader define the meaning of an unfamiliar word. When this happens, one strategy that readers may employ is **substitution**. A good reader will brainstorm some possible synonyms for the given word, and he or she will substitute these words into the sentence. If the sentence and the surrounding passage continue to make sense, then the substitution has revealed at least some information about the unfamiliar word. Consider the sentence: *Frank's admonition rang in her ears as she climbed the mountain.* A reader unfamiliar with *admonition* might come up with some substitutions like *vow, promise, advice, complaint,* or *compliment.* All of these words make general sense of the sentence, though their meanings are diverse. However, this process has suggested that an admonition is some sort of message. The substitution strategy is rarely able to pinpoint a precise definition, but this process can be effective as a last resort.

Occasionally, you will be able to define an unfamiliar word by looking at the descriptive words in the context. Consider the following sentence: *Fred dragged the recalcitrant boy kicking and screaming up the stairs.* The words *dragged, kicking,* and *screaming* all suggest that the boy does not want to go up the stairs. The reader may assume that *recalcitrant* means something like unwilling or protesting. In this example, an unfamiliar adjective was identified.

Additionally, using description to define an unfamiliar noun is a common practice compared to unfamiliar adjectives, as in this sentence: *Don's wrinkled frown and constantly shaking fist identified him as a curmudgeon of the first order.* Don is described as having a *wrinkled frown and constantly shaking fist*, suggesting that a *curmudgeon* must be a grumpy person. Contrasts do not always provide detailed information about the unfamiliar word, but they at least give the reader some clues.

WORDS WITH MULTIPLE MEANINGS

When a word has more than one meaning, readers can have difficulty determining how the word is being used in a given sentence. For instance, the verb *cleave*, can mean either *join* or *separate*. When

readers come upon this word, they will have to select the definition that makes the most sense. Consider the following sentence: *Hermione's knife cleaved the bread cleanly*. Since a knife cannot join bread together, the word must indicate separation. A slightly more difficult example would be the sentence: *The birds cleaved to one another as they flew from the oak tree.* Immediately, the presence of the words *to one another* should suggest that in this sentence *cleave* is being used to mean *join*. Discovering the intent of a word with multiple meanings requires the same tricks as defining an unknown word: look for contextual clues and evaluate the substituted words.

CONTEXT CLUES TO HELP DETERMINE MEANINGS OF WORDS

If readers simply bypass unknown words, they can reach unclear conclusions about what they read. However, looking for the definition of every unfamiliar word in the dictionary can slow their reading progress. Moreover, the dictionary may list multiple definitions for a word, so readers must search the word's context for meaning. Hence context is important to new vocabulary regardless of reader methods. Four types of context clues are examples, definitions, descriptive words, and opposites. Authors may use a certain word, and then follow it with several different examples of what it describes. Sometimes authors actually supply a definition of a word they use, which is especially true in informational and technical texts. Authors may use descriptive words that elaborate upon a vocabulary word they just used. Authors may also use opposites with negation that help define meaning.

EXAMPLES AND DEFINITIONS

An author may use a word and then give examples that illustrate its meaning. Consider this text: "Teachers who do not know how to use sign language can help students who are deaf or hard of hearing understand certain instructions by using gestures instead, like pointing their fingers to indicate which direction to look or go; holding up a hand, palm outward, to indicate stopping; holding the hands flat, palms up, curling a finger toward oneself in a beckoning motion to indicate 'come here'; or curling all fingers toward oneself repeatedly to indicate 'come on', 'more', or 'continue.'" The author of this text has used the word "gestures" and then followed it with examples, so a reader unfamiliar with the word could deduce from the examples that "gestures" means "hand motions." Readers can find examples by looking for signal words "for example," "for instance," "like," "such as," and "e.g."

While readers sometimes have to look for definitions of unfamiliar words in a dictionary or do some work to determine a word's meaning from its surrounding context, at other times an author may make it easier for readers by defining certain words. For example, an author may write, "The company did not have sufficient capital, that is, available money, to continue operations." The author defined "capital" as "available money," and heralded the definition with the phrase "that is." Another way that authors supply word definitions is with appositives. Rather than being introduced by a signal phrase like "that is," "namely," or "meaning," an appositive comes after the vocabulary word it defines and is enclosed within two commas. For example, an author may write, "The Indians introduced the Pilgrims to pemmican, cakes they made of lean meat dried and mixed with fat, which proved greatly beneficial to keep settlers from starving while trapping." In this example, the appositive phrase following "pemmican" and preceding "which" defines the word "pemmican."

DESCRIPTIONS

When readers encounter a word they do not recognize in a text, the author may expand on that word to illustrate it better. While the author may do this to make the prose more picturesque and vivid, the reader can also take advantage of this description to provide context clues to the meaning of the unfamiliar word. For example, an author may write, "The man sitting next to me on the airplane was obese. His shirt stretched across his vast expanse of flesh, strained almost to bursting."

65

The descriptive second sentence elaborates on and helps to define the previous sentence's word "obese" to mean extremely fat. A reader unfamiliar with the word "repugnant" can decipher its meaning through an author's accompanying description: "The way the child grimaced and shuddered as he swallowed the medicine showed that its taste was particularly repugnant."

<u>OPPOSITES</u>

Text authors sometimes introduce a contrasting or opposing idea before or after a concept they present. They may do this to emphasize or heighten the idea they present by contrasting it with something that is the reverse. However, readers can also use these context clues to understand familiar words. For example, an author may write, "Our conversation was not cheery. We sat and talked very solemnly about his experience and a number of similar events." The reader who is not familiar with the word "solemnly" can deduce by the author's preceding use of "not cheery" that "solemn" means the opposite of cheery or happy, so it must mean serious or sad. Or if someone writes, "Don't condemn his entire project because you couldn't find anything good to say about it," readers unfamiliar with "condemn" can understand from the sentence structure that it means the opposite of saying anything good, so it must mean reject, dismiss, or disapprove. "Entire" adds another context clue, meaning total or complete rejection.

SYNTAX TO DETERMINE PART OF SPEECH AND MEANINGS OF WORDS

Syntax refers to sentence structure and word order. Suppose that a reader encounters an unfamiliar word when reading a text. To illustrate, consider an invented word like "splunch." If this word is used in a sentence like "Please splunch that ball to me," the reader can assume from syntactic context that "splunch" is a verb. We would not use a noun, adjective, adverb, or preposition with the object "that ball," and the prepositional phrase "to me" further indicates "splunch" represents an action. However, in the sentence, "Please hand that splunch to me," the reader can assume that "splunch" is a noun. Demonstrative adjectives like "that" modify nouns. Also, we hand someone some*thing*—a thing being a noun; we do not hand someone a verb, adjective, or adverb. Some sentences contain further clues. For example, from the sentence, "The princess wore the glittering splunch on her head," the reader can deduce that it is a crown, tiara, or something similar from the syntactic context, without knowing the word.

SYNTAX TO INDICATE DIFFERENT MEANINGS OF SIMILAR SENTENCES

The syntax, or structure, of a sentence affords grammatical cues that aid readers in comprehending the meanings of words, phrases, and sentences in the texts that they read. Seemingly minor differences in how the words or phrases in a sentence are ordered can make major differences in meaning. For example, two sentences can use exactly the same words but have different meanings based on the word order:

- "The man with a broken arm sat in a chair."
- "The man sat in a chair with a broken arm."

While both sentences indicate that a man sat in a chair, differing syntax indicates whether the man's or chair's arm was broken.

> **Review Video: <u>Syntax</u>**
> Visit mometrix.com/academy and enter code: 242280

DETERMINING MEANING OF PHRASES AND PARAGRAPHS

Like unknown words, the meanings of phrases, paragraphs, and entire works can also be difficult to discern. Each of these can be better understood with added context. However, for larger groups of words, more context is needed. Unclear phrases are similar to unclear words, and the same methods can be used to understand their meaning. However, it is also important to consider how the individual words in the phrase work together. Paragraphs are a bit more complicated. Just as words must be compared to other words in a sentence, paragraphs must be compared to other paragraphs in a composition or a section.

DETERMINING MEANING IN VARIOUS TYPES OF COMPOSITIONS

To understand the meaning of an entire composition, the type of composition must be considered. **Expository writing** is generally organized so that each paragraph focuses on explaining one idea, or part of an idea, and its relevance. **Persuasive writing** uses paragraphs for different purposes to organize the parts of the argument. **Unclear paragraphs** must be read in the context of the paragraphs around them for their meaning to be fully understood. The meaning of full texts can also be unclear at times. The purpose of composition is also important for understanding the meaning of a text. To quickly understand the broad meaning of a text, look to the introductory and concluding paragraphs. Fictional texts are different. Some fictional works have implicit meanings, but some do not. The target audience must be considered for understanding texts that do have an implicit meaning, as most children's fiction will clearly state any lessons or morals. For other fiction, the application of literary theories and criticism may be helpful for understanding the text.

RESOURCES FOR DETERMINING WORD MEANING AND USAGE

While these strategies are useful for determining the meaning of unknown words and phrases, sometimes additional resources are needed to properly use the terms in different contexts. Some words have multiple definitions, and some words are inappropriate in particular contexts or modes of writing. The following tools are helpful for understanding all meanings and proper uses for words and phrases.

- **Dictionaries** provide the meaning of a multitude of words in a language. Many dictionaries include additional information about each word, such as its etymology, its synonyms, or variations of the word.
- **Glossaries** are similar to dictionaries, as they provide the meanings of a variety of terms. However, while dictionaries typically feature an extensive list of words and comprise an entire publication, glossaries are often included at the end of a text and only include terms and definitions that are relevant to the text they follow.
- **Spell Checkers** are used to detect spelling errors in typed text. Some spell checkers may also detect the misuse of plural or singular nouns, verb tenses, or capitalization. While spell checkers are a helpful tool, they are not always reliable or attuned to the author's intent, so it is important to review the spell checker's suggestions before accepting them.
- **Style Manuals** are guidelines on the preferred punctuation, format, and grammar usage according to different fields or organizations. For example, the Associated Press Stylebook is a style guide often used for media writing. The guidelines within a style guide are not always applicable across different contexts and usages, as the guidelines often cover grammatical or formatting situations that are not objectively correct or incorrect.

Elements of Story

PLOT AND STORY STRUCTURE
PLOT AND STORY STRUCTURE

The **plot** includes the events that happen in a story and the order in which they are told to the reader. There are several types of plot structures, as stories can be told in many ways. The most common plot structure is the chronological plot, which presents the events to the reader in the same order they occur for the characters in the story. Chronological plots usually have five main parts, the **exposition**, **rising action**, the **climax**, **falling action**, and the **resolution**. This type of plot structure guides the reader through the story's events as the characters experience them and is the easiest structure to understand and identify. While this is the most common plot structure, many stories are nonlinear, which means the plot does not sequence events in the same order the characters experience them. Such stories might include elements like flashbacks that cause the story to be nonlinear.

> **Review Video: How to Make a Story Map**
> Visit mometrix.com/academy and enter code: 261719

EXPOSITION

The **exposition** is at the beginning of the story and generally takes place before the rising action begins. The purpose of the exposition is to give the reader context for the story, which the author may do by introducing one or more characters, describing the setting or world, or explaining the events leading up to the point where the story begins. The exposition may still include events that contribute to the plot, but the **rising action** and main conflict of the story are not part of the exposition. Some narratives skip the exposition and begin the story with the beginning of the rising action, which causes the reader to learn the context as the story intensifies.

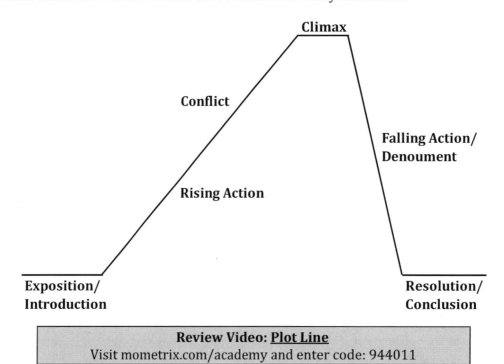

> **Review Video: Plot Line**
> Visit mometrix.com/academy and enter code: 944011

CONFLICT

A **conflict** is a problem to be solved. Literary plots typically include one conflict or more. Characters' attempts to resolve conflicts drive the narrative's forward movement. **Conflict resolution** is often the protagonist's primary occupation. Physical conflicts like exploring, wars, and escapes tend to make plots most suspenseful and exciting. Emotional, mental, or moral conflicts tend to make stories more personally gratifying or rewarding for many audiences. Conflicts can be external or internal. A major type of internal conflict is some inner personal battle, or **man versus self**. Major types of external conflicts include **man versus nature**, **man versus man**, and **man**

versus society. Readers can identify conflicts in literary plots by identifying the protagonist and antagonist and asking why they conflict, what events develop the conflict, where the climax occurs, and how they identify with the characters.

Read the following paragraph and discuss the type of conflict present:

> Timothy was shocked out of sleep by the appearance of a bear just outside his tent. After panicking for a moment, he remembered some advice he had read in preparation for this trip: he should make noise so the bear would not be startled. As Timothy started to hum and sing, the bear wandered away.

There are three main types of conflict in literature: **man versus man**, **man versus nature**, and **man versus self**. This paragraph is an example of man versus nature. Timothy is in conflict with the bear. Even though no physical conflict like an attack exists, Timothy is pitted against the bear. Timothy uses his knowledge to "defeat" the bear and keep himself safe. The solution to the conflict is that Timothy makes noise, the bear wanders away, and Timothy is safe.

> **Review Video: <u>Conflict</u>**
> Visit mometrix.com/academy and enter code: 559550
>
> **Review Video: <u>Determining Relationships in a Story</u>**
> Visit mometrix.com/academy and enter code: 929925

RISING ACTION

The **rising action** is the part of the story where conflict **intensifies**. The rising action begins with an event that prompts the main conflict of the story. This may also be called the **inciting incident**. The main conflict generally occurs between the protagonist and an antagonist, but this is not the only type of conflict that may occur in a narrative. After this event, the protagonist works to resolve the main conflict by preparing for an altercation, pursuing a goal, fleeing an antagonist, or doing some other action that will end the conflict. The rising action is composed of several additional events that increase the story's tension. Most often, other developments will occur alongside the growth of the main conflict, such as character development or the development of minor conflicts. The rising action ends with the **climax**, which is the point of highest tension in the story.

CLIMAX

The **climax** is the event in the narrative that marks the height of the story's conflict or tension. The event that takes place at the story's climax will end the rising action and bring about the results of the main conflict. If the conflict was between a good protagonist and an evil antagonist, the climax may be a final battle between the two characters. If the conflict is an adventurer looking for heavily guarded treasure, the climax may be the adventurer's encounter with the final obstacle that protects the treasure. The climax may be made of multiple scenes, but can usually be summarized as one event. Once the conflict and climax are complete, the **falling action** begins.

FALLING ACTION

The **falling action** shows what happens in the story between the climax and the resolution. The falling action often composes a much smaller portion of the story than the rising action does. While the climax includes the end of the main conflict, the falling action may show the results of any minor conflicts in the story. For example, if the protagonist encountered a troll on the way to find some treasure, and the troll demanded the protagonist share the treasure after retrieving it, the falling action would include the protagonist returning to share the treasure with the troll. Similarly, any unexplained major events are usually made clear during the falling action. Once all significant

69

elements of the story are resolved or addressed, the story's resolution will occur. The **resolution** is the end of the story, which shows the final result of the plot's events and shows what life is like for the main characters once they are no longer experiencing the story's conflicts.

RESOLUTION

The way the conflict is **resolved** depends on the type of conflict. The plot of any book starts with the lead up to the conflict, then the conflict itself, and finally the solution, or **resolution**, to the conflict. In **man versus man** conflicts, the conflict is often resolved by two parties coming to some sort of agreement or by one party triumphing over the other party. In **man versus nature** conflicts, the conflict is often resolved by man coming to some realization about some aspect of nature. In **man versus self** conflicts, the conflict is often resolved by the character growing or coming to an understanding about part of himself.

THEME

A **theme** is a central idea demonstrated by a passage. Often, a theme is a lesson or moral contained in the text, but it does not have to be. It also is a unifying idea that is used throughout the text; it can take the form of a common setting, idea, symbol, design, or recurring event. A passage can have two or more themes that convey its overall idea. The theme or themes of a passage are often based on **universal themes**. They can frequently be expressed using well-known sayings about life, society, or human nature, such as "Hard work pays off" or "Good triumphs over evil." Themes are not usually stated **explicitly**. The reader must figure them out by carefully reading the passage. Themes are created through descriptive language or events in the plot. The events of a story help shape the themes of a passage.

EXAMPLE

Explain why "if you care about something, you need to take care of it" accurately describes the theme of the following excerpt.

> Luca collected baseball cards, but he wasn't very careful with them. He left them around the house. His dog liked to chew. One day, Luca and his friend Bart were looking at his collection. Then they went outside. When Luca got home, he saw his dog chewing on his cards. They were ruined.

This excerpt tells the story of a boy who is careless with his baseball cards and leaves them lying around. His dog ends up chewing them and ruining them. The lesson is that if you care about something, you need to take care of it. This is the theme, or point, of the story. Some stories have more than one theme, but this is not really true of this excerpt. The reader needs to figure out the theme based on what happens in the story. Sometimes, as in the case of fables, the theme is stated directly in the text. However, this is not usually the case.

Review Video: Themes in Literature
Visit mometrix.com/academy and enter code: 732074

CHARACTER DEVELOPMENT AND DIALOGUE
CHARACTER DEVELOPMENT

When depicting characters or figures in a written text, authors generally use actions, dialogue, and descriptions as characterization techniques. Characterization can occur in both fiction and nonfiction and is used to show a character or figure's personality, demeanor, and thoughts. This helps create a more engaging experience for the reader by providing a more concrete picture of a

character or figure's tendencies and features. Characterizations also gives authors the opportunity to integrate elements such as dialects, activities, attire, and attitudes into their writing.

To understand the meaning of a story, it is vital to understand the characters as the author describes them. We can look for contradictions in what a character thinks, says, and does. We can notice whether the author's observations about a character differ from what other characters in the story say about that character. A character may be dynamic, meaning they change significantly during the story, or static, meaning they remain the same from beginning to end. Characters may be two-dimensional, not fully developed, or may be well developed with characteristics that stand out vividly. Characters may also symbolize universal properties. Additionally, readers can compare and contrast characters to analyze how each one developed.

A well-known example of character development can be found in Charles Dickens's *Great Expectations*. The novel's main character, Pip, is introduced as a young boy, and he is depicted as innocent, kind, and humble. However, as Pip grows up and is confronted with the social hierarchy of Victorian England, he becomes arrogant and rejects his loved ones in pursuit of his own social advancement. Once he achieves his social goals, he realizes the merits of his former lifestyle, and lives with the wisdom he gained in both environments and life stages. Dickens shows Pip's ever-changing character through his interactions with others and his inner thoughts, which evolve as his personal values and personality shift.

> **Review Video: Character Changes**
> Visit mometrix.com/academy and enter code: 408719

DIALOGUE

Effectively written dialogue serves at least one, but usually several, purposes. It advances the story and moves the plot, develops the characters, sheds light on the work's theme or meaning, and can, often subtly, account for the passage of time not otherwise indicated. It can alter the direction that the plot is taking, typically by introducing some new conflict or changing existing ones. **Dialogue** can establish a work's narrative voice and the characters' voices and set the tone of the story or of particular characters. When fictional characters display enlightenment or realization, dialogue can give readers an understanding of what those characters have discovered and how. Dialogue can illuminate the motivations and wishes of the story's characters. By using consistent thoughts and syntax, dialogue can support character development. Skillfully created, it can also represent real-life speech rhythms in written form. Via conflicts and ensuing action, dialogue also provides drama.

DIALOGUE IN FICTION

In fictional works, effectively written dialogue does more than just break up or interrupt sections of narrative. While **dialogue** may supply exposition for readers, it must nonetheless be believable. Dialogue should be dynamic, not static, and it should not resemble regular prose. Authors should not use dialogue to write clever similes or metaphors, or to inject their own opinions. Nor should they use dialogue at all when narrative would be better. Most importantly, dialogue should not slow the plot movement. Dialogue must seem natural, which means careful construction of phrases rather than actually duplicating natural speech, which does not necessarily translate well to the written word. Finally, all dialogue must be pertinent to the story, rather than just added conversation.

Reading

Craft and Comprehension

MAIN IDEAS AND SUPPORTING DETAILS
IDENTIFYING TOPICS AND MAIN IDEAS

One of the most important skills in reading comprehension is the identification of **topics** and **main ideas**. There is a subtle difference between these two features. The topic is the subject of a text (i.e., what the text is all about). The main idea, on the other hand, is the most important point being made by the author. The topic is usually expressed in a few words at the most while the main idea often needs a full sentence to be completely defined. As an example, a short passage might be written on the topic of penguins, and the main idea could be written as *Penguins are different from other birds in many ways*. In most nonfiction writing, the topic and the main idea will be **stated directly** and often appear in a sentence at the very beginning or end of the text. When being tested on an understanding of the author's topic, you may be able to skim the passage for the general idea by reading only the first sentence of each paragraph. A body paragraph's first sentence is often—but not always—the main **topic sentence** which gives you a summary of the content in the paragraph.

However, there are cases in which the reader must figure out an **unstated** topic or main idea. In these instances, you must read every sentence of the text and try to come up with an overarching idea that is supported by each of those sentences.

Note: The main idea should not be confused with the thesis statement. While the main idea gives a brief, general summary of a text, the thesis statement provides a **specific perspective** on an issue that the author supports with evidence.

> **Review Video: Topics and Main Ideas**
> Visit mometrix.com/academy and enter code: 407801

SUPPORTING DETAILS

Supporting details are smaller pieces of evidence that provide backing for the main point. In order to show that a main idea is correct or valid, an author must add details that prove their point. All texts contain details, but they are only classified as supporting details when they serve to reinforce some larger point. Supporting details are most commonly found in informative and persuasive texts. In some cases, they will be clearly indicated with terms like *for example* or *for instance*, or they will be enumerated with terms like *first*, *second*, and *last*. However, you need to be prepared for texts that do not contain those indicators. As a reader, you should consider whether the author's supporting details really back up his or her main point. Details can be factual and correct, yet they may not be **relevant** to the author's point. Conversely, details can be relevant, but be ineffective because they are based on opinion or assertions that cannot be proven.

> **Review Video: Supporting Details**
> Visit mometrix.com/academy and enter code: 396297

AUTHOR'S PURPOSE
AUTHOR'S PURPOSE

Usually, identifying the author's **purpose** is easier than identifying his or her **position**. In most cases, the author has no interest in hiding his or her purpose. A text that is meant to entertain, for instance, should be written to please the reader. Most narratives, or stories, are written to entertain, though they may also inform or persuade. Informative texts are easy to identify, while the most difficult purpose of a text to identify is persuasion because the author has an interest in

72

making this purpose hard to detect. When a reader discovers that the author is trying to persuade, he or she should be skeptical of the argument. For this reason, persuasive texts often try to establish an entertaining tone and hope to amuse the reader into agreement. On the other hand, an informative tone may be implemented to create an appearance of authority and objectivity.

An author's purpose is evident often in the **organization** of the text (e.g., section headings in bold font points to an informative text). However, you may not have such organization available to you in your exam. Instead, if the author makes his or her main idea clear from the beginning, then the likely purpose of the text is to **inform**. If the author begins by making a claim and provides various arguments to support that claim, then the purpose is probably to **persuade**. If the author tells a story or wants to gain the reader's attention more than to push a particular point or deliver information, then his or her purpose is most likely to **entertain**. As a reader, you must judge authors on how well they accomplish their purpose. In other words, you need to consider the type of passage (e.g., technical, persuasive, etc.) that the author has written and if the author has followed the requirements of the passage type.

> **Review Video: Understanding the Author's Intent**
> Visit mometrix.com/academy and enter code: 511819

INFORMATIONAL TEXTS

An **informational text** is written to educate and enlighten readers. Informational texts are almost always nonfiction and are rarely structured as a story. The intention of an informational text is to deliver information in the most comprehensible way. So, look for the structure of the text to be very clear. In an informational text, the thesis statement is one or two sentences that normally appears at the end of the first paragraph. The author may use some colorful language, but he or she is likely to put more emphasis on clarity and precision. Informational essays do not typically appeal to the emotions. They often contain facts and figures and rarely include the opinion of the author; however, readers should remain aware of the possibility for bias as those facts are presented. Sometimes a persuasive essay can resemble an informative essay, especially if the author maintains an even tone and presents his or her views as if they were established fact.

> **Review Video: Informational Text**
> Visit mometrix.com/academy and enter code: 924964

PERSUASIVE WRITING

In a persuasive essay, the author is attempting to change the reader's mind or **convince** him or her of something that he or she did not believe previously. There are several identifying characteristics of **persuasive writing**. One is **opinion presented as fact**. When authors attempt to persuade readers, they often present their opinions as if they were fact. Readers must be on guard for statements that sound factual but which cannot be subjected to research, observation, or experiment. Another characteristic of persuasive writing is **emotional language**. An author will often try to play on the emotions of readers by appealing to their sympathy or sense of morality. When an author uses colorful or evocative language with the intent of arousing the reader's passions, then the author may be attempting to persuade. Finally, in many cases, a persuasive text will give an **unfair explanation of opposing positions**, if these positions are mentioned at all.

ENTERTAINING TEXTS

The success or failure of an author's intent to **entertain** is determined by those who read the author's work. Entertaining texts may be either fiction or nonfiction, and they may describe real or imagined people, places, and events. Entertaining texts are often narratives or poems. A text that is

written to entertain is likely to contain **colorful language** that engages the imagination and the emotions. Such writing often features a great deal of figurative language, which typically enlivens the subject matter with images and analogies.

Though an entertaining text is not usually written to persuade or inform, authors may accomplish both of these tasks in their work. An entertaining text may *appeal to the reader's emotions* and cause him or her to think differently about a particular subject. In any case, entertaining texts tend to showcase the personality of the author more than other types of writing.

DESCRIPTIVE TEXT

In a sense, almost all writing is descriptive, insofar as an author seeks to describe events, ideas, or people to the reader. Some texts, however, are primarily concerned with **description**. A descriptive text focuses on a particular subject and attempts to depict the subject in a way that will be clear to readers. Descriptive texts contain many adjectives and adverbs (i.e., words that give shades of meaning and create a more detailed mental picture for the reader). A descriptive text fails when it is unclear to the reader. A descriptive text will certainly be informative and may be persuasive and entertaining as well.

> **Review Video: Descriptive Texts**
> Visit mometrix.com/academy and enter code: 174903

EXPRESSION OF FEELINGS

When an author intends to **express feelings**, he or she may use **expressive and bold language**. An author may write with emotion for any number of reasons. Sometimes, authors will express feelings because they are describing a personal situation of great pain or happiness. In other situations, authors will attempt to persuade the reader and will use emotion to stir up the passions. This kind of expression is easy to identify when the writer uses phrases like *I felt* and *I sense*. However, readers may find that the author will simply describe feelings without introducing them. As a reader, you must know the importance of recognizing when an author is expressing emotion and not to become overwhelmed by sympathy or passion. Readers should maintain some **detachment** so that they can still evaluate the strength of the author's argument or the quality of the writing.

> **Review Video: Emotional Language in Literature**
> Visit mometrix.com/academy and enter code: 759390

EXPOSITORY PASSAGE

An **expository** passage aims to **inform** and enlighten readers. Expository passages are nonfiction and usually center around a simple, easily defined topic. Since the goal of exposition is to teach, such a passage should be as clear as possible. Often, an expository passage contains helpful organizing words, like *first, next, for example*, and *therefore*. These words keep the reader **oriented** in the text. Although expository passages do not need to feature colorful language and artful writing, they are often more effective with these features. For a reader, the challenge of expository passages is to maintain steady attention. Expository passages are not always about subjects that will naturally interest a reader, so the writer is often more concerned with **clarity** and **comprehensibility** than with engaging the reader. By reading actively, you can ensure a good habit of focus when reading an expository passage.

> **Review Video: Expository Passages**
> Visit mometrix.com/academy and enter code: 256515

74

NARRATIVE PASSAGE

A **narrative** passage is a story that can be fiction or nonfiction. However, there are a few elements that a text must have in order to be classified as a narrative. First, the text must have a **plot** (i.e., a series of events). Narratives often proceed in a clear sequence, but this is not a requirement. If the narrative is good, then these events will be interesting to readers. Second, a narrative has **characters**. These characters could be people, animals, or even inanimate objects—so long as they participate in the plot. Third, a narrative passage often contains **figurative language** which is meant to stimulate the imagination of readers by making comparisons and observations. For instance, a *metaphor*, a common piece of figurative language, is a description of one thing in terms of another. *The moon was a frosty snowball* is an example of a metaphor. In the literal sense this is obviously untrue, but the comparison suggests a certain mood for the reader.

TECHNICAL PASSAGE

A **technical** passage is written to *describe* a complex object or process. Technical writing is common in medical and technological fields, in which complex ideas of mathematics, science, and engineering need to be explained *simply* and *clearly*. To ease comprehension, a technical passage usually proceeds in a very logical order. Technical passages often have clear headings and subheadings, which are used to keep the reader oriented in the text. Additionally, you will find that these passages divide sections up with numbers or letters. Many technical passages look more like an outline than a piece of prose. The amount of **jargon** or difficult vocabulary will vary in a technical passage depending on the intended audience. As much as possible, technical passages try to avoid language that the reader will have to research in order to understand the message, yet readers will find that jargon cannot always be avoided.

> **Review Video: Technical Passages**
> Visit mometrix.com/academy and enter code: 478923

COMMON ORGANIZATIONS OF TEXTS

ORGANIZATION OF THE TEXT

The way a text is organized can help readers understand the author's intent and his or her conclusions. There are various ways to organize a text, and each one has a purpose and use. Usually, authors will organize information logically in a passage so the reader can follow and locate the information within the text. However, since not all passages are written with the same logical structure, you need to be familiar with several different types of passage structure.

> **Review Video: Organizational Methods to Structure Text**
> Visit mometrix.com/academy and enter code: 606263
>
> **Review Video: Sequence of Events in a Story**
> Visit mometrix.com/academy and enter code: 807512

CHRONOLOGICAL

When using **chronological** order, the author presents information in the order that it happened. For example, biographies are typically written in chronological order. The subject's birth and childhood are presented first, followed by their adult life, and lastly the events leading up to the person's death.

CAUSE AND EFFECT

One of the most common text structures is **cause and effect**. A **cause** is an act or event that makes something happen, and an **effect** is the thing that happens as a result of the cause. A cause-and-

75

effect relationship is not always explicit, but there are some terms in English that signal causes, such as *since, because,* and *due to.* Furthermore, terms that signal effects include *consequently, therefore, this leads to.* As an example, consider the sentence *Because the sky was clear, Ron did not bring an umbrella.* The cause is the clear sky, and the effect is that Ron did not bring an umbrella. However, readers may find that sometimes the cause-and-effect relationship will not be clearly noted. For instance, the sentence *He was late and missed the meeting* does not contain any signaling words, but the sentence still contains a cause (he was late) and an effect (he missed the meeting).

> **Review Video: Cause and Effect**
> Visit mometrix.com/academy and enter code: 868099
>
> **Review Video: Rhetorical Strategy of Cause and Effect Analysis**
> Visit mometrix.com/academy and enter code: 725944

MULTIPLE EFFECTS

Be aware of the possibility for a single cause to have **multiple effects.** (e.g., *Single cause*: Because you left your homework on the table, your dog engulfed the assignment. *Multiple effects*: As a result, you receive a failing grade, your parents do not allow you to go out with your friends, you miss out on the new movie, and one of your classmates spoils it for you before you have another chance to watch it).

MULTIPLE CAUSES

Also, there is the possibility for a single effect to have **multiple causes.** (e.g., *Single effect*: Alan has a fever. *Multiple causes*: An unexpected cold front came through the area, and Alan forgot to take his multi-vitamin to avoid getting sick.) Additionally, an effect can in turn be the cause of another effect, in what is known as a cause-and-effect chain. (e.g., As a result of her disdain for procrastination, Lynn prepared for her exam. This led to her passing her test with high marks. Hence, her resume was accepted and her application was approved.)

CAUSE AND EFFECT IN PERSUASIVE ESSAYS

Persuasive essays, in which an author tries to make a convincing argument and change the minds of readers, usually include cause-and-effect relationships. However, these relationships should not always be taken at face value. Frequently, an author will assume a cause or take an effect for granted. To read a persuasive essay effectively, readers need to judge the cause-and-effect relationships that the author is presenting. For instance, imagine an author wrote the following: *The parking deck has been unprofitable because people would prefer to ride their bikes.* The relationship is clear: the cause is that people prefer to ride their bikes, and the effect is that the parking deck has been unprofitable. However, readers should consider whether this argument is conclusive. Perhaps there are other reasons for the failure of the parking deck: a down economy, excessive fees, etc. Too often, authors present causal relationships as if they are fact rather than opinion. Readers should be on the alert for these dubious claims.

PROBLEM-SOLUTION

Some nonfiction texts are organized to **present a problem** followed by a solution. For this type of text, the problem is often explained before the solution is offered. In some cases, as when the problem is well known, the solution may be introduced briefly at the beginning. Other passages may focus on the solution, and the problem will be referenced only occasionally. Some texts will outline multiple solutions to a problem, leaving readers to choose among them. If the author has an interest or an allegiance to one solution, he or she may fail to mention or describe accurately some of the other solutions. Readers should be careful of the author's agenda when reading a problem-

solution text. Only by understanding the author's perspective and interests can one develop a proper judgment of the proposed solution.

COMPARE AND CONTRAST

Many texts follow the **compare-and-contrast** model in which the similarities and differences between two ideas or things are explored. Analysis of the similarities between ideas is called **comparison**. In an ideal comparison, the author places ideas or things in an equivalent structure, i.e., the author presents the ideas in the same way. If an author wants to show the similarities between cricket and baseball, then he or she may do so by summarizing the equipment and rules for each game. Be mindful of the similarities as they appear in the passage and take note of any differences that are mentioned. Often, these small differences will only reinforce the more general similarity.

> **Review Video: Compare and Contrast**
> Visit mometrix.com/academy and enter code: 798319

Thinking critically about ideas and conclusions can seem like a daunting task. One way to ease this task is to understand the basic elements of ideas and writing techniques. Looking at the ways different ideas relate to each other can be a good way for readers to begin their analysis. For instance, sometimes authors will write about two ideas that are in opposition to each other. Or, one author will provide his or her ideas on a topic, and another author may respond in opposition. The analysis of these opposing ideas is known as **contrast**. Contrast is often marred by the author's obvious partiality to one of the ideas. A discerning reader will be put off by an author who does not engage in a fair fight. In an analysis of opposing ideas, both ideas should be presented in clear and reasonable terms. If the author does prefer a side, you need to read carefully to determine the areas where the author shows or avoids this preference. In an analysis of opposing ideas, you should proceed through the passage by marking the major differences point by point with an eye that is looking for an explanation of each side's view. For instance, in an analysis of capitalism and communism, there is an importance in outlining each side's view on labor, markets, prices, personal responsibility, etc. Additionally, as you read through the passages, you should note whether the opposing views present each side in a similar manner.

SEQUENCE

Readers must be able to identify a text's **sequence**, or the order in which things happen. Often, when the sequence is very important to the author, the text is indicated with signal words like *first*, *then*, *next*, and *last*. However, a sequence can be merely implied and must be noted by the reader. Consider the sentence *He walked through the garden and gave water and fertilizer to the plants*. Clearly, the man did not walk through the garden before he collected water and fertilizer for the plants. So, the implied sequence is that he first collected water, then he collected fertilizer, next he walked through the garden, and last he gave water or fertilizer as necessary to the plants. Texts do not always proceed in an orderly sequence from first to last. Sometimes they begin at the end and start over at the beginning. As a reader, you can enhance your understanding of the passage by taking brief notes to clarify the sequence.

> **Review Video: Sequence**
> Visit mometrix.com/academy and enter code: 489027

MAKING AND EVALUATING PREDICTIONS

MAKING PREDICTIONS

When we read literature, **making predictions** about what will happen in the writing reinforces our purpose for reading and prepares us mentally. A **prediction** is a guess about what will happen next. Readers constantly make predictions based on what they have read and what they already know. We can make predictions before we begin reading and during our reading. Consider the following sentence: *Staring at the computer screen in shock, Kim blindly reached over for the brimming glass of water on the shelf to her side.* The sentence suggests that Kim is distracted, and that she is not looking at the glass that she is going to pick up. So, a reader might predict that Kim is going to knock over the glass. Of course, not every prediction will be accurate: perhaps Kim will pick the glass up cleanly. Nevertheless, the author has certainly created the expectation that the water might be spilled.

As we read on, we can test the accuracy of our predictions, revise them in light of additional reading, and confirm or refute our predictions. Predictions are always subject to revision as the reader acquires more information. A reader can make predictions by observing the title and illustrations; noting the structure, characters, and subject; drawing on existing knowledge relative to the subject; and asking "why" and "who" questions. Connecting reading to what we already know enables us to learn new information and construct meaning. For example, before third-graders read a book about Johnny Appleseed, they may start a KWL chart—a list of what they *Know*, what they *Want* to know or learn, and what they have *Learned* after reading. Activating existing background knowledge and thinking about the text before reading improves comprehension.

> **Review Video: <u>Predictive Reading</u>**
> Visit mometrix.com/academy and enter code: 437248

Test-taking tip: To respond to questions requiring future predictions, your answers should be based on evidence of past or present behavior and events.

EVALUATING PREDICTIONS

When making predictions, readers should be able to explain how they developed their prediction. One way readers can defend their thought process is by citing textual evidence. Textual evidence to evaluate reader predictions about literature includes specific synopses of the work, paraphrases of the work or parts of it, and direct quotations from the work. These references to the text must support the prediction by indicating, clearly or unclearly, what will happen later in the story. A text may provide these indications through literary devices such as foreshadowing. Foreshadowing is anything in a text that gives the reader a hint about what is to come by emphasizing the likelihood of an event or development. Foreshadowing can occur through descriptions, exposition, and dialogue. Foreshadowing in dialogue usually occurs when a character gives a warning or expresses a strong feeling that a certain event will occur. Foreshadowing can also occur through irony. However, unlike other forms of foreshadowing, the events that seem the most likely are the opposite of what actually happens. Instances of foreshadowing and irony can be summarized, paraphrased, or quoted to defend a reader's prediction.

> **Review Video: <u>Textual Evidence for Predictions</u>**
> Visit mometrix.com/academy and enter code: 261070

MAKING INFERENCES AND DRAWING CONCLUSIONS

Inferences are logical conclusions that readers make based on their observations and previous knowledge. An inference is based on both what is found in a passage or a story and what is known

78

from personal experience. For instance, a story may say that a character is frightened and can hear howling in the distance. Based on both what is in the text and personal knowledge, it is a logical conclusion that the character is frightened because he hears the sound of wolves. A good inference is supported by the information in a passage.

IMPLICIT AND EXPLICIT INFORMATION

By inferring, readers construct meanings from text that are personally relevant. By combining their own schemas or concepts and their background information pertinent to the text with what they read, readers interpret it according to both what the author has conveyed and their own unique perspectives. Inferences are different from **explicit information**, which is clearly stated in a passage. Authors do not always explicitly spell out every meaning in what they write; many meanings are implicit. Through inference, readers can comprehend implied meanings in the text, and also derive personal significance from it, making the text meaningful and memorable to them. Inference is a natural process in everyday life. When readers infer, they can draw conclusions about what the author is saying, predict what may reasonably follow, amend these predictions as they continue to read, interpret the import of themes, and analyze the characters' feelings and motivations through their actions.

EXAMPLE OF DRAWING CONCLUSIONS FROM INFERENCES

Read the excerpt and decide why Jana finally relaxed.

> Jana loved her job, but the work was very demanding. She had trouble relaxing. She called a friend, but she still thought about work. She ordered a pizza, but eating it did not help. Then, her kitten jumped on her lap and began to purr. Jana leaned back and began to hum a little tune. She felt better.

You can draw the conclusion that Jana relaxed because her kitten jumped on her lap. The kitten purred, and Jana leaned back and hummed a tune. Then she felt better. The excerpt does not explicitly say that this is the reason why she was able to relax. The text leaves the matter unclear, but the reader can infer or make a "best guess" that this is the reason she is relaxing. This is a logical conclusion based on the information in the passage. It is the best conclusion a reader can make based on the information he or she has read. Inferences are based on the information in a passage, but they are not directly stated in the passage.

Test-taking tip: While being tested on your ability to make correct inferences, you must look for **contextual clues**. An answer can be true, but not the best or most correct answer. The contextual clues will help you find the answer that is the **best answer** out of the given choices. Be careful in your reading to understand the context in which a phrase is stated. When asked for the implied meaning of a statement made in the passage, you should immediately locate the statement and read the **context** in which the statement was made. Also, look for an answer choice that has a similar phrase to the statement in question.

> **Review Video: <u>Inference</u>**
> Visit mometrix.com/academy and enter code: 379203
>
> **Review Video: <u>How to Support a Conclusion</u>**
> Visit mometrix.com/academy and enter code: 281653

CRITICAL READING SKILLS
OPINIONS, FACTS, AND FALLACIES

Critical thinking skills are mastered through understanding various types of writing and the different purposes authors can have for writing different passages. Every author writes for a purpose. When you understand their purpose and how they accomplish their goal, you will be able to analyze their writing and determine whether or not you agree with their conclusions.

Readers must always be aware of the difference between fact and opinion. A **fact** can be subjected to analysis and proven to be true. An **opinion**, on the other hand, is the author's personal thoughts or feelings and may not be altered by research or evidence. If the author writes that the distance from New York City to Boston is about two hundred miles, then he or she is stating a fact. If the author writes that New York City is too crowded, then he or she is giving an opinion because there is no objective standard for overpopulation. Opinions are often supported by facts. For instance, an author might use a comparison between the population density of New York City and that of other major American cities as evidence of an overcrowded population. An opinion supported by facts tends to be more convincing. On the other hand, when authors support their opinions with other opinions, readers should employ critical thinking and approach the argument with skepticism.

> **Review Video: Distinguishing Fact and Opinion**
> Visit mometrix.com/academy and enter code: 870899

RELIABLE SOURCES

When you read an argumentative passage, you need to be sure that facts are presented to the reader from **reliable sources**. An opinion is what the author thinks about a given topic. An opinion is not common knowledge or proven by expert sources, instead the information is the personal beliefs and thoughts of the author. To distinguish between fact and opinion, a reader needs to consider the type of source that is presenting information, the information that backs-up a claim, and the author's motivation to have a certain point-of-view on a given topic. For example, if a panel of scientists has conducted multiple studies on the effectiveness of taking a certain vitamin, then the results are more likely to be factual than those of a company that is selling a vitamin and simply claims that taking the vitamin can produce positive effects. The company is motivated to sell their product, and the scientists are using the scientific method to prove a theory. Remember, if you find sentences that contain phrases such as "I think…", then the statement is an opinion.

BIASES

In their attempts to persuade, writers often make mistakes in their thought processes and writing choices. These processes and choices are important to understand so you can make an informed decision about the author's credibility. Every author has a point of view, but authors demonstrate a **bias** when they ignore reasonable counterarguments or distort opposing viewpoints. A bias is evident whenever the author's claims are presented in a way that is unfair or inaccurate. Bias can be intentional or unintentional, but readers should be skeptical of the author's argument in either case. Remember that a biased author may still be correct. However, the author will be correct in spite of, not because of, his or her bias.

A **stereotype** is a bias applied specifically to a group of people or a place. Stereotyping is considered to be particularly abhorrent because it promotes negative, misleading generalizations

about people. Readers should be very cautious of authors who use stereotypes in their writing. These faulty assumptions typically reveal the author's ignorance and lack of curiosity.

Review Video: Bias and Stereotype
Visit mometrix.com/academy and enter code: 644829

PERSUASION AND RHETORIC
PERSUASIVE TECHNIQUES

To **appeal using reason**, writers present logical arguments, such as using "If... then... because" statements. To **appeal to emotions**, authors may ask readers how they would feel about something or to put themselves in another's place, present their argument as one that will make the audience feel good, or tell readers how they should feel. To **appeal to character**, **morality**, or **ethics**, authors present their points to readers as the right or most moral choices. Authors cite expert opinions to show readers that someone very knowledgeable about the subject or viewpoint agrees with the author's claims. **Testimonials**, usually via anecdotes or quotations regarding the author's subject, help build the audience's trust in an author's message through positive support from ordinary people. **Bandwagon appeals** claim that everybody else agrees with the author's argument and persuade readers to conform and agree, also. Authors **appeal to greed** by presenting their choice as cheaper, free, or more valuable for less cost. They **appeal to laziness** by presenting their views as more convenient, easy, or relaxing. Authors also anticipate potential objections and argue against them before audiences think of them, thereby depicting those objections as weak.

Authors can use **comparisons** like analogies, similes, and metaphors to persuade audiences. For example, a writer might represent excessive expenses as "hemorrhaging" money, which the author's recommended solution will stop. Authors can use negative word connotations to make some choices unappealing to readers, and positive word connotations to make others more appealing. Using **humor** can relax readers and garner their agreement. However, writers must take care: ridiculing opponents can be a successful strategy for appealing to readers who already agree with the author, but can backfire by angering other readers. **Rhetorical questions** need no answer, but create effect that can force agreement, such as asking the question, "Wouldn't you rather be paid more than less?" **Generalizations** persuade readers by being impossible to disagree with. Writers can easily make generalizations that appear to support their viewpoints, like saying, "We all want peace, not war" regarding more specific political arguments. **Transfer** and **association** persuade by example: if advertisements show attractive actors enjoying their products, audiences imagine they will experience the same. **Repetition** can also sometimes effectively persuade audiences.

Review Video: Using Rhetorical Strategies for Persuasion
Visit mometrix.com/academy and enter code: 302658

CLASSICAL AUTHOR APPEALS

In his *On Rhetoric,* ancient Greek philosopher Aristotle defined three basic types of appeal used in writing, which he called *pathos, ethos,* and *logos. **Pathos*** means suffering or experience and refers to appeals to the emotions (the English word *pathetic* comes from this root). Writing that is meant to entertain audiences, by making them either happy, as with comedy, or sad, as with tragedy, uses *pathos.* Aristotle's *Poetics* states that evoking the emotions of terror and pity is one of the criteria for writing tragedy. ***Ethos*** means character and connotes ideology (the English word *ethics* comes from this root). Writing that appeals to credibility, based on academic, professional, or personal merit, uses *ethos.* ***Logos*** means "I say" and refers to a plea, opinion, expectation, word or speech, account, opinion, or reason (the English word *logic* comes from this root.) Aristotle used it to mean persuasion that appeals to the audience through reasoning and logic to influence their opinions.

RHETORICAL DEVICES

- An **anecdote** is a brief story authors may relate to their argument, which can illustrate their points in a more real and relatable way.
- **Aphorisms** concisely state common beliefs and may rhyme. For example, Benjamin Franklin's "Early to bed and early to rise / Makes a man healthy, wealthy, and wise" is an aphorism.
- **Allusions** refer to literary or historical figures to impart symbolism to a thing or person and to create reader resonance. In John Steinbeck's *Of Mice and Men,* protagonist George's last name is Milton. This alludes to John Milton, who wrote *Paradise Lost,* and symbolizes George's eventual loss of his dream.
- **Satire** exaggerates, ridicules, or pokes fun at human flaws or ideas, as in the works of Jonathan Swift and Mark Twain.
- A **parody** is a form of satire that imitates another work to ridicule its topic or style.
- A **paradox** is a statement that is true despite appearing contradictory.
- **Hyperbole** is overstatement using exaggerated language.
- An **oxymoron** combines seeming contradictions, such as "deafening silence."
- **Analogies** compare two things that share common elements.
- **Similes** (stated comparisons using the words *like* or *as*) and **metaphors** (stated comparisons that do not use *like* or *as*) are considered forms of analogy.
- When using logic to reason with audiences, **syllogism** refers either to deductive reasoning or a deceptive, very sophisticated, or subtle argument.
- **Deductive reasoning** moves from general to specific, **inductive reasoning** from specific to general.
- **Diction** is author word choice that establishes tone and effect.
- **Understatement** achieves effects like contrast or irony by downplaying or describing something more subtly than warranted.
- **Chiasmus** uses parallel clauses, the second reversing the order of the first. Examples include T. S. Eliot's "Has the Church failed mankind, or has mankind failed the Church?" and John F. Kennedy's "Ask not what your country can do for you; ask what you can do for your country."
- **Anaphora** regularly repeats a word or phrase at the beginnings of consecutive clauses or phrases to add emphasis to an idea. A classic example of anaphora was Winston Churchill's emphasis of determination: "[W]e shall fight on the beaches, we shall fight on the landing grounds, we shall fight in the fields and in the streets, we shall fight in the hills; we shall never surrender..."

READING COMPREHENSION AND CONNECTING WITH TEXTS

COMPARING TWO STORIES

When presented with two different stories, there will be **similarities** and **differences** between the two. A reader needs to make a list, or other graphic organizer, of the points presented in each story. Once the reader has written down the main point and supporting points for each story, the two sets of ideas can be compared. The reader can then present each idea and show how it is the same or different in the other story. This is called **comparing and contrasting ideas**.

The reader can compare ideas by stating, for example: "In Story 1, the author believes that humankind will one day land on Mars, whereas in Story 2, the author believes that Mars is too far away for humans to ever step foot on." Note that the two viewpoints are different in each story that the reader is comparing. A reader may state that: "Both stories discussed the likelihood of humankind landing on Mars." This statement shows how the viewpoint presented in both stories is based on the same topic, rather than how each viewpoint is different. The reader will complete a comparison of two stories with a conclusion.

> **Review Video: How to Compare and Contrast**
> Visit mometrix.com/academy and enter code: 833765

OUTLINING A PASSAGE

As an aid to drawing conclusions, **outlining** the information contained in the passage should be a familiar skill to readers. An effective outline will reveal the structure of the passage and will lead to solid conclusions. An effective outline will have a title that refers to the basic subject of the text, though the title does not need to restate the main idea. In most outlines, the main idea will be the first major section. Each major idea in the passage will be established as the head of a category. For instance, the most common outline format calls for the main ideas of the passage to be indicated with Roman numerals. In an effective outline of this kind, each of the main ideas will be represented by a Roman numeral and none of the Roman numerals will designate minor details or secondary ideas. Moreover, all supporting ideas and details should be placed in the appropriate place on the outline. An outline does not need to include every detail listed in the text, but it should feature all of those that are central to the argument or message. Each of these details should be listed under the corresponding main idea.

> **Review Video: Outlining as an Aid to Drawing Conclusions**
> Visit mometrix.com/academy and enter code: 584445

USING GRAPHIC ORGANIZERS

Ideas from a text can also be organized using **graphic organizers**. A graphic organizer is a way to simplify information and take key points from the text. A graphic organizer such as a timeline may have an event listed for a corresponding date on the timeline, while an outline may have an event listed under a key point that occurs in the text. Each reader needs to create the type of graphic organizer that works the best for him or her in terms of being able to recall information from a story. Examples include a spider-map, which takes a main idea from the story and places it in a bubble with supporting points branching off the main idea. An outline is useful for diagramming the main and supporting points of the entire story, and a Venn diagram compares and contrasts characteristics of two or more ideas.

> **Review Video: Graphic Organizers**
> Visit mometrix.com/academy and enter code: 665513

83

MAKING LOGICAL CONCLUSIONS ABOUT A PASSAGE

A reader should always be drawing conclusions from the text. Sometimes conclusions are **implied** from written information, and other times the information is **stated directly** within the passage. One should always aim to draw conclusions from information stated within a passage, rather than to draw them from mere implications. At times an author may provide some information and then describe a counterargument. Readers should be alert for direct statements that are subsequently rejected or weakened by the author. Furthermore, you should always read through the entire passage before drawing conclusions. Many readers are trained to expect the author's conclusions at either the beginning or the end of the passage, but many texts do not adhere to this format.

Drawing conclusions from information implied within a passage requires confidence on the part of the reader. **Implications** are things that the author does not state directly, but readers can assume based on what the author does say. Consider the following passage: *I stepped outside and opened my umbrella. By the time I got to work, the cuffs of my pants were soaked.* The author never states that it is raining, but this fact is clearly implied. Conclusions based on implication must be well supported by the text. In order to draw a solid conclusion, readers should have **multiple pieces of evidence**. If readers have only one piece, they must be assured that there is no other possible explanation than their conclusion. A good reader will be able to draw many conclusions from information implied by the text, which will be a great help on the exam.

DRAWING CONCLUSIONS

A common type of inference that a reader has to make is **drawing a conclusion**. The reader makes this conclusion based on the information provided within a text. Certain facts are included to help a reader come to a specific conclusion. For example, a story may open with a man trudging through the snow on a cold winter day, dragging a sled behind him. The reader can logically **infer** from the setting of the story that the man is wearing heavy winter clothes in order to stay warm. Information is implied based on the setting of a story, which is why **setting** is an important element of the text. If the same man in the example was trudging down a beach on a hot summer day, dragging a surf board behind him, the reader would assume that the man is not wearing heavy clothes. The reader makes inferences based on their own experiences and the information presented to them in the story.

Test-taking tip: When asked to identify a conclusion that may be drawn, look for critical "hedge" phrases, such as *likely, may, can,* and *will often,* among many others. When you are being tested on this knowledge, remember the question that writers insert into these hedge phrases to cover every possibility. Often an answer will be wrong simply because there is no room for exception. Extreme positive or negative answers (such as always or never) are usually not correct. When answering these questions, the reader **should not** use any outside knowledge that is not gathered directly or reasonably inferred from the passage. Correct answers can be derived straight from the passage.

EXAMPLE

Read the following sentence from *Little Women* by Louisa May Alcott and draw a conclusion based upon the information presented:

> *You know the reason Mother proposed not having any presents this Christmas was because it is going to be a hard winter for everyone; and she thinks we ought not to spend money for pleasure, when our men are suffering so in the army.*

Based on the information in the sentence, the reader can conclude, or **infer**, that the men are away at war while the women are still at home. The pronoun *our* gives a clue to the reader that the character is speaking about men she knows. In addition, the reader can assume that the character is

speaking to a brother or sister, since the term "Mother" is used by the character while speaking to another person. The reader can also come to the conclusion that the characters celebrate Christmas, since it is mentioned in the **context** of the sentence. In the sentence, the mother is presented as an unselfish character who is opinionated and thinks about the wellbeing of other people.

SUMMARIZING

A helpful tool is the ability to **summarize** the information that you have read in a paragraph or passage format. This process is similar to creating an effective outline. First, a summary should accurately define the main idea of the passage, though the summary does not need to explain this main idea in exhaustive detail. The summary should continue by laying out the most important supporting details or arguments from the passage. All of the significant supporting details should be included, and none of the details included should be irrelevant or insignificant. Also, the summary should accurately report all of these details. Too often, the desire for brevity in a summary leads to the sacrifice of clarity or accuracy. Summaries are often difficult to read because they omit all of the graceful language, digressions, and asides that distinguish great writing. However, an effective summary should communicate the same overall message as the original text.

> **Review Video: Summarizing Text**
> Visit mometrix.com/academy and enter code: 172903

PARAPHRASING

Paraphrasing is another method that the reader can use to aid in comprehension. When paraphrasing, one puts what they have read into their own words by rephrasing what the author has written, or one "translates" all of what the author shared into their own words by including as many details as they can.

EVALUATING A PASSAGE

It is important to understand the logical conclusion of the ideas presented in an informational text. **Identifying a logical conclusion** can help you determine whether you agree with the writer or not. Coming to this conclusion is much like making an inference: the approach requires you to combine the information given by the text with what you already know and make a logical conclusion. If the author intended for the reader to draw a certain conclusion, then you can expect the author's argumentation and detail to be leading in that direction.

One way to approach the task of drawing conclusions is to make brief **notes** of all the points made by the author. When the notes are arranged on paper, they may clarify the logical conclusion. Another way to approach conclusions is to consider whether the reasoning of the author raises any pertinent questions. Sometimes you will be able to draw several conclusions from a passage. On occasion these will be conclusions that were never imagined by the author. Therefore, be aware that these conclusions must be **supported directly by the text**.

EVALUATION OF SUMMARIES

A summary of a literary passage is a condensation in the reader's own words of the passage's main points. Several guidelines can be used in evaluating a summary. The summary should be complete yet concise. It should be accurate, balanced, fair, neutral, and objective, excluding the reader's own opinions or reactions. It should reflect in similar proportion how much each point summarized was covered in the original passage. Summary writers should include tags of attribution, like "Macaulay argues that" to reference the original author whose ideas are represented in the summary. Summary writers should not overuse quotations; they should only quote central concepts or phrases they cannot precisely convey in words other than those of the original author. Another

85

aspect of evaluating a summary is considering whether it can stand alone as a coherent, unified composition. In addition, evaluation of a summary should include whether its writer has cited the original source of the passage they have summarized so that readers can find it.

MAKING CONNECTIONS TO ENHANCE COMPREHENSION

Reading involves thinking. For good comprehension, readers make **text-to-self**, **text-to-text**, and **text-to-world connections**. Making connections helps readers understand text better and predict what might occur next based on what they already know, such as how characters in the story feel or what happened in another text. Text-to-self connections with the reader's life and experiences make literature more personally relevant and meaningful to readers. Readers can make connections before, during, and after reading—including whenever the text reminds them of something similar they have encountered in life or other texts. The genre, setting, characters, plot elements, literary structure and devices, and themes an author uses allow a reader to make connections to other works of literature or to people and events in their own lives. Venn diagrams and other graphic organizers help visualize connections. Readers can also make double-entry notes: key content, ideas, events, words, and quotations on one side, and the connections with these on the other.

READING ARGUMENTATIVE WRITING

AUTHOR'S ARGUMENT IN ARGUMENTATIVE WRITING

In argumentative writing, the argument is a belief, position, or opinion that the author wants to convince readers to believe as well. For the first step, readers should identify the **issue**. Some issues are controversial, meaning people disagree about them. Gun control, foreign policy, and the death penalty are all controversial issues. The next step is to determine the **author's position** on the issue. That position or viewpoint constitutes the author's argument. Readers should then identify the **author's assumptions**: things he or she accepts, believes, or takes for granted without needing proof. Inaccurate or illogical assumptions produce flawed arguments and can mislead readers. Readers should identify what kinds of **supporting evidence** the author offers, such as research results, personal observations or experiences, case studies, facts, examples, expert testimony and opinions, and comparisons. Readers should decide how relevant this support is to the argument.

> **Review Video: Argumentative Writing**
> Visit mometrix.com/academy and enter code: 561544

EVALUATING AN AUTHOR'S ARGUMENT

The first three reader steps to **evaluate an author's argument** are to identify the **author's assumptions**, identify the **supporting evidence**, and decide **whether the evidence is relevant**. For example, if an author is not an expert on a particular topic, then that author's personal experience or opinion might not be relevant. The fourth step is to assess the **author's objectivity**. For example, consider whether the author introduces clear, understandable supporting evidence and facts to support the argument. The fifth step is evaluating whether the author's **argument is complete**. When authors give sufficient support for their arguments and also anticipate and respond effectively to opposing arguments or objections to their points, their arguments are complete. However, some authors omit information that could detract from their arguments. If instead they stated this information and refuted it, it would strengthen their arguments. The sixth step in evaluating an author's argumentative writing is to assess whether the **argument is valid**. Providing clear, logical reasoning makes an author's argument valid. Readers should ask themselves whether the author's points follow a sequence that makes sense, and whether each point leads to the next. The seventh step is to determine whether the author's **argument is credible**, meaning that it is convincing and believable. Arguments that are not valid are not

86

credible, so step seven depends on step six. Readers should be mindful of their own biases as they evaluate and should not expect authors to conclusively prove their arguments, but rather to provide effective support and reason.

EVALUATING AN AUTHOR'S METHOD OF APPEAL

To evaluate the effectiveness of an appeal, it is important to consider the author's purpose for writing. Any appeals an author uses in their argument must be relevant to the argument's goal. For example, a writer that argues for the reclassification of Pluto, but primarily uses appeals to emotion, will not have an effective argument. This writer should focus on using appeals to logic and support their argument with provable facts. While most arguments should include appeals to logic, emotion, and credibility, some arguments only call for one or two of these types of appeal. Evidence can support an appeal, but the evidence must be relevant to truly strengthen the appeal's effectiveness. If the writer arguing for Pluto's reclassification uses the reasons for Jupiter's classification as evidence, their argument would be weak. This information may seem relevant because it is related to the classification of planets. However, this classification is highly dependent on the size of the celestial object, and Jupiter is significantly bigger than Pluto. This use of evidence is illogical and does not support the appeal. Even when appropriate evidence and appeals are used, appeals and arguments lose their effectiveness when they create logical fallacies.

EVIDENCE

The term **text evidence** refers to information that supports a main point or minor points and can help lead the reader to a conclusion about the text's credibility. Information used as text evidence is precise, descriptive, and factual. A main point is often followed by supporting details that provide evidence to back up a claim. For example, a passage may include the claim that winter occurs during opposite months in the Northern and Southern hemispheres. Text evidence for this claim may include examples of countries where winter occurs in opposite months. Stating that the tilt of the Earth as it rotates around the sun causes winter to occur at different times in separate hemispheres is another example of text evidence. Text evidence can come from common knowledge, but it is also valuable to include text evidence from credible, relevant outside sources.

Review Video: Textual Evidence
Visit mometrix.com/academy and enter code: 486236

Evidence that supports the thesis and additional arguments needs to be provided. Most arguments must be supported by facts or statistics. A fact is something that is known with certainty, has been verified by several independent individuals, and can be proven to be true. In addition to facts, examples and illustrations can support an argument by adding an emotional component. With this component, you persuade readers in ways that facts and statistics cannot. The emotional component is effective when used alongside objective information that can be confirmed.

CREDIBILITY

The text used to support an argument can be the argument's downfall if the text is not credible. A text is **credible**, or believable, when its author is knowledgeable and objective, or unbiased. The author's motivations for writing the text play a critical role in determining the credibility of the text and must be evaluated when assessing that credibility. Reports written about the ozone layer by an environmental scientist and a hairdresser will have a different level of credibility.

Review Video: Author Credibility
Visit mometrix.com/academy and enter code: 827257

APPEAL TO EMOTION

Sometimes, authors will appeal to the reader's emotion in an attempt to persuade or to distract the reader from the weakness of the argument. For instance, the author may try to inspire the pity of the reader by delivering a heart-rending story. An author also might use the bandwagon approach, in which he suggests that his opinion is correct because it is held by the majority. Some authors resort to name-calling, in which insults and harsh words are delivered to the opponent in an attempt to distract. In advertising, a common appeal is the celebrity testimonial, in which a famous person endorses a product. Of course, the fact that a famous person likes something should not really mean anything to the reader. These and other emotional appeals are usually evidence of poor reasoning and a weak argument.

> **Review Video: Emotional Language in Literature**
> Visit mometrix.com/academy and enter code: 759390

COUNTER ARGUMENTS

When authors give both sides to the argument, they build trust with their readers. As a reader, you should start with an undecided or neutral position. If an author presents only his or her side to the argument, then they are not exhibiting credibility and are weakening their argument.

Building common ground with readers can be effective for persuading neutral, skeptical, or opposed readers. Sharing values with undecided readers can allow people to switch positions without giving up what they feel is important. People who may oppose a position need to feel that they can change their minds without betraying who they are as a person. This appeal to having an open mind can be a powerful tool in arguing a position without antagonizing other views. Objections can be countered on a point-by-point basis or in a summary paragraph. Be mindful of how an author points out flaws in counter arguments. If they are unfair to the other side of the argument, then you should lose trust with the author.

Types of Non-Literary Texts

READING INFORMATIONAL TEXTS
LANGUAGE USE
LITERAL AND FIGURATIVE LANGUAGE

As in fictional literature, informational text also uses both **literal language**, which means just what it says, and **figurative language**, which imparts more than literal meaning. For example, an informational text author might use a simile or direct comparison, such as writing that a racehorse "ran like the wind." Informational text authors also use metaphors or implied comparisons, such as "the cloud of the Great Depression." Imagery may also appear in informational texts to increase the reader's understanding of ideas and concepts discussed in the text.

EXPLICIT AND IMPLICIT INFORMATION

When informational text states something explicitly, the reader is told by the author exactly what is meant, which can include the author's interpretation or perspective of events. For example, a professor writes, "I have seen students go into an absolute panic just because they weren't able to complete the exam in the time they were allotted." This explicitly tells the reader that the students were afraid, and by using the words "just because," the writer indicates their fear was exaggerated out of proportion relative to what happened. However, another professor writes, "I have had students come to me, their faces drained of all color, saying 'We weren't able to finish the exam.'" This is an example of implicit meaning: the second writer did not state explicitly that the students

were panicked. Instead, he wrote a description of their faces being "drained of all color." From this description, the reader can infer that the students were so frightened that their faces paled.

> **Review Video: Explicit and Implicit Information**
> Visit mometrix.com/academy and enter code: 735771

MAKING INFERENCES ABOUT INFORMATIONAL TEXT

With informational text, reader comprehension depends not only on recalling important statements and details, but also on reader inferences based on examples and details. Readers add information from the text to what they already know to draw inferences about the text. These inferences help the readers to fill in the information that the text does not explicitly state, enabling them to understand the text better. When reading a nonfictional autobiography or biography, for example, the most appropriate inferences might concern the events in the book, the actions of the subject of the autobiography or biography, and the message the author means to convey. When reading a nonfictional expository (informational) text, the reader would best draw inferences about problems and their solutions, and causes and their effects. When reading a nonfictional persuasive text, the reader will want to infer ideas supporting the author's message and intent.

STRUCTURES OR ORGANIZATIONAL PATTERNS IN INFORMATIONAL TEXTS

Informational text can be **descriptive**, appealing to the five senses and answering the questions what, who, when, where, and why. Another method of structuring informational text is sequence and order. **Chronological** texts relate events in the sequence that they occurred, from start to finish, while how-to texts organize information into a series of instructions in the sequence in which the steps should be followed. **Comparison-contrast** structures of informational text describe various ideas to their readers by pointing out how things or ideas are similar and how they are different. **Cause and effect** structures of informational text describe events that occurred and identify the causes or reasons that those events occurred. **Problem and solution** structures of informational texts introduce and describe problems and offer one or more solutions for each problem described.

DETERMINING AN INFORMATIONAL AUTHOR'S PURPOSE

Informational authors' purposes are why they write texts. Readers must determine authors' motivations and goals. Readers gain greater insight into a text by considering the author's motivation. This develops critical reading skills. Readers perceive writing as a person's voice, not simply printed words. Uncovering author motivations and purposes empowers readers to know what to expect from the text, read for relevant details, evaluate authors and their work critically, and respond effectively to the motivations and persuasions of the text. The main idea of a text is what the reader is supposed to understand from reading it; the purpose of the text is why the author has written it and what the author wants readers to do with its information. Authors state some purposes clearly, while other purposes may be unstated but equally significant. When stated purposes contradict other parts of a text, the author may have a hidden agenda. Readers can better evaluate a text's effectiveness, whether they agree or disagree with it, and why they agree or disagree through identifying unstated author purposes.

IDENTIFYING AUTHOR'S POINT OF VIEW OR PURPOSE

In some informational texts, readers find it easy to identify the author's point of view and purpose, such as when the author explicitly states his or her position and reason for writing. But other texts are more difficult, either because of the content or because the authors give neutral or balanced viewpoints. This is particularly true in scientific texts, in which authors may state the purpose of

89

their research in the report, but never state their point of view except by interpreting evidence or data.

To analyze text and identify point of view or purpose, readers should ask themselves the following four questions:

1. With what main point or idea does this author want to persuade readers to agree?
2. How does this author's word choice affect the way that readers consider this subject?
3. How do this author's choices of examples and facts affect the way that readers consider this subject?
4. What is it that this author wants to accomplish by writing this text?

<table>
<tr><td>

Review Video: <u>Understanding the Author's Intent</u>
Visit mometrix.com/academy and enter code: 511819

Review Video: <u>Author's Position</u>
Visit mometrix.com/academy and enter code: 827954
</td></tr>
</table>

EVALUATING ARGUMENTS MADE BY INFORMATIONAL TEXT WRITERS

When evaluating an informational text, the first step is to identify the argument's conclusion. Then identify the author's premises that support the conclusion. Try to paraphrase premises for clarification and make the conclusion and premises fit. List all premises first, sequentially numbered, then finish with the conclusion. Identify any premises or assumptions not stated by the author but required for the stated premises to support the conclusion. Read word assumptions sympathetically, as the author might. Evaluate whether premises reasonably support the conclusion. For inductive reasoning, the reader should ask if the premises are true, if they support the conclusion, and if so, how strongly. For deductive reasoning, the reader should ask if the argument is valid or invalid. If all premises are true, then the argument is valid unless the conclusion can be false. If it can, then the argument is invalid. An invalid argument can be made valid through alterations such as the addition of needed premises.

USE OF RHETORIC IN INFORMATIONAL TEXTS

There are many ways authors can support their claims, arguments, beliefs, ideas, and reasons for writing in informational texts. For example, authors can appeal to readers' sense of **logic** by communicating their reasoning through a carefully sequenced series of logical steps to help "prove" the points made. Authors can appeal to readers' **emotions** by using descriptions and words that evoke feelings of sympathy, sadness, anger, righteous indignation, hope, happiness, or any other emotion to reinforce what they express and share with their audience. Authors may appeal to the **moral** or **ethical values** of readers by using words and descriptions that can convince readers that something is right or wrong. By relating personal anecdotes, authors can supply readers with more accessible, realistic examples of points they make, as well as appealing to their emotions. They can provide supporting evidence by reporting case studies. They can also illustrate their points by making analogies to which readers can better relate.

ORGANIZATIONAL FEATURES IN TEXTS
TEXT FEATURES IN INFORMATIONAL TEXTS

- The **title of a text** gives readers some idea of its content.
- The **table of contents** is a list near the beginning of a text, showing the book's sections and chapters and their coinciding page numbers. This gives readers an overview of the whole text and helps them find specific chapters easily.

- An **appendix**, at the back of the book or document, includes important information that is not present in the main text.
- Also at the back, an **index** lists the book's important topics alphabetically with their page numbers to help readers find them easily.
- **Glossaries**, usually found at the backs of books, list technical terms alphabetically with their definitions to aid vocabulary learning and comprehension. Boldface print is used to emphasize certain words, often identifying words included in the text's glossary where readers can look up their definitions.
- **Headings** separate sections of text and show the topic of each.
- **Subheadings** divide subject headings into smaller, more specific categories to help readers organize information.
- **Footnotes**, at the bottom of the page, give readers more information, such as citations or links.
- **Bullet points** list items separately, making facts and ideas easier to see and understand.
- A **sidebar** is a box of information to one side of the main text giving additional information, often on a more focused or in-depth example of a topic.

VISUAL FEATURES IN TEXTS

- **Illustrations** and **photographs** are pictures that visually emphasize important points in text.
- The **captions** below the illustrations explain what those images show.
- **Charts** and **tables** are visual forms of information that make something easier to understand quickly.
- **Diagrams** are drawings that show relationships or explain a process.
- **Graphs** visually show the relationships among multiple sets of information plotted along vertical and horizontal axes.
- **Maps** show geographical information visually to help readers understand the relative locations of places covered in the text.
- **Timelines** are visual graphics that show historical events in chronological order to help readers see their sequence.

> **Review Video: Informational Text**
> Visit mometrix.com/academy and enter code: 924964

TECHNICAL LANGUAGE

TECHNICAL LANGUAGE

Technical language is more impersonal than literary and vernacular language. Passive voice makes the tone impersonal. For example, instead of writing, "We found this a central component of protein metabolism," scientists write, "This was found a central component of protein metabolism." While science professors have traditionally instructed students to avoid active voice because it leads to first-person ("I" and "we") usage, science editors today find passive voice dull and weak. Many journal articles combine both. Tone in technical science writing should be detached, concise, and professional. While one may normally write, "This chemical has to be available for proteins to be digested," professionals write technically, "The presence of this chemical is required for the enzyme to break the covalent bonds of proteins." The use of technical language appeals to both technical and non-technical audiences by displaying the author or speaker's understanding of the subject and suggesting their credibility regarding the message they are communicating.

TECHNICAL MATERIAL FOR NON-TECHNICAL READERS

Writing about **technical subjects** for **non-technical readers** differs from writing for colleagues because authors place more importance on delivering a critical message than on imparting the maximum technical content possible. Technical authors also must assume that non-technical audiences do not have the expertise to comprehend extremely scientific or technical messages, concepts, and terminology. They must resist the temptation to impress audiences with their scientific knowledge and expertise and remember that their primary purpose is to communicate a message that non-technical readers will understand, feel, and respond to. Non-technical and technical styles include similarities. Both should formally cite any references or other authors' work utilized in the text. Both must follow intellectual property and copyright regulations. This includes the author's protecting his or her own rights, or a public domain statement, as he or she chooses.

> **Review Video: Technical Passages**
> Visit mometrix.com/academy and enter code: 478923

NON-TECHNICAL AUDIENCES

Writers of technical or scientific material may need to write for many non-technical audiences. Some readers have no technical or scientific background, and those who do may not be in the same field as the authors. Government and corporate policymakers and budget managers need technical information they can understand for decision-making. Citizens affected by technology or science are a different audience. Non-governmental organizations can encompass many of the preceding groups. Elementary and secondary school programs also need non-technical language for presenting technical subject matter. Additionally, technical authors will need to use non-technical language when collecting consumer responses to surveys, presenting scientific or para-scientific material to the public, writing about the history of science, and writing about science and technology in developing countries.

USE OF EVERYDAY LANGUAGE

Authors of technical information sometimes must write using non-technical language that readers outside their disciplinary fields can comprehend. They should use not only non-technical terms, but also normal, everyday language to accommodate readers whose native language is different than the language the text is written in. For example, instead of writing that "eustatic changes like thermal expansion are causing hazardous conditions in the littoral zone," an author would do better to write that "a rising sea level is threatening the coast." When technical terms cannot be avoided, authors should also define or explain them using non-technical language. Although authors must cite references and acknowledge their use of others' work, they should avoid the kinds of references or citations that they would use in scientific journals—unless they reinforce author messages. They should not use endnotes, footnotes, or any other complicated referential techniques because non-technical journal publishers usually do not accept them. Including high-resolution illustrations, photos, maps, or satellite images and incorporating multimedia into digital publications will enhance non-technical writing about technical subjects. Technical authors may publish using non-technical language in e-journals, trade journals, specialty newsletters, and daily newspapers.

TYPES OF TECHNICAL WRITING
TYPES OF PRINTED COMMUNICATION
MEMO

A memo (short for *memorandum*) is a common form of written communication. There is a standard format for these documents. It is typical for there to be a **heading** at the top indicating the author,

date, and recipient. In some cases, this heading will also include the author's title and the name of his or her institution. Below this information will be the **body** of the memo. These documents are typically written by and for members of the same organization. They usually contain a plan of action, a request for information on a specific topic, or a response to such a request. Memos are considered to be official documents, so they are usually written in a **formal** style. Many memos are organized with numbers or bullet points, which make it easier for the reader to identify key ideas.

POSTED ANNOUNCEMENT

People post **announcements** for all sorts of occasions. Many people are familiar with notices for lost pets, yard sales, and landscaping services. In order to be effective, these announcements need to *contain all of the information* the reader requires to act on the message. For instance, a lost pet announcement needs to include a good description of the animal and a contact number for the owner. A yard sale notice should include the address, date, and hours of the sale, as well as a brief description of the products that will be available there. When composing an announcement, it is important to consider the perspective of the **audience**—what will they need to know in order to respond to the message? Although a posted announcement can have color and decoration to attract the eye of the passerby, it must also convey the necessary information clearly.

CLASSIFIED ADVERTISEMENT

Classified advertisements, or **ads**, are used to sell or buy goods, to attract business, to make romantic connections, and to do countless other things. They are an inexpensive, and sometimes free, way to make a brief **pitch**. Classified ads used to be found only in newspapers or special advertising circulars, but there are now online listings as well. The style of these ads has remained basically the same. An ad usually begins with a word or phrase indicating what is being **sold** or **sought**. Then, the listing will give a brief **description** of the product or service. Because space is limited and costly in newspapers, classified ads there will often contain abbreviations for common attributes. For instance, two common abbreviations are *bk* for *black*, and *obo* for *or best offer*. Classified ads will then usually conclude by listing the **price** (or the amount the seeker is willing to pay), followed by **contact information** like a telephone number or email address.

SCALE READINGS OF STANDARD MEASUREMENT INSTRUMENTS

The scales used on **standard measurement instruments** are fairly easy to read with a little practice. Take the **ruler** as an example. A typical ruler has different units along each long edge. One side measures inches, and the other measures centimeters. The units are specified close to the zero reading for the ruler. Note that the ruler does not begin measuring from its outermost edge. The zero reading is a black line a tiny distance inside of the edge. On the inches side, each inch is indicated with a long black line and a number. Each half-inch is noted with a slightly shorter line. Quarter-inches are noted with still shorter lines, eighth-inches are noted with even shorter lines, and sixteenth-inches are noted with the shortest lines of all. On the centimeter side, the second-largest black lines indicate half-centimeters, and the smaller lines indicate tenths of centimeters, otherwise known as millimeters.

VISUAL INFORMATION IN INFORMATIONAL TEXTS
CHARTS, GRAPHS, AND VISUALS
PIE CHART

A pie chart, also known as a circle graph, is useful for depicting how a single unit or category is divided. The standard pie chart is a circle with designated wedges. Each wedge is **proportional** in size to a part of the whole. For instance, consider Shawna, a student at City College, who uses a pie chart to represent her budget. If she spends half of her money on rent, then the pie chart will represent that amount with a line through the center of the pie. If she spends a quarter of her money on food, there will be a line extending from the edge of the circle to the center at a right angle to the line depicting rent. This illustration would make it clear that the student spends twice the amount of money on rent as she does on food.

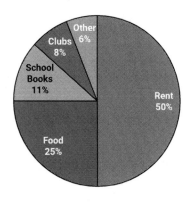

A pie chart is effective at showing how a single entity is divided into parts. They are not effective at demonstrating the relationships between parts of different wholes. For example, an unhelpful use of a pie chart would be to compare the respective amounts of state and federal spending devoted to infrastructure since these values are only meaningful in the context of the entire budget.

BAR GRAPH

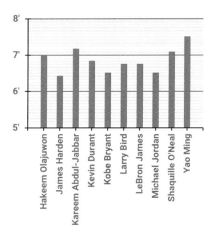

The bar graph is one of the most common visual representations of information. **Bar graphs** are used to illustrate sets of numerical **data**. The graph has a vertical axis (along which numbers are listed) and a horizontal axis (along which categories, words, or some other indicators are placed). One example of a bar graph is a depiction of the respective heights of famous basketball players: the vertical axis would contain numbers ranging from five to eight feet, and the horizontal axis would contain the names of the players. The length of the bar above the player's name would illustrate his height, and the top of the bar would stop perpendicular to the height listed along the left side. In this representation, one would see that Yao Ming is taller than Michael Jordan because Yao's bar would be higher.

LINE GRAPH

A line graph is a type of graph that is typically used for measuring trends over time. The graph is set up along a vertical and a horizontal **axis**. The variables being measured are listed along the left side and the bottom side of the axes. Points are then plotted along the graph as they correspond with their values for each variable. For instance, consider a line graph measuring a person's income for each month of the year. If the person earned $1500 in January, there should be a point directly above January (perpendicular to the horizontal axis) and directly to the right of $1500 (perpendicular to the vertical axis). Once all of the lines are plotted, they are connected with a line from left to right. This line provides a nice visual illustration of the general **trends** of the data, if they exist. For instance, using the earlier example, if the line sloped up, then one would see that the person's income had increased over the course of the year.

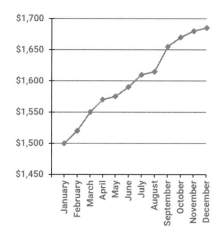

PICTOGRAPHS

A **pictograph** is a graph, generally in the horizontal orientation, that uses pictures or symbols to represent the data. Each pictograph must have a key that defines the picture or symbol and gives the quantity each picture or symbol represents. Pictures or symbols on a pictograph are not always shown as whole elements. In this case, the fraction of the picture or symbol shown represents the same fraction of the quantity a whole picture or symbol stands for.

> **Review Video: Pictographs**
> Visit mometrix.com/academy and enter code: 147860

Chapter Quiz

Ready to see how well you retained what you just read? Scan the QR code to go directly to the chapter quiz interface for this study guide. If you're using a computer, simply visit the bonus page at **mometrix.com/bonus948/pert** and click the Chapter Quizzes link.

Writing

Transform passive reading into active learning! After immersing yourself in this chapter, put your comprehension to the test by taking a quiz. The insights you gained will stay with you longer this way. Scan the QR code to go directly to the chapter quiz interface for this study guide. If you're using a computer, simply visit the bonus page at **mometrix.com/bonus948/pert** and click the Chapter Quizzes link.

Grammar and Usage

PARTS OF SPEECH

NOUNS

A noun is a person, place, thing, or idea. The two main types of nouns are **common** and **proper** nouns. Nouns can also be categorized as abstract (i.e., general) or concrete (i.e., specific).

COMMON NOUNS

Common nouns are generic names for people, places, and things. Common nouns are not usually capitalized.

Examples of common nouns:

People: boy, girl, worker, manager

Places: school, bank, library, home

Things: dog, cat, truck, car

> **Review Video: Nouns**
> Visit mometrix.com/academy and enter code: 344028

PROPER NOUNS

Proper nouns name specific people, places, or things. All proper nouns are capitalized.

Examples of proper nouns:

People: Abraham Lincoln, George Washington, Martin Luther King, Jr.

Places: Los Angeles, California; New York; Asia

Things: Statue of Liberty, Earth, Lincoln Memorial

Note: Some nouns can be either common or proper depending on their use. For example, when referring to the planet that we live on, *Earth* is a proper noun and is capitalized. When referring to the dirt, rocks, or land on our planet, *earth* is a common noun and is not capitalized.

GENERAL AND SPECIFIC NOUNS

General nouns are the names of conditions or ideas. **Specific nouns** name people, places, and things that are understood by using your senses.

General nouns:

Condition: beauty, strength

Idea: truth, peace

Specific nouns:

People: baby, friend, father

Places: town, park, city hall

Things: rainbow, cough, apple, silk, gasoline

COLLECTIVE NOUNS

Collective nouns are the names for a group of people, places, or things that may act as a whole. The following are examples of collective nouns: *class, company, dozen, group, herd, team,* and *public*. Collective nouns usually require an article, which denotes the noun as being a single unit. For instance, a choir is a group of singers. Even though there are many singers in a choir, the word choir is grammatically treated as a single unit. If we refer to the members of the group, and not the group itself, it is no longer a collective noun.

Incorrect: The *choir are* going to compete nationally this year.

Correct: The *choir is* going to compete nationally this year.

Incorrect: The *members* of the choir *is* competing nationally this year.

Correct: The *members* of the choir *are* competing nationally this year.

PRONOUNS

Pronouns are words that are used to stand in for nouns. A pronoun may be classified as personal, intensive, relative, interrogative, demonstrative, indefinite, and reciprocal.

Personal: *Nominative* is the case for nouns and pronouns that are the subject of a sentence. *Objective* is the case for nouns and pronouns that are an object in a sentence. *Possessive* is the case for nouns and pronouns that show possession or ownership.

Singular

	Nominative	Objective	Possessive
First Person	I	me	my, mine
Second Person	you	you	your, yours
Third Person	he, she, it	him, her, it	his, her, hers, its

Plural

	Nominative	Objective	Possessive
First Person	we	us	our, ours
Second Person	you	you	your, yours
Third Person	they	them	their, theirs

97

Intensive: I myself, you yourself, he himself, she herself, the (thing) itself, we ourselves, you yourselves, they themselves

Relative: which, who, whom, whose

Interrogative: what, which, who, whom, whose

Demonstrative: this, that, these, those

Indefinite: all, any, each, everyone, either/neither, one, some, several

Reciprocal: each other, one another

Review Video: <u>Nouns and Pronouns</u>
Visit mometrix.com/academy and enter code: 312073

VERBS

A verb is a word or group of words that indicates action or being. In other words, the verb shows something's action or state of being or the action that has been done to something. If you want to write a sentence, then you need a verb. Without a verb, you have no sentence.

TRANSITIVE AND INTRANSITIVE VERBS

A **transitive verb** is a verb whose action indicates a receiver. **Intransitive verbs** do not indicate a receiver of an action. In other words, the action of the verb does not point to an object.

Transitive: He drives a car. | She feeds the dog.

Intransitive: He runs every day. | She voted in the last election.

A dictionary will tell you whether a verb is transitive or intransitive. Some verbs can be transitive or intransitive.

ACTION VERBS AND LINKING VERBS

Action verbs show what the subject is doing. In other words, an action verb shows action. Unlike most types of words, a single action verb, in the right context, can be an entire sentence. **Linking verbs** link the subject of a sentence to a noun or pronoun, or they link a subject with an adjective. You always need a verb if you want a complete sentence. However, linking verbs on their own cannot be a complete sentence.

Common linking verbs include *appear, be, become, feel, grow, look, seem, smell, sound,* and *taste.* However, any verb that shows a condition and connects to a noun, pronoun, or adjective that describes the subject of a sentence is a linking verb.

Action: He sings. | Run! | Go! | I talk with him every day. | She reads.

Linking:

Incorrect: I am.

Correct: I am John. | The roses smell lovely. | I feel tired.

Note: Some verbs are followed by words that look like prepositions, but they are a part of the verb and a part of the verb's meaning. These are known as phrasal verbs, and examples include *call off*, *look up*, and *drop off*.

> **Review Video: Action Verbs and Linking Verbs**
> Visit mometrix.com/academy and enter code: 743142

VOICE

Transitive verbs may be in active voice or passive voice. The difference between active voice and passive voice is whether the subject is acting or being acted upon. When the subject of the sentence is doing the action, the verb is in **active voice**. When the subject is being acted upon, the verb is in **passive voice**.

Active: Jon drew the picture. (The subject *Jon* is doing the action of *drawing a picture*.)

Passive: The picture is drawn by Jon. (The subject *picture* is receiving the action from Jon.)

VERB TENSES

Verb **tense** is a property of a verb that indicates when the action being described takes place (past, present, or future) and whether or not the action is completed (simple or perfect). Describing an action taking place in the present (*I talk*) requires a different verb tense than describing an action that took place in the past (*I talked*). Some verb tenses require an auxiliary (helping) verb. These helping verbs include *am, are, is | have, has, had | was, were, will* (or *shall*).

Present: I talk	Present perfect: I have talked
Past: I talked	Past perfect: I had talked
Future: I will talk	Future perfect: I will have talked

Present: The action is happening at the current time.

Example: He *walks* to the store every morning.

To show that something is happening right now, use the progressive present tense: I *am walking*.

Past: The action happened in the past.

Example: She *walked* to the store an hour ago.

Future: The action will happen later.

Example: I *will walk* to the store tomorrow.

Present perfect: The action started in the past and continues into the present or took place previously at an unspecified time.

Example: I *have walked* to the store three times today.

Past perfect: The action was completed at some point in the past. This tense is usually used to describe an action that was completed before some other reference time or event.

Example: I *had eaten* already before they arrived.

Writing

Future perfect: The action will be completed before some point in the future. This tense may be used to describe an action that has already begun or has yet to begin.

Example: The project *will have been completed* by the deadline.

> **Review Video: Present Perfect, Past Perfect, and Future Perfect Verb Tenses**
> Visit mometrix.com/academy and enter code: 269472

CONJUGATING VERBS

When you need to change the form of a verb, you are **conjugating** a verb. The key forms of a verb are present tense (sing/sings), past tense (sang), present participle (singing), and past participle (sung). By combining these forms with helping verbs, you can make almost any verb tense. The following table demonstrate some of the different ways to conjugate a verb:

Tense	First Person	Second Person	Third Person Singular	Third Person Plural
Simple Present	I sing	You sing	He, she, it sings	They sing
Simple Past	I sang	You sang	He, she, it sang	They sang
Simple Future	I will sing	You will sing	He, she, it will sing	They will sing
Present Progressive	I am singing	You are singing	He, she, it is singing	They are singing
Past Progressive	I was singing	You were singing	He, she, it was singing	They were singing
Present Perfect	I have sung	You have sung	He, she, it has sung	They have sung
Past Perfect	I had sung	You had sung	He, she, it had sung	They had sung

MOOD

There are three **moods** in English: the indicative, the imperative, and the subjunctive.

The **indicative mood** is used for facts, opinions, and questions.

Fact: You can do this.

Opinion: I think that you can do this.

Question: Do you know that you can do this?

The **imperative** is used for orders or requests.

Order: You are going to do this!

Request: Will you do this for me?

The **subjunctive mood** is for wishes and statements that go against fact.

Wish: I wish that I were famous.

Statement against fact: If I were you, I would do this. (This goes against fact because I am not you. You have the chance to do this, and I do not have the chance.)

100

ADJECTIVES

An **adjective** is a word that is used to modify a noun or pronoun. An adjective answers a question: *Which one? What kind?* or *How many?* Usually, adjectives come before the words that they modify, but they may also come after a linking verb.

Which one? The *third* suit is my favorite.

What kind? This suit is *navy blue*.

How many? I am going to buy *four* pairs of socks to match the suit.

> **Review Video: Descriptive Text**
> Visit mometrix.com/academy and enter code: 174903

ARTICLES

Articles are adjectives that are used to distinguish nouns as definite or indefinite. *A*, *an*, and *the* are the only articles. **Definite** nouns are preceded by *the* and indicate a specific person, place, thing, or idea. **Indefinite** nouns are preceded by *a* or *an* and do not indicate a specific person, place, thing, or idea.

Note: *An* comes before words that start with a vowel sound. For example, "Are you going to get an **u**mbrella?"

Definite: I lost *the* bottle that belongs to me.

Indefinite: Does anyone have *a* bottle to share?

> **Review Video: Function of Articles in a Sentence**
> Visit mometrix.com/academy and enter code: 449383

COMPARISON WITH ADJECTIVES

Some adjectives are relative and other adjectives are absolute. Adjectives that are **relative** can show the comparison between things. **Absolute** adjectives can also show comparison, but they do so in a different way. Let's say that you are reading two books. You think that one book is perfect, and the other book is not exactly perfect. It is not possible for one book to be more perfect than the other. Either you think that the book is perfect, or you think that the book is imperfect. In this case, perfect and imperfect are absolute adjectives.

Relative adjectives will show the different **degrees** of something or someone to something else or someone else. The three degrees of adjectives include positive, comparative, and superlative.

The **positive** degree is the normal form of an adjective.

Example: This work is *difficult*. | She is *smart*.

The **comparative** degree compares one person or thing to another person or thing.

Example: This work is *more difficult* than your work. | She is *smarter* than me.

101

The **superlative** degree compares more than two people or things.

Example: This is the *most difficult* work of my life. | She is the *smartest* lady in school.

ADVERBS

An **adverb** is a word that is used to **modify** a verb, an adjective, or another adverb. Usually, adverbs answer one of these questions: *When? Where? How?* and *Why?* The negatives *not* and *never* are considered adverbs. Adverbs that modify adjectives or other adverbs **strengthen** or **weaken** the words that they modify.

Examples:

He walks *quickly* through the crowd.

The water flows *smoothly* on the rocks.

Note: Adverbs are usually indicated by the morpheme *-ly*, which has been added to the root word. For instance, *quick* can be made into an adverb by adding *-ly* to construct *quickly*. Some words that end in *-ly* do not follow this rule and can behave as other parts of speech. Examples of adjectives ending in *-ly* include: *early, friendly, holy, lonely, silly*, and *ugly*. To know if a word that ends in *-ly* is an adjective or adverb, check your dictionary. Also, while many adverbs end in *-ly*, you need to remember that not all adverbs end in *-ly*.

Examples:

He is *never* angry.

You are *too* irresponsible to travel alone.

COMPARISON WITH ADVERBS

The rules for comparing adverbs are the same as the rules for adjectives.

The **positive** degree is the standard form of an adverb.

Example: He arrives *soon*. | She speaks *softly* to her friends.

The **comparative** degree compares one person or thing to another person or thing.

Example: He arrives *sooner* than Sarah. | She speaks *more softly* than him.

The **superlative** degree compares more than two people or things.

Example: He arrives *soonest* of the group. | She speaks the *most softly* of any of her friends.

PREPOSITIONS

A **preposition** is a word placed before a noun or pronoun that shows the relationship between that noun or pronoun and another word in the sentence.

Common prepositions:

about	before	during	on	under
after	beneath	for	over	until
against	between	from	past	up
among	beyond	in	through	with
around	by	of	to	within
at	down	off	toward	without

Examples:

The napkin is *in* the drawer.

The Earth rotates *around* the Sun.

The needle is *beneath* the haystack.

Can you find "me" *among* the words?

> **Review Video: Prepositions**
> Visit mometrix.com/academy and enter code: 946763

CONJUNCTIONS

Conjunctions join words, phrases, or clauses and they show the connection between the joined pieces. **Coordinating conjunctions** connect equal parts of sentences. **Correlative conjunctions** show the connection between pairs. **Subordinating conjunctions** join subordinate (i.e., dependent) clauses with independent clauses.

COORDINATING CONJUNCTIONS

The **coordinating conjunctions** include: *and, but, yet, or, nor, for,* and *so*

Examples:

The rock was small, *but* it was heavy.

She drove in the night, *and* he drove in the day.

Writing

CORRELATIVE CONJUNCTIONS

The **correlative conjunctions** are: *either...or* | *neither...nor* | *not only...but also*

Examples:

Either you are coming *or* you are staying.

He *not only* ran three miles *but also* swam 200 yards.

> **Review Video: Coordinating and Correlative Conjunctions**
> Visit mometrix.com/academy and enter code: 390329
>
> **Review Video: Adverb Equal Comparisons**
> Visit mometrix.com/academy and enter code: 231291

SUBORDINATING CONJUNCTIONS

Common **subordinating conjunctions** include:

after	since	whenever
although	so that	where
because	unless	wherever
before	until	whether
in order that	when	while

Examples:

I am hungry *because* I did not eat breakfast.

He went home *when* everyone left.

> **Review Video: Subordinating Conjunctions**
> Visit mometrix.com/academy and enter code: 958913

INTERJECTIONS

Interjections are words of exclamation (i.e., audible expression of great feeling) that are used alone or as a part of a sentence. Often, they are used at the beginning of a sentence for an introduction. Sometimes, they can be used in the middle of a sentence to show a change in thought or attitude.

Common Interjections: Hey! | Oh, | Ouch! | Please! | Wow!

AGREEMENT AND SENTENCE STRUCTURE
SUBJECTS AND PREDICATES
SUBJECTS

The **subject** of a sentence names who or what the sentence is about. The subject may be directly stated in a sentence, or the subject may be the implied *you*. The **complete subject** includes the simple subject and all of its modifiers. To find the complete subject, ask *Who* or *What* and insert the verb to complete the question. The answer, including any modifiers (adjectives, prepositional phrases, etc.), is the complete subject. To find the **simple subject**, remove all of the modifiers in the complete subject. Being able to locate the subject of a sentence helps with many problems, such as those involving sentence fragments and subject-verb agreement.

Examples:

simple
subject

The small, red ⏞car⏞ is the one that he wants for Christmas.
⏟_____⏟
complete
subject

simple
subject

The young ⏞artist⏞ is coming over for dinner.
⏟_____⏟
complete
subject

In **imperative** sentences, the verb's subject is understood (e.g., [You] Run to the store), but is not actually present in the sentence. Normally, the subject comes before the verb. However, the subject comes after the verb in sentences that begin with *There are* or *There was*.

Direct:

John knows the way to the park.	Who knows the way to the park?	John
The cookies need ten more minutes.	What needs ten minutes?	The cookies
By five o'clock, Bill will need to leave.	Who needs to leave?	Bill
There are five letters on the table for him.	What is on the table?	Five letters
There were coffee and doughnuts in the house.	What was in the house?	Coffee and doughnuts

Implied:

Go to the post office for me.	Who is going to the post office?	You
Come and sit with me, please?	Who needs to come and sit?	You

PREDICATES

In a sentence, you always have a predicate and a subject. The subject tells who or what the sentence is about, and the **predicate** explains or describes the subject. The predicate includes the verb or verb phrase and any direct or indirect objects of the verb, as well as any words or phrases modifying these.

Think about the sentence *He sings*. In this sentence, we have a subject (He) and a predicate (sings). This is all that is needed for a sentence to be complete. Most sentences contain more information, but if this is all the information that you are given, then you have a complete sentence.

Now, let's look at another sentence: *John and Jane sing on Tuesday nights at the dance hall.*

subject   predicate

John and Jane sing on Tuesday nights at the dance hall.

> **Review Video: Complete Predicate**
> Visit mometrix.com/academy and enter code: 293942

SUBJECT-VERB AGREEMENT

Verbs must **agree** with their subjects in number and in person. To agree in number, singular subjects need singular verbs and plural subjects need plural verbs. A **singular** noun refers to **one** person, place, or thing. A **plural** noun refers to **more than one** person, place, or thing. To agree in person, the correct verb form must be chosen to match the first, second, or third person subject. The present tense ending *-s* or *-es* is used on a verb if its subject is third person singular; otherwise, the verb's ending is not modified.

> **Review Video: Subject-Verb Agreement**
> Visit mometrix.com/academy and enter code: 479190

NUMBER AGREEMENT EXAMPLES:

singular singular
subject verb

Single Subject and Verb: Dan calls home.

Dan is one person. So, the singular verb *calls* is needed.

plural   plural
subject verb

Plural Subject and Verb: Dan and Bob call home.

More than one person needs the plural verb *call*.

PERSON AGREEMENT EXAMPLES:

First Person: I *am* walking.

Second Person: You *are* walking.

Third Person: He *is* walking.

COMPLICATIONS WITH SUBJECT-VERB AGREEMENT
WORDS BETWEEN SUBJECT AND VERB

Words that come between the simple subject and the verb have no bearing on subject-verb agreement.

Examples:

singular   singular
subject   verb

The joy of my life returns home tonight.

106

The phrase *of my life* does not influence the verb *returns*.

The $\overset{\overset{\text{singular}}{\text{subject}}}{\text{question}}$ that still remains unanswered $\overset{\overset{\text{singular}}{\text{verb}}}{\text{is}}$ "Who are you?"

Don't let the phrase *"that still remains…"* trouble you. The subject *question* goes with *is*.

COMPOUND SUBJECTS

A compound subject is formed when two or more nouns joined by *and*, *or*, or *nor* jointly act as the subject of the sentence.

JOINED BY AND

When a compound subject is joined by *and*, it is treated as a plural subject and requires a plural verb.

Examples:

$\overset{\overset{\text{plural}}{\text{subject}}}{\text{You and Jon}}$ $\overset{\overset{\text{plural}}{\text{verb}}}{\text{are}}$ invited to come to my house.

The $\overset{\overset{\text{plural}}{\text{subject}}}{\text{pencil and paper}}$ $\overset{\overset{\text{plural}}{\text{verb}}}{\text{belong}}$ to me.

JOINED BY OR/NOR

For a compound subject joined by *or* or *nor*, the verb must agree in number with the part of the subject that is closest to the verb (italicized in the examples below).

Examples:

$\overset{\text{subject}}{\text{Today or tomorrow}}$ $\overset{\text{verb}}{\text{is}}$ the day.

$\overset{\text{subject}}{\text{Stan or Phil}}$ $\overset{\text{verb}}{\text{wants}}$ to read the book.

Neither the $\overset{\text{subject}}{\text{pen nor the book}}$ $\overset{\text{verb}}{\text{is}}$ on the desk.

Either the $\overset{\text{subject}}{\text{blanket or pillows}}$ $\overset{\text{verb}}{\text{arrive}}$ this afternoon.

INDEFINITE PRONOUNS AS SUBJECT

An indefinite pronoun is a pronoun that does not refer to a specific noun. Some indefinite pronouns function as only singular, some function as only plural, and some can function as either singular or plural depending on how they are used.

ALWAYS SINGULAR

Pronouns such as *each*, *either*, *everybody*, *anybody*, *somebody*, and *nobody* are always singular.

Examples:

singular
subject   singular
verb

Each of the runners has a different bib number.

singular singular
verb   subject

Is either of you ready for the game?

Note: The words *each* and *either* can also be used as adjectives (e.g., *each* person is unique). When one of these adjectives modifies the subject of a sentence, it is always a singular subject.

singular   singular
subject   verb

Everybody grows a day older every day.

singular   singular
subject   verb

Anybody is welcome to bring a tent.

ALWAYS PLURAL

Pronouns such as *both*, *several*, and *many* are always plural.

Examples:

plural
subject   plural
verb

Both of the siblings were too tired to argue.

plural   plural
subject verb

Many have tried, but none have succeeded.

DEPEND ON CONTEXT

Pronouns such as *some*, *any*, *all*, *none*, *more*, and *most* can be either singular or plural depending on what they are representing in the context of the sentence.

Examples:

singular   singular
subject   verb

All of my dog's food was still there in his bowl.

plural   plural
subject   verb

By the end of the night, all of my guests were already excited about coming to my next party.

OTHER CASES INVOLVING PLURAL OR IRREGULAR FORM

Some nouns are **singular in meaning but plural in form**: news, mathematics, physics, and economics.

> The *news is* coming on now.

> *Mathematics is* my favorite class.

Some nouns are plural in form and meaning, and have **no singular equivalent**: scissors and pants.

> Do these *pants come* with a shirt?

> The *scissors are* for my project.

Mathematical operations are **irregular** in their construction, but are normally considered to be **singular in meaning**.

> *One plus one is* two.

> *Three times three is* nine.

Note: Look to your **dictionary** for help when you aren't sure whether a noun with a plural form has a singular or plural meaning.

COMPLEMENTS

A complement is a noun, pronoun, or adjective that is used to give more information about the subject or object in the sentence.

DIRECT OBJECTS

A direct object is a noun or pronoun that tells who or what **receives** the action of the verb. A sentence will only include a direct object if the verb is a transitive verb. If the verb is an intransitive verb or a linking verb, there will be no direct object. When you are looking for a direct object, find the verb and ask *who* or *what*.

Examples:

> I took *the blanket.*

> Jane read *books.*

INDIRECT OBJECTS

An indirect object is a noun or pronoun that indicates what or whom the action had an **influence** on. If there is an indirect object in a sentence, then there will also be a direct object. When you are looking for the indirect object, find the verb and ask *to/for whom or what.*

Examples:

indirect   direct
object   object

We taught the old dog a new trick.

indirect   direct
object   object

I gave them a math lesson.

Review Video: Direct and Indirect Objects
Visit mometrix.com/academy and enter code: 817385

PREDICATE NOMINATIVES AND PREDICATE ADJECTIVES

As we looked at previously, verbs may be classified as either action verbs or linking verbs. A linking verb is so named because it links the subject to words in the predicate that describe or define the subject. These words are called predicate nominatives (if nouns or pronouns) or predicate adjectives (if adjectives).

Examples:

subject   predicate nominative

My father is a lawyer.

subject   predicate adjective

Your mother is patient.

PRONOUN USAGE

The **antecedent** is the noun that has been replaced by a pronoun. A pronoun and its antecedent **agree** when they have the same number (singular or plural) and gender (male, female, or neutral).

Examples:

antecedent   pronoun

Singular agreement: John came into town, and he played for us.

antecedent   pronoun

Plural agreement: John and Rick came into town, and they played for us.

To determine which is the correct pronoun to use in a compound subject or object, try each pronoun **alone** in place of the compound in the sentence. Your knowledge of pronouns will tell you which one is correct.

Example:

Bob and (I, me) will be going.

Test: (1) *I will be going* or (2) *Me will be going*. The second choice cannot be correct because *me* cannot be used as the subject of a sentence. Instead, *me* is used as an object.

Answer: Bob and I will be going.

When a pronoun is used with a noun immediately following (as in "we boys"), try the sentence **without the added noun**.

Example:

(We/Us) boys played football last year.

Test: (1) *We played football last ye*ar or (2) *Us played football last year*. Again, the second choice cannot be correct because *us* cannot be used as a subject of a sentence. Instead, *us* is used as an object.

Answer: We boys played football last year.

Review Video: <u>Pronoun Usage</u> Visit mometrix.com/academy and enter code: 666500 **Review Video: <u>Pronoun-Antecedent Agreement</u>** Visit mometrix.com/academy and enter code: 919704

A pronoun should point clearly to the **antecedent**. Here is how a pronoun reference can be unhelpful if it is puzzling or not directly stated.

antecedent   pronoun
Unhelpful: Ron and Jim went to the store, and he bought soda.

Who bought soda? Ron or Jim?

antecedent   pronoun
Helpful: Jim went to the store, and he bought soda.

The sentence is clear. Jim bought the soda.

Some pronouns change their form by their placement in a sentence. A pronoun that is a **subject** in a sentence comes in the **subjective case**. Pronouns that serve as **objects** appear in the **objective case**. Finally, the pronouns that are used as **possessives** appear in the **possessive case**.

Examples:

Subjective case: *He* is coming to the show.

The pronoun *He* is the subject of the sentence.

Objective case: Josh drove *him* to the airport.

The pronoun *him* is the object of the sentence.

Possessive case: The flowers are *mine*.

The pronoun *mine* shows ownership of the flowers.

The word *who* is a subjective-case pronoun that can be used as a **subject**. The word *whom* is an objective-case pronoun that can be used as an **object**. The words *who* and *whom* are common in subordinate clauses or in questions.

Writing

111

Examples:

subject   verb
He knows who wants to come.

object   verb
He knows the man whom we want at the party.

CLAUSES

A clause is a group of words that contains both a subject and a predicate (verb). There are two types of clauses: independent and dependent. An **independent clause** contains a complete thought, while a **dependent (or subordinate) clause** does not. A dependent clause includes a subject and a verb, and may also contain objects or complements, but it cannot stand as a complete thought without being joined to an independent clause. Dependent clauses function within sentences as adjectives, adverbs, or nouns.

Example:

independent   dependent
clause   clause
I am running because I want to stay in shape.

The clause *I am running* is an independent clause: it has a subject and a verb, and it gives a complete thought. The clause *because I want to stay in shape* is a dependent clause: it has a subject and a verb, but it does not express a complete thought. It adds detail to the independent clause to which it is attached.

> **Review Video: Clauses**
> Visit mometrix.com/academy and enter code: 940170
>
> **Review Video: Independent and Dependent Clauses**
> Visit mometrix.com/academy and enter code: 556903

TYPES OF DEPENDENT CLAUSES

ADJECTIVE CLAUSES

An **adjective clause** is a dependent clause that modifies a noun or a pronoun. Adjective clauses begin with a relative pronoun (*who, whose, whom, which,* and *that*) or a relative adverb (*where, when,* and *why*).

Also, adjective clauses usually come immediately after the noun that the clause needs to explain or rename. This is done to ensure that it is clear which noun or pronoun the clause is modifying.

Examples:

independent   adjective
clause   clause
I learned the reason why I won the award.

independent   adjective
clause   clause
This is the place where I started my first job.

An adjective clause can be an essential or nonessential clause. An essential clause is very important to the sentence. **Essential clauses** explain or define a person or thing. **Nonessential clauses** give

112

more information about a person or thing but are not necessary to define them. Nonessential clauses are set off with commas while essential clauses are not.

Examples:

essential
clause

A person who works hard at first can often rest later in life.

nonessential
clause

Neil Armstrong, who walked on the moon, is my hero.

> **Review Video: Adjective Clauses and Phrases**
> Visit mometrix.com/academy and enter code: 520888

ADVERB CLAUSES

An **adverb clause** is a dependent clause that modifies a verb, adjective, or adverb. In sentences with multiple dependent clauses, adverb clauses are usually placed immediately before or after the independent clause. An adverb clause is introduced with words such as *after, although, as, before, because, if, since, so, unless, when, where*, and *while*.

Examples:

adverb
clause

When you walked outside, I called the manager.

adverb
clause

I will go with you unless you want to stay.

NOUN CLAUSES

A **noun clause** is a dependent clause that can be used as a subject, object, or complement. Noun clauses begin with words such as *how, that, what, whether, which, who*, and *why*. These words can also come with an adjective clause. Unless the noun clause is being used as the subject of the sentence, it should come after the verb of the independent clause.

Examples:

noun
clause

The real mystery is how you avoided serious injury.

noun
clause

What you learn from each other depends on your honesty with others.

SUBORDINATION

When two related ideas are not of equal importance, the ideal way to combine them is to make the more important idea an independent clause and the less important idea a dependent or subordinate clause. This is called **subordination**.

Writing

113

Example:

> **Separate ideas**: The team had a perfect regular season. The team lost the championship.

> **Subordinated**: Despite having a perfect regular season, *the team lost the championship.*

PHRASES

A phrase is a group of words that functions as a single part of speech, usually a noun, adjective, or adverb. A **phrase** is not a complete thought and does not contain a subject and predicate, but it adds detail or explanation to a sentence, or renames something within the sentence.

PREPOSITIONAL PHRASES

One of the most common types of phrases is the prepositional phrase. A **prepositional phrase** begins with a preposition and ends with a noun or pronoun that is the object of the preposition. Normally, the prepositional phrase functions as an **adjective** or an **adverb** within the sentence.

Examples:

> prepositional
> phrase
> The picnic is on the blanket.

> prepositional
> phrase
> I am sick with a fever today.

> prepositional
> phrase
> Among the many flowers, John found a four-leaf clover.

VERBAL PHRASES

A **verbal** is a word or phrase that is formed from a verb but does not function as a verb. Depending on its particular form, it may be used as a noun, adjective, or adverb. A verbal does **not** replace a verb in a sentence.

Examples:

> verb
> Correct: Walk a mile daily.

> This is a complete sentence with the implied subject *you.*

> verbal
> Incorrect: To walk a mile.

> This is not a sentence since there is no functional verb.

There are three types of verbal: **participles**, **gerunds**, and **infinitives**. Each type of verbal has a corresponding **phrase** that consists of the verbal itself along with any complements or modifiers.

PARTICIPLES

A **participle** is a type of verbal that always functions as an adjective. The present participle always ends with *-ing*. Past participles end with *-d, -ed, -n,* or *-t.* Participles are combined with helping verbs to form certain verb tenses, but a participle by itself cannot function as a verb.

Examples:

verb	present participle	past participle
dance	dancing	danced

Participial phrases most often come right before or right after the noun or pronoun that they modify.

Examples:

participial phrase
Shipwrecked on an island, the boys started to fish for food.

participial phrase
Having been seated for five hours, we got out of the car to stretch our legs.

participial phrase
Praised for their work, the group accepted the first-place trophy.

GERUNDS

A **gerund** is a type of verbal that always functions as a **noun**. Like present participles, gerunds always end with *-ing*, but they can be easily distinguished from participles by the part of speech they represent (participles always function as adjectives). Since a gerund or gerund phrase always functions as a noun, it can be used as the subject of a sentence, the predicate nominative, or the object of a verb or preposition.

Examples:

gerund
We want to be known for teaching the poor.
object of preposition

gerund
Coaching this team is the best job of my life.
subject

gerund
We like practicing our songs in the basement.
object of verb

INFINITIVES

An **infinitive** is a type of verbal that can function as a noun, an adjective, or an adverb. An infinitive is made of the word *to* and the basic form of the verb. As with all other types of verbal phrases, an infinitive phrase includes the verbal itself and all of its complements or modifiers.

115

Examples:

infinitive
To join the team is my goal in life.
noun

infinitive
The animals have enough food to eat for the night.
adjective

infinitive
People lift weights to exercise their muscles.
adverb

> **Review Video: Verbals**
> Visit mometrix.com/academy and enter code: 915480

APPOSITIVE PHRASES

An **appositive** is a word or phrase that is used to explain or rename nouns or pronouns. Noun phrases, gerund phrases, and infinitive phrases can all be used as appositives.

Examples:

appositive
Terriers, hunters at heart, have been dressed up to look like lap dogs.

The noun phrase *hunters at heart* renames the noun *terriers*.

appositive
His plan, to save and invest his money, was proven as a safe approach.

The infinitive phrase explains what the plan is.

Appositive phrases can be **essential** or **nonessential**. An appositive phrase is essential if the person, place, or thing being described or renamed is too general for its meaning to be understood without the appositive.

Examples:

essential
Two of America's Founding Fathers, George Washington and Thomas Jefferson, served as presidents.

nonessential
George Washington and Thomas Jefferson, two Founding Fathers, served as presidents.

ABSOLUTE PHRASES

An absolute phrase is a phrase that consists of **a noun followed by a participle**. An absolute phrase provides **context** to what is being described in the sentence, but it does not modify or explain any particular word; it is essentially independent.

116

Examples:

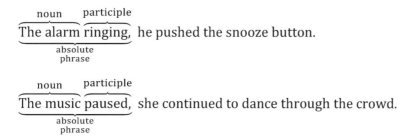

PARALLELISM

When multiple items or ideas are presented in a sentence in series, such as in a list, the items or ideas must be stated in grammatically equivalent ways. For example, if two ideas are listed in parallel and the first is stated in gerund form, the second cannot be stated in infinitive form. (e.g., *I enjoy <u>reading</u> and <u>to study</u>*. [incorrect]) An infinitive and a gerund are not grammatically equivalent. Instead, you should write *I enjoy <u>reading</u> and <u>studying</u>* OR *I like <u>to read</u> and <u>to study</u>*. In lists of more than two, all items must be parallel.

Example:

Incorrect: He stopped at the office, grocery store, and the pharmacy before heading home.

The first and third items in the list of places include the article *the*, so the second item needs it as well.

Correct: He stopped at the office, *the* grocery store, and the pharmacy before heading home.

Example:

Incorrect: While vacationing in Europe, she went biking, skiing, and climbed mountains.

The first and second items in the list are gerunds, so the third item must be as well.

Correct: While vacationing in Europe, she went biking, skiing, and *mountain climbing*.

> **Review Video: Parallel Sentence Construction**
> Visit mometrix.com/academy and enter code: 831988

SENTENCE PURPOSE

There are four types of sentences: declarative, imperative, interrogative, and exclamatory.

A **declarative** sentence states a fact and ends with a period.

The football game starts at seven o'clock.

An **imperative** sentence tells someone to do something and generally ends with a period. An urgent command might end with an exclamation point instead.

Don't forget to buy your ticket.

An **interrogative** sentence asks a question and ends with a question mark.

Are you going to the game on Friday?

117

An **exclamatory** sentence shows strong emotion and ends with an exclamation point.

I can't believe we won the game!

SENTENCE STRUCTURE

Sentences are classified by structure based on the type and number of clauses present. The four classifications of sentence structure are the following:

Simple: A simple sentence has one independent clause with no dependent clauses. A simple sentence may have **compound elements** (i.e., compound subject or verb).

Examples:

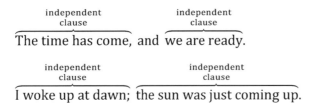

Compound: A compound sentence has two or more independent clauses with no dependent clauses. Usually, the independent clauses are joined with a comma and a coordinating conjunction or with a semicolon.

Examples:

independent clause — independent clause
The time has come, and we are ready.

independent clause — independent clause
I woke up at dawn; the sun was just coming up.

Complex: A complex sentence has one independent clause and at least one dependent clause.

Examples:

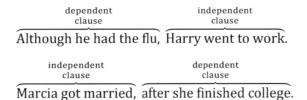

dependent clause — independent clause
Although he had the flu, Harry went to work.

independent clause — dependent clause
Marcia got married, after she finished college.

118

Compound-Complex: A compound-complex sentence has at least two independent clauses and at least one dependent clause.

Examples:

independent   dependent   independent
clause   clause   clause

John is my friend who went to India, and he brought back souvenirs.

independent   independent   dependent
clause   clause   clause

You may not realize this, but we heard the music that you played last night.

> **Review Video: Sentence Structure**
> Visit mometrix.com/academy and enter code: 700478

Sentence variety is important to consider when writing an essay or speech. A variety of sentence lengths and types creates rhythm, makes a passage more engaging, and gives writers an opportunity to demonstrate their writing style. Writing that uses the same length or type of sentence without variation can be boring or difficult to read. To evaluate a passage for effective sentence variety, it is helpful to note whether the passage contains diverse sentence structures and lengths. It is also important to pay attention to the way each sentence starts and avoid beginning with the same words or phrases.

SENTENCE FRAGMENTS

Recall that a group of words must contain at least one **independent clause** in order to be considered a sentence. If it doesn't contain even one independent clause, it is called a **sentence fragment**.

The appropriate process for **repairing** a sentence fragment depends on what type of fragment it is. If the fragment is a dependent clause, it can sometimes be as simple as removing a subordinating word (e.g., when, because, if) from the beginning of the fragment. Alternatively, a dependent clause can be incorporated into a closely related neighboring sentence. If the fragment is missing some required part, like a subject or a verb, the fix might be as simple as adding the missing part.

Examples:

> **Fragment**: Because he wanted to sail the Mediterranean.
>
> **Removed subordinating word**: He wanted to sail the Mediterranean.
>
> **Combined with another sentence**: Because he wanted to sail the Mediterranean, he booked a Greek island cruise.

RUN-ON SENTENCES

Run-on sentences consist of multiple independent clauses that have not been joined together properly. Run-on sentences can be corrected in several different ways:

Join clauses properly: This can be done with a comma and coordinating conjunction, with a semicolon, or with a colon or dash if the second clause is explaining something in the first.

Writing

Example:

>   **Incorrect**: I went on the trip, we visited lots of castles.

>   **Corrected**: I went on the trip, and we visited lots of castles.

Split into separate sentences: This correction is most effective when the independent clauses are very long or when they are not closely related.

Example:

>   **Incorrect**: The drive to New York takes ten hours, my uncle lives in Boston.

>   **Corrected**: The drive to New York takes ten hours. My uncle lives in Boston.

Make one clause dependent: This is the easiest way to make the sentence correct and more interesting at the same time. It's often as simple as adding a subordinating word between the two clauses or before the first clause.

Example:

>   **Incorrect**: I finally made it to the store and I bought some eggs.

>   **Corrected**: When I finally made it to the store, I bought some eggs.

Reduce to one clause with a compound verb: If both clauses have the same subject, remove the subject from the second clause, and you now have just one clause with a compound verb.

Example:

>   **Incorrect**: The drive to New York takes ten hours, it makes me very tired.

>   **Corrected**: The drive to New York takes ten hours and makes me very tired.

Note: While these are the simplest ways to correct a run-on sentence, often the best way is to completely reorganize the thoughts in the sentence and rewrite it.

Review Video: <u>Fragments and Run-on Sentences</u>
Visit mometrix.com/academy and enter code: 541989

DANGLING AND MISPLACED MODIFIERS

DANGLING MODIFIERS

A dangling modifier is a dependent clause or verbal phrase that does not have a clear logical connection to a word in the sentence.

Example:

Incorrect: $\overbrace{\text{Reading each magazine article,}}^{\text{dangling modifier}}$ the stories caught my attention.

The word *stories* cannot be modified by *Reading each magazine article*. People can read, but stories cannot read. Therefore, the subject of the sentence must be a person.

Corrected: $\overbrace{\text{Reading each magazine article,}}^{\text{gerund phrase}}$ I was entertained by the stories.

Example:

Incorrect: $\overbrace{\text{Ever since childhood,}}^{\text{dangling modifier}}$ my grandparents have visited me for Christmas.

The speaker in this sentence can't have been visited by her grandparents when *they* were children, since she wouldn't have been born yet. Either the modifier should be clarified or the sentence should be rearranged to specify whose childhood is being referenced.

Clarified: $\overbrace{\text{Ever since I was a child,}}^{\text{dependent clause}}$ my grandparents have visited for Christmas.

Rearranged: $\overbrace{\text{Ever since childhood,}}^{\text{adverb phrase}}$ I have enjoyed my grandparents visiting for Christmas.

MISPLACED MODIFIERS

Because modifiers are grammatically versatile, they can be put in many different places within the structure of a sentence. The danger of this versatility is that a modifier can accidentally be placed where it is modifying the wrong word or where it is not clear which word it is modifying.

Example:

Incorrect: She read the book to a crowd $\overbrace{\text{that was filled with beautiful pictures.}}^{\text{modifier}}$

The book was filled with beautiful pictures, not the crowd.

Corrected: She read the book $\overbrace{\text{that was filled with beautiful pictures}}^{\text{modifier}}$ to a crowd.

121

Example:

Ambiguous: Derek saw a bus nearly hit a man $\overbrace{\text{on his way to work}}^{\text{modifier}}$.

Was Derek on his way to work or was the other man?

Derek: $\overbrace{\text{On his way to work,}}^{\text{modifier}}$ Derek saw a bus nearly hit a man.

The other man: Derek saw a bus nearly hit a man $\overbrace{\text{who was on his way to work}}^{\text{modifier}}$.

SPLIT INFINITIVES

A split infinitive occurs when a modifying word comes between the word *to* and the verb that pairs with *to*.

Example: To *clearly* explain vs. *To explain* clearly | To *softly* sing vs. *To sing* softly

Though considered improper by some, split infinitives may provide better clarity and simplicity in some cases than the alternatives. As such, avoiding them should not be considered a universal rule.

DOUBLE NEGATIVES

Standard English allows **two negatives** only when a **positive** meaning is intended. (e.g., The team was *not displeased* with their performance.) Double negatives to emphasize negation are not used in standard English.

Negative modifiers (e.g., never, no, and not) should not be paired with other negative modifiers or negative words (e.g., none, nobody, nothing, or neither). The modifiers *hardly, barely*, and *scarcely* are also considered negatives in standard English, so they should not be used with other negatives.

PUNCTUATION
END PUNCTUATION
PERIODS

Use a period to end all sentences except direct questions and exclamations. Periods are also used for abbreviations.

Examples: 3 p.m. | 2 a.m. | Mr. Jones | Mrs. Stevens | Dr. Smith | Bill, Jr. | Pennsylvania Ave.

Note: An abbreviation is a shortened form of a word or phrase.

QUESTION MARKS

Question marks should be used following a **direct question**. A polite request can be followed by a period instead of a question mark.

Direct Question: What is for lunch today? | How are you? | Why is that the answer?

Polite Requests: Can you please send me the item tomorrow. | Will you please walk with me on the track.

Review Video: Question Marks
Visit mometrix.com/academy and enter code: 118471

EXCLAMATION MARKS

Exclamation marks are used after a word group or sentence that shows much feeling or has special importance. Exclamation marks should not be overused. They are saved for proper **exclamatory interjections**.

Example: We're going to the finals! | You have a beautiful car! | "That's crazy!" she yelled.

COMMAS

The comma is a punctuation mark that can help you understand connections in a sentence. Not every sentence needs a comma. However, if a sentence needs a comma, you need to put it in the right place. A comma in the wrong place (or an absent comma) will make a sentence's meaning unclear.

These are some of the rules for commas:

Use Case	Example
Before a **coordinating conjunction** joining independent clauses	Bob caught three fish, and I caught two fish.
After an **introductory phrase**	After the final out, we went to a restaurant to celebrate.
After an **adverbial clause**	Studying the stars, I was awed by the beauty of the sky.
Between **items in a series**	I will bring the turkey, the pie, and the coffee.
For **interjections**	Wow, you know how to play this game.
After *yes* and *no* responses	No, I cannot come tomorrow.
Separate **nonessential modifiers**	John Frank, who coaches the team, was promoted today.
Separate **nonessential appositives**	Thomas Edison, an American inventor, was born in Ohio.
Separate **nouns of direct address**	You, John, are my only hope in this moment.
Separate **interrogative tags**	This is the last time, correct?
Separate **contrasts**	You are my friend, not my enemy.
Writing **dates**	July 4, 1776, is an important date to remember.
Writing **addresses**	He is meeting me at 456 Delaware Avenue, Washington, D.C., tomorrow morning.
Writing **geographical names**	Paris, France, is my favorite city.
Writing **titles**	John Smith, PhD, will be visiting your class today.
Separate **expressions like *he said***	"You can start," she said, "with an apology."

A comma is also used **between coordinate adjectives** not joined with *and*. However, not all adjectives are coordinate (i.e., equal or parallel). To determine if your adjectives are coordinate, try connecting them with *and* or reversing their order. If it still sounds right, they are coordinate.

Incorrect: The kind, brown dog followed me home.

Correct: The kind, loyal dog followed me home.

SEMICOLONS

The semicolon is used to join closely related independent clauses without the need for a coordinating conjunction. Semicolons are also used in place of commas to separate list elements that have internal commas. Some rules for semicolons include:

Use Case	Example
Between closely connected independent clauses **not connected with a coordinating conjunction**	You are right; we should go with your plan.
Between independent clauses **linked with a transitional word**	I think that we can agree on this; however, I am not sure about my friends.
Between items in a **series that has internal punctuation**	I have visited New York, New York; Augusta, Maine; and Baltimore, Maryland.

> **Review Video: How to Use Semicolons**
> Visit mometrix.com/academy and enter code: 370605

COLONS

The colon is used to call attention to the words that follow it. When used in a sentence, a colon should only come at the **end** of a **complete sentence**. The rules for colons are as follows:

Use Case	Example
After an independent clause to **make a list**	I want to learn many languages: Spanish, German, and Italian.
For **explanations**	There is one thing that stands out on your resume: responsibility.
To give a **quote**	He started with an idea: "We are able to do more than we imagine."
After the **greeting in a formal letter**	To Whom It May Concern:
Show **hours and minutes**	It is 3:14 p.m.
Separate a **title and subtitle**	The essay is titled "America: A Short Introduction to a Modern Country."

> **Review Video: Using Colons**
> Visit mometrix.com/academy and enter code: 868673

PARENTHESES

Parentheses are used for additional information. Also, they can be used to put labels for letters or numbers in a series. Parentheses should be not be used very often. If they are overused, parentheses can be a distraction instead of a help.

Examples:

> **Extra Information**: The rattlesnake (see Image 2) is a dangerous snake of North and South America.

> **Series**: Include in the email (1) your name, (2) your address, and (3) your question for the author.

> **Review Video: Parentheses**
> Visit mometrix.com/academy and enter code: 947743

QUOTATION MARKS

Use quotation marks to close off **direct quotations** of a person's spoken or written words. Do not use quotation marks around indirect quotations. An indirect quotation gives someone's message without using the person's exact words. Use **single quotation marks** to close off a quotation inside a quotation.

> **Direct Quote**: Nancy said, "I am waiting for Henry to arrive."

> **Indirect Quote**: Henry said that he is going to be late to the meeting.

> **Quote inside a Quote**: The teacher asked, "Has everyone read 'The Gift of the Magi'?"

Quotation marks should be used around the titles of **short works**: newspaper and magazine articles, poems, short stories, songs, television episodes, radio programs, and subdivisions of books or websites.

Examples:

> "Rip Van Winkle" (short story by Washington Irving)

> "O Captain! My Captain!" (poem by Walt Whitman)

Although it is not standard usage, quotation marks are sometimes used to highlight **irony** or the use of words to mean something other than their dictionary definition. This type of usage should be employed sparingly, if at all.

Examples:

The boss warned Frank that he was walking on "thin ice."	Frank is not walking on real ice. Instead, he is being warned to avoid mistakes.
The teacher thanked the young man for his "honesty."	The quotation marks around *honesty* show that the teacher does not believe the young man's explanation.

Review Video: Quotation Marks
Visit mometrix.com/academy and enter code: 884918

Periods and commas are put **inside** quotation marks. Colons and semicolons are put **outside** the quotation marks. Question marks and exclamation points are placed inside quotation marks when they are part of a quote. When the question or exclamation mark goes with the whole sentence, the mark is left outside of the quotation marks.

Examples:

Period and comma	We read "The Gift of the Magi," "The Skylight Room," and "The Cactus."
Semicolon	They watched "The Nutcracker"; then, they went home.
Exclamation mark that is a part of a quote	The crowd cheered, "Victory!"
Question mark that goes with the whole sentence	Is your favorite short story "The Tell-Tale Heart"?

Writing

APOSTROPHES

An apostrophe is used to show **possession** or the **deletion of letters in contractions**. An apostrophe is not needed with the possessive pronouns *his, hers, its, ours, theirs, whose,* and *yours.*

Singular Nouns: David's car | a book's theme | my brother's board game

Plural Nouns that end with *-s*: the scissors' handle | boys' basketball

Plural Nouns that end without *-s*: Men's department | the people's adventure

> **Review Video: When to Use an Apostrophe**
> Visit mometrix.com/academy and enter code: 213068
>
> **Review Video: Punctuation Errors in Possessive Pronouns**
> Visit mometrix.com/academy and enter code: 221438

HYPHENS

Hyphens are used to **separate compound words**. Use hyphens in the following cases:

Use Case	Example
Compound numbers from 21 to 99 when written out in words	This team needs twenty-five points to win the game.
Written-out fractions that are used as adjectives	The recipe says that we need a three-fourths cup of butter.
Compound adjectives that come before a noun	The well-fed dog took a nap.
Unusual compound words that would be hard to read or easily confused with other words	This is the best anti-itch cream on the market.

Note: This is not a complete set of the rules for hyphens. A dictionary is the best tool for knowing if a compound word needs a hyphen.

> **Review Video: Hyphens**
> Visit mometrix.com/academy and enter code: 981632

DASHES

Dashes are used to show a **break** or a **change in thought** in a sentence or to act as parentheses in a sentence. When typing, use two hyphens to make a dash. Do not put a space before or after the dash. The following are the functions of dashes:

Use Case	Example
Set off parenthetical statements or an **appositive with internal punctuation**	The three trees—oak, pine, and magnolia—are coming on a truck tomorrow.
Show a **break or change in tone or thought**	The first question—how silly of me—does not have a correct answer.

ELLIPSIS MARKS

The ellipsis mark has **three** periods (…) to show when **words have been removed** from a quotation. If a **full sentence or more** is removed from a quoted passage, you need to use **four** periods to show the removed text and the end punctuation mark. The ellipsis mark should not be used at the beginning of a quotation. The ellipsis mark should also not be used at the end of a quotation unless some words have been deleted from the end of the final quoted sentence.

Example:

"Then he picked up the groceries...paid for them...later he went home."

BRACKETS

There are two main reasons to use brackets:

Use Case	Example
Placing **parentheses inside of parentheses**	The hero of this story, Paul Revere (a silversmith and industrialist [see Ch. 4]), rode through towns of Massachusetts to warn of advancing British troops.
Adding **clarification or detail to a quotation** that is not part of the quotation	The father explained, "My children are planning to attend my alma mater [State University]."

> **Review Video: Brackets**
> Visit mometrix.com/academy and enter code: 727546

COMMON USAGE MISTAKES
WORD CONFUSION
WHICH, THAT, AND WHO

The words *which*, *that*, and *who* can act as **relative pronouns** to help clarify or describe a noun.

Which is used for things only.

Example: Andrew's car, *which is old and rusty,* broke down last week.

That is used for people or things. *That* is usually informal when used to describe people.

Example: Is this the only book *that Louis L'Amour wrote?*

Example: Is Louis L'Amour the author *that wrote Western novels?*

Who is used for people or for animals that have an identity or personality.

Example: Mozart was the composer *who wrote those operas.*

Example: John's dog, *who is called Max,* is large and fierce.

HOMOPHONES

Homophones are words that sound alike (or similar) but have different **spellings** and **definitions**. A homophone is a type of **homonym**, which is a pair or group of words that are pronounced or spelled the same, but do not mean the same thing.

TO, TOO, AND TWO

To can be an adverb or a preposition for showing direction, purpose, and relationship. See your dictionary for the many other ways to use *to* in a sentence.

>   Examples: I went to the store. | I want to go with you.

Too is an adverb that means *also, as well, very,* or *in excess.*

>   Examples: I can walk a mile too. | You have eaten too much.

Two is a number.

>   Example: You have two minutes left.

THERE, THEIR, AND THEY'RE

There can be an adjective, adverb, or pronoun. Often, *there* is used to show a place or to start a sentence.

>   Examples: I went there yesterday. | There is something in his pocket.

Their is a pronoun that is used to show ownership.

>   Examples: He is their father. | This is their fourth apology this week.

They're is a contraction of *they are.*

>   Example: Did you know that they're in town?

KNEW AND NEW

Knew is the past tense of *know.*

>   Example: I knew the answer.

New is an adjective that means something is current, has not been used, or is modern.

>   Example: This is my new phone.

THEN AND THAN

Then is an adverb that indicates sequence or order:

>   Example: I'm going to run to the library and then come home.

Than is special-purpose word used only for comparisons:

>   Example: Susie likes chips more than candy.

ITS AND IT'S

Its is a pronoun that shows ownership.

>   Example: The guitar is in its case.

It's is a contraction of *it is*.

> Example: It's an honor and a privilege to meet you.

Note: The *h* in honor is silent, so *honor* starts with the vowel sound *o*, which must have the article *an*.

YOUR AND YOU'RE

Your is a pronoun that shows ownership.

> Example: This is your moment to shine.

You're is a contraction of *you are*.

> Example: Yes, you're correct.

SAW AND SEEN

Saw is the past-tense form of *see*.

> Example: I saw a turtle on my walk this morning.

Seen is the past participle of *see*.

> Example: I have seen this movie before.

AFFECT AND EFFECT

There are two main reasons that *affect* and *effect* are so often confused: 1) both words can be used as either a noun or a verb, and 2) unlike most homophones, their usage and meanings are closely related to each other. Here is a quick rundown of the four usage options:

Affect (n): feeling, emotion, or mood that is displayed

> Example: The patient had a flat *affect*. (i.e., his face showed little or no emotion)

Affect (v): to alter, to change, to influence

> Example: The sunshine *affects* the plant's growth.

Effect (n): a result, a consequence

> Example: What *effect* will this weather have on our schedule?

Effect (v): to bring about, to cause to be

> Example: These new rules will *effect* order in the office.

The noun form of *affect* is rarely used outside of technical medical descriptions, so if a noun form is needed on the test, you can safely select *effect*. The verb form of *effect* is not as rare as the noun form of *affect*, but it's still not all that likely to show up on your test. If you need a verb and you can't decide which to use based on the definitions, choosing *affect* is your best bet.

HOMOGRAPHS

Homographs are words that share the same spelling, but have different meanings and sometimes different pronunciations. To figure out which meaning is being used, you should be looking for

129

context clues. The context clues give hints to the meaning of the word. For example, the word *spot* has many meanings. It can mean "a place" or "a stain or blot." In the sentence "After my lunch, I saw a spot on my shirt," the word *spot* means "a stain or blot." The context clues of "After my lunch" and "on my shirt" guide you to this decision. A homograph is another type of homonym.

BANK

      (noun): an establishment where money is held for savings or lending

      (verb): to collect or pile up

CONTENT

      (noun): the topics that will be addressed within a book

      (adjective): pleased or satisfied

      (verb): to make someone pleased or satisfied

FINE

      (noun): an amount of money that acts a penalty for an offense

      (adjective): very small or thin

      (adverb): in an acceptable way

      (verb): to make someone pay money as a punishment

INCENSE

      (noun): a material that is burned in religious settings and makes a pleasant aroma

      (verb): to frustrate or anger

LEAD

      (noun): the first or highest position

      (noun): a heavy metallic element

      (verb): to direct a person or group of followers

      (adjective): containing lead

OBJECT

      (noun): a lifeless item that can be held and observed

      (verb): to disagree

PRODUCE

      (noun): fruits and vegetables

      (verb): to make or create something

REFUSE

      (noun): garbage or debris that has been thrown away

      (verb): to not allow

SUBJECT

> (noun): an area of study

> (verb): to force or subdue

TEAR

> (noun): a fluid secreted by the eyes

> (verb): to separate or pull apart

COMMONLY MISUSED WORDS AND PHRASES

A LOT

The phrase *a lot* should always be written as two words; never as *alot*.

> **Correct**: That's a lot of chocolate!

> **Incorrect**: He does that alot.

CAN

The word *can* is used to describe things that are possible occurrences; the word *may* is used to described things that are allowed to happen.

> **Correct**: May I have another piece of pie?

> **Correct**: I can lift three of these bags of mulch at a time.

> **Incorrect**: Mom said we can stay up thirty minutes later tonight.

COULD HAVE

The phrase *could of* is often incorrectly substituted for the phrase *could have*. Similarly, *could of*, *may of*, and *might of* are sometimes used in place of the correct phrases *could have*, *may have*, and *might have*.

> **Correct**: If I had known, I would have helped out.

> **Incorrect**: Well, that could of gone much worse than it did.

MYSELF

The word *myself* is a reflexive pronoun, often incorrectly used in place of *I* or *me*.

> **Correct**: He let me do it myself.

> **Incorrect**: The job was given to Dave and myself.

OFF

The phrase *off of* is a redundant expression that should be avoided. In most cases, it can be corrected simply by removing *of*.

> **Correct**: My dog chased the squirrel off its perch on the fence.

> **Incorrect**: He finally moved his plate off of the table.

Writing

131

SUPPOSED TO

The phrase *suppose to* is sometimes used incorrectly in place of the phrase *supposed to*.

Correct: I was supposed to go to the store this afternoon.

Incorrect: When are we suppose to get our grades?

TRY TO

The phrase *try and* is often used in informal writing and conversation to replace the correct phrase *try to*.

Correct: It's a good policy to try to satisfy every customer who walks in the door.

Incorrect: Don't try and do too much.

Writing Process

THE WRITING PROCESS

BRAINSTORMING

Brainstorming is a technique that is used to find a creative approach to a subject. This can be accomplished by simple **free-association** with a topic. For example, with paper and pen, write every thought that you have about the topic in a word or phrase. This is done without critical thinking. You should put everything that comes to your mind about the topic on your scratch paper. Then, you need to read the list over a few times. Next, look for patterns, repetitions, and clusters of ideas. This allows a variety of fresh ideas to come as you think about the topic.

FREE WRITING

Free writing is a more structured form of brainstorming. The method involves taking a limited amount of time (e.g., 2 to 3 minutes) to write everything that comes to mind about the topic in complete sentences. When time expires, review everything that has been written down. Many of your sentences may make little or no sense, but the insights and observations that can come from free writing make this method a valuable approach. Usually, free writing results in a fuller expression of ideas than brainstorming because thoughts and associations are written in complete sentences. However, both techniques can be used to complement each other.

PLANNING

Planning is the process of organizing a piece of writing before composing a draft. Planning can include creating an outline or a graphic organizer, such as a Venn diagram, a spider-map, or a flowchart. These methods should help the writer identify their topic, main ideas, and the general organization of the composition. Preliminary research can also take place during this stage. Planning helps writers organize all of their ideas and decide if they have enough material to begin their first draft. However, writers should remember that the decisions they make during this step will likely change later in the process, so their plan does not have to be perfect.

DRAFTING

Writers may then use their plan, outline, or graphic organizer to compose their first draft. They may write subsequent drafts to improve their writing. Writing multiple drafts can help writers consider different ways to communicate their ideas and address errors that may be difficult to correct without rewriting a section or the whole composition. Most writers will vary in how many drafts

132

they choose to write, as there is no "right" number of drafts. Writing drafts also takes away the pressure to write perfectly on the first try, as writers can improve with each draft they write.

REVISING, EDITING, AND PROOFREADING

Once a writer completes a draft, they can move on to the revising, editing, and proofreading steps to improve their draft. These steps begin with making broad changes that may apply to large sections of a composition and then making small, specific corrections. **Revising** is the first and broadest of these steps. Revising involves ensuring that the composition addresses an appropriate audience, includes all necessary material, maintains focus throughout, and is organized logically. Revising may occur after the first draft to ensure that the following drafts improve upon errors from the first draft. Some revision should occur between each draft to avoid repeating these errors. The **editing** phase of writing is narrower than the revising phase. Editing a composition should include steps such as improving transitions between paragraphs, ensuring each paragraph is on topic, and improving the flow of the text. The editing phase may also include correcting grammatical errors that cannot be fixed without significantly altering the text. **Proofreading** involves fixing misspelled words, typos, other grammatical errors, and any remaining surface-level flaws in the composition.

RECURSIVE WRITING PROCESS

However you approach writing, you may find comfort in knowing that the revision process can occur in any order. The **recursive writing process** is not as difficult as the phrase may make it seem. Simply put, the recursive writing process means that you may need to revisit steps after completing other steps. It also implies that the steps are not required to take place in any certain order. Indeed, you may find that planning, drafting, and revising can all take place at about the same time. The writing process involves moving back and forth between planning, drafting, and revising, followed by more planning, more drafting, and more revising until the writing is satisfactory.

> **Review Video: Recursive Writing Process**
> Visit mometrix.com/academy and enter code: 951611

OUTLINING AND ORGANIZING IDEAS
ESSAYS

Essays usually focus on one topic, subject, or goal. There are several types of essays, including informative, persuasive, and narrative. An essay's structure and level of formality depend on the type of essay and its goal. While narrative essays typically do not include outside sources, other types of essays often require some research and the integration of primary and secondary sources.

The basic format of an essay typically has three major parts: the introduction, the body, and the conclusion. The body is further divided into the writer's main points. Short and simple essays may have three main points, while essays covering broader ranges and going into more depth can have almost any number of main points, depending on length.

An essay's introduction should answer three questions:

1. What is the **subject** of the essay?

    If a student writes an essay about a book, the answer would include the title and author of the book and any additional information needed—such as the subject or argument of the book.

2. How does the essay **address** the subject?

To answer this, the writer identifies the essay's organization by briefly summarizing main points and the evidence supporting them.

3. What will the essay **prove**?
   This is the thesis statement, usually the opening paragraph's last sentence, clearly stating the writer's message.

The body elaborates on all the main points related to the thesis, introducing one main point at a time, and includes supporting evidence with each main point. Each body paragraph should state the point in a topic sentence, which is usually the first sentence in the paragraph. The paragraph should then explain the point's meaning, support it with quotations or other evidence, and then explain how this point and the evidence are related to the thesis. The writer should then repeat this procedure in a new paragraph for each additional main point.

The conclusion reiterates the content of the introduction, including the thesis, to remind the reader of the essay's main argument or subject. The essay writer may also summarize the highlights of the argument or description contained in the body of the essay, following the same sequence originally used in the body. For example, a conclusion might look like: Point 1 + Point 2 + Point 3 = Thesis, or Point 1 → Point 2 → Point 3 → Thesis Proof. Good organization makes essays easier for writers to compose and provides a guide for readers to follow. Well-organized essays hold attention better and are more likely to get readers to accept their theses as valid.

MAIN IDEAS, SUPPORTING DETAILS, AND OUTLINING A TOPIC

A writer often begins the first paragraph of a paper by stating the **main idea** or point, also known as the **topic sentence**. The rest of the paragraph supplies particular details that develop and support the main point. One way to visualize the relationship between the main point and supporting information is by considering a table: the tabletop is the main point, and each of the table's legs is a supporting detail or group of details. Both professional authors and students can benefit from planning their writing by first making an outline of the topic. Outlines facilitate quick identification of the main point and supporting details without having to wade through the additional language that will exist in the fully developed essay, article, or paper. Outlining can also help readers to analyze a piece of existing writing for the same reason. The outline first summarizes the main idea in one sentence. Then, below that, it summarizes the supporting details in a numbered list. Writing the paper then consists of filling in the outline with detail, writing a paragraph for each supporting point, and adding an introduction and conclusion.

INTRODUCTION

The purpose of the introduction is to capture the reader's attention and announce the essay's main idea. Normally, the introduction contains 50-80 words, or 3-5 sentences. An introduction can begin with an interesting quote, a question, or a strong opinion—something that will **engage** the reader's interest and prompt them to keep reading. If you are writing your essay to a specific prompt, your introduction should include a **restatement or summarization** of the prompt so that the reader will have some context for your essay. Finally, your introduction should briefly state your **thesis or main idea**: the primary thing you hope to communicate to the reader through your essay. Don't try to include all of the details and nuances of your thesis, or all of your reasons for it, in the introduction. That's what the rest of the essay is for!

> **Review Video: Introduction**
> Visit mometrix.com/academy and enter code: 961328

THESIS STATEMENT

The thesis is the main idea of the essay. A temporary thesis, or working thesis, should be established early in the writing process because it will serve to keep the writer focused as ideas develop. This temporary thesis is subject to change as you continue to write.

The temporary thesis has two parts: a **topic** (i.e., the focus of your essay based on the prompt) and a **comment**. The comment makes an important point about the topic. A temporary thesis should be interesting and specific. Also, you need to limit the topic to a manageable scope. These three questions are useful tools to measure the effectiveness of any temporary thesis:

- Does the focus of my essay have enough interest to hold an audience?
- Is the focus of my essay specific enough to generate interest?
- Is the focus of my essay manageable for the time limit? Too broad? Too narrow?

The thesis should be a generalization rather than a fact because the thesis prepares readers for facts and details that support the thesis. The process of bringing the thesis into sharp focus may help in outlining major sections of the work. Once the thesis and introduction are complete, you can address the body of the work.

> **Review Video: Thesis Statements**
> Visit mometrix.com/academy and enter code: 691033

SUPPORTING THE THESIS

Throughout your essay, the thesis should be **explained clearly and supported** adequately by additional arguments. The thesis sentence needs to contain a clear statement of the purpose of your essay and a comment about the thesis. With the thesis statement, you have an opportunity to state what is noteworthy of this particular treatment of the prompt. Each sentence and paragraph should build on and support the thesis.

When you respond to the prompt, use parts of the passage to support your argument or defend your position. Using supporting evidence from the passage strengths your argument because readers can see your attention to the entire passage and your response to the details and facts within the passage. You can use facts, details, statistics, and direct quotations from the passage to uphold your position. Be sure to point out which information comes from the original passage and base your argument around that evidence.

BODY

In an essay's introduction, the writer establishes the thesis and may indicate how the rest of the piece will be structured. In the body of the piece, the writer **elaborates** upon, **illustrates**, and **explains** the **thesis statement**. How writers arrange supporting details and their choices of paragraph types are development techniques. Writers may give examples of the concept introduced in the thesis statement. If the subject includes a cause-and-effect relationship, the author may explain its causality. A writer will explain or analyze the main idea of the piece throughout the body, often by presenting arguments for the veracity or credibility of the thesis statement. Writers may use development to define or clarify ambiguous terms. Paragraphs within the body may be organized using natural sequences, like space and time. Writers may employ **inductive reasoning,** using multiple details to establish a generalization or causal relationship, or **deductive reasoning**, proving a generalized hypothesis or proposition through a specific example or case.

PARAGRAPHS

After the introduction of a passage, a series of body paragraphs will carry a message through to the conclusion. Each paragraph should be **unified around a main point**. Normally, a good topic sentence summarizes the paragraph's main point. A topic sentence is a general sentence that gives an introduction to the paragraph.

The sentences that follow support the topic sentence. However, though it is usually the first sentence, the topic sentence can come as the final sentence to the paragraph if the earlier sentences give a clear explanation of the paragraph's topic. This allows the topic sentence to function as a concluding sentence. Overall, the paragraphs need to stay true to the main point. This means that any unnecessary sentences that do not advance the main point should be removed.

The main point of a paragraph requires adequate development (i.e., a substantial paragraph that covers the main point). A paragraph of two or three sentences does not cover a main point. This is especially true when the main point of the paragraph gives strong support to the argument of the thesis. An occasional short paragraph is fine as a transitional device. However, a well-developed argument will have paragraphs with more than a few sentences.

METHODS OF DEVELOPING PARAGRAPHS

Common methods of adding substance to paragraphs include examples, illustrations, analogies, and cause and effect.

- **Examples** are supporting details to the main idea of a paragraph or a passage. When authors write about something that their audience may not understand, they can provide an example to show their point. When authors write about something that is not easily accepted, they can give examples to prove their point.
- **Illustrations** are extended examples that require several sentences. Well-selected illustrations can be a great way for authors to develop a point that may not be familiar to their audience.
- **Analogies** make comparisons between items that appear to have nothing in common. Analogies are employed by writers to provoke fresh thoughts about a subject. These comparisons may be used to explain the unfamiliar, to clarify an abstract point, or to argue a point. Although analogies are effective literary devices, they should be used carefully in arguments. Two things may be alike in some respects but completely different in others.
- **Cause and effect** is an excellent device to explain the connection between an action or situation and a particular result. One way that authors can use cause and effect is to state the effect in the topic sentence of a paragraph and add the causes in the body of the paragraph. This method can give an author's paragraphs structure, which always strengthens writing.

TYPES OF PARAGRAPHS

A **paragraph of narration** tells a story or a part of a story. Normally, the sentences are arranged in chronological order (i.e., the order that the events happened). However, flashbacks (i.e., an anecdote from an earlier time) can be included.

A **descriptive paragraph** makes a verbal portrait of a person, place, or thing. When specific details are used that appeal to one or more of the senses (i.e., sight, sound, smell, taste, and touch), authors give readers a sense of being present in the moment.

A **process paragraph** is related to time order (i.e., First, you open the bottle. Second, you pour the liquid, etc.). Usually, this describes a process or teaches readers how to perform a process.

Comparing two things draws attention to their similarities and indicates a number of differences. When authors contrast, they focus only on differences. Both comparing and contrasting may be done point-by-point, noting both the similarities and differences of each point, or in sequential paragraphs, where you discuss all the similarities and then all the differences, or vice versa.

BREAKING TEXT INTO PARAGRAPHS

For most forms of writing, you will need to use multiple paragraphs. As such, determining when to start a new paragraph is very important. Reasons for starting a new paragraph include:

- To mark off the introduction and concluding paragraphs
- To signal a shift to a new idea or topic
- To indicate an important shift in time or place
- To explain a point in additional detail
- To highlight a comparison, contrast, or cause and effect relationship

PARAGRAPH LENGTH

Most readers find that their comfort level for a paragraph is between 100 and 200 words. Shorter paragraphs cause too much starting and stopping and give a choppy effect. Paragraphs that are too long often test the attention span of readers. Two notable exceptions to this rule exist. In scientific or scholarly papers, longer paragraphs suggest seriousness and depth. In journalistic writing, constraints are placed on paragraph size by the narrow columns in a newspaper format.

The first and last paragraphs of a text will usually be the introduction and conclusion. These special-purpose paragraphs are likely to be shorter than paragraphs in the body of the work. Paragraphs in the body of the essay follow the subject's outline (e.g., one paragraph per point in short essays and a group of paragraphs per point in longer works). Some ideas require more development than others, so it is good for a writer to remain flexible. A paragraph of excessive length may be divided, and shorter ones may be combined.

CONCLUSION

Two important principles to consider when writing a conclusion are strength and closure. A strong conclusion gives the reader a sense that the author's main points are meaningful and important, and that the supporting facts and arguments are convincing, solid, and well developed. When a conclusion achieves closure, it gives the impression that the writer has stated all necessary information and points and completed the work, rather than simply stopping after a specified length. Some things to avoid when writing concluding paragraphs include:

- Introducing a completely new idea
- Beginning with obvious or unoriginal phrases like "In conclusion" or "To summarize"
- Apologizing for one's opinions or writing
- Repeating the thesis word for word rather than rephrasing it
- Believing that the conclusion must always summarize the piece

Writing

COHERENCE IN WRITING

COHERENT PARAGRAPHS

A smooth flow of sentences and paragraphs without gaps, shifts, or bumps will lead to paragraph **coherence**. Ties between old and new information can be smoothed using several methods:

- **Linking ideas clearly**, from the topic sentence to the body of the paragraph, is essential for a smooth transition. The topic sentence states the main point, and this should be followed by specific details, examples, and illustrations that support the topic sentence. The support may be direct or indirect. In **indirect support**, the illustrations and examples may support a sentence that in turn supports the topic directly.
- The **repetition of key words** adds coherence to a paragraph. To avoid dull language, variations of the key words may be used.
- **Parallel structures** are often used within sentences to emphasize the similarity of ideas and connect sentences giving similar information.
- Maintaining a **consistent verb tense** throughout the paragraph helps. Shifting tenses affects the smooth flow of words and can disrupt the coherence of the paragraph.

SEQUENCE WORDS AND PHRASES

When a paragraph opens with the topic sentence, the second sentence may begin with a phrase like *first of all*, introducing the first supporting detail or example. The writer may introduce the second supporting item with words or phrases like *also*, *in addition*, and *besides*. The writer might introduce succeeding pieces of support with wording like, *another thing*, *moreover*, *furthermore*, or *not only that, but*. The writer may introduce the last piece of support with *lastly*, *finally*, or *last but not least*. Writers get off the point by presenting off-target items not supporting the main point. For example, a main point *my dog is not smart* is supported by the statement, *he's six years old and still doesn't answer to his name*. But *he cries when I leave for school* is not supportive, as it does not indicate lack of intelligence. Writers stay on point by presenting only supportive statements that are directly relevant to and illustrative of their main point.

TRANSITIONS

Transitions between sentences and paragraphs guide readers from idea to idea and indicate relationships between sentences and paragraphs. Writers should be judicious in their use of transitions, inserting them sparingly. They should also be selected to fit the author's purpose—transitions can indicate time, comparison, and conclusion, among other purposes. Tone is also important to consider when using transitional phrases, varying the tone for different audiences. For example, in a scholarly essay, *in summary* would be preferable to the more informal *in short*.

When working with transitional words and phrases, writers usually find a natural flow that indicates when a transition is needed. In reading a draft of the text, it should become apparent where the flow is disrupted. At this point, the writer can add transitional elements during the

138

revision process. Revising can also afford an opportunity to delete transitional devices that seem heavy handed or unnecessary.

> **Review Video: Transitions in Writing**
> Visit mometrix.com/academy and enter code: 233246

TYPES OF TRANSITIONAL WORDS

Time	afterward, immediately, earlier, meanwhile, recently, lately, now, since, soon, when, then, until, before, etc.
Sequence	too, first, second, further, moreover, also, again, and, next, still, besides, finally
Comparison	similarly, in the same way, likewise, also, again, once more
Contrasting	but, although, despite, however, instead, nevertheless, on the one hand... on the other hand, regardless, yet, in contrast
Cause and Effect	because, consequently, thus, therefore, then, to this end, since, so, as a result, if... then, accordingly
Examples	for example, for instance, such as, to illustrate, indeed, in fact, specifically
Place	near, far, here, there, to the left/right, next to, above, below, beyond, opposite, beside
Concession	granted that, naturally, of course, it may appear, although it is true that
Repetition, Summary, or Conclusion	as mentioned earlier, as noted, in other words, in short, on the whole, to summarize, therefore, as a result, to conclude, in conclusion
Addition	and, also, furthermore, moreover
Generalization	in broad terms, broadly speaking, in general

> **Review Video: Transition Words**
> Visit mometrix.com/academy and enter code: 707563
>
> **Review Video: How to Effectively Connect Sentences**
> Visit mometrix.com/academy and enter code: 948325

WRITING STYLE AND FORM

WRITING STYLE AND LINGUISTIC FORM

Linguistic form encodes the literal meanings of words and sentences. It comes from the phonological, morphological, syntactic, and semantic parts of a language. **Writing style** consists of different ways of encoding the meaning and indicating figurative and stylistic meanings. An author's writing style can also be referred to as his or her **voice**.

Writers' stylistic choices accomplish three basic effects on their audiences:

- They **communicate meanings** beyond linguistically dictated meanings,
- They communicate the **author's attitude**, such as persuasive or argumentative effects accomplished through style, and
- They communicate or **express feelings**.

Within style, component areas include:

- Narrative structure
- Viewpoint

Writing

- Focus
- Sound patterns
- Meter and rhythm
- Lexical and syntactic repetition and parallelism
- Writing genre
- Representational, realistic, and mimetic effects
- Representation of thought and speech
- Meta-representation (representing representation)
- Irony
- Metaphor and other indirect meanings
- Representation and use of historical and dialectal variations
- Gender-specific and other group-specific speech styles, both real and fictitious
- Analysis of the processes for inferring meaning from writing

TONE

Tone may be defined as the writer's **attitude** toward the topic, and to the audience. This attitude is reflected in the language used in the writing. The tone of a work should be **appropriate to the topic** and to the intended audience. While it may be fine to use slang or jargon in some pieces, other texts should not contain such terms. Tone can range from humorous to serious and any level in between. It may be more or less formal, depending on the purpose of the writing and its intended audience. All these nuances in tone can flavor the entire writing and should be kept in mind as the work evolves.

Review Video: Style, Tone, and Mood
Visit mometrix.com/academy and enter code: 416961

WORD SELECTION

A writer's choice of words is a signature of their style. Careful thought about the use of words can improve a piece of writing. A passage can be an exciting piece to read when attention is given to the use of vivid or specific nouns rather than general ones.

Example:

General: His kindness will never be forgotten.

Specific: His thoughtful gifts and bear hugs will never be forgotten.

ACTIVE AND PASSIVE LANGUAGE

Attention should also be given to the kind of verbs that are used in sentences. Active verbs (e.g., run, swim) are about an action. Whenever possible, an **active verb should replace a linking verb** to provide clear examples for arguments and to strengthen a passage overall. When using an active verb, one should be sure that the verb is used in the active voice instead of the passive voice. Verbs are in the active voice when the subject is the one doing the action. A verb is in the passive voice when the subject is the recipient of an action.

Example:

Passive: The winners were called to the stage by the judges.

Active: The judges called the winners to the stage.

140

CONCISENESS

Conciseness is writing that communicates a message in the fewest words possible. Writing concisely is valuable because short, uncluttered messages allow the reader to understand the author's message more easily and efficiently. Planning is important in writing concise messages. If you have in mind what you need to write beforehand, it will be easier to make a message short and to the point. Do not state the obvious.

Revising is also important. After the message is written, make sure you have effective, pithy sentences that efficiently get your point across. When reviewing the information, imagine a conversation taking place, and concise writing will likely result.

APPROPRIATE KINDS OF WRITING FOR DIFFERENT TASKS, PURPOSES, AND AUDIENCES

When preparing to write a composition, consider the audience and purpose to choose the best type of writing. Four common types of writing are persuasive, expository, and narrative. **Persuasive**, or argumentative writing, is used to convince the audience to take action or agree with the author's claims. **Expository** writing is meant to inform the audience of the author's observations or research on a topic. **Narrative** writing is used to tell the audience a story and often allows more room for creativity. **Descriptive** writing is when a writer provides a substantial amount of detail to the reader so he or she can visualize the topic. While task, purpose, and audience inform a writer's mode of writing, these factors also impact elements such as tone, vocabulary, and formality.

For example, students who are writing to persuade their parents to grant them some additional privilege, such as permission for a more independent activity, should use more sophisticated vocabulary and diction that sounds more mature and serious to appeal to the parental audience. However, students who are writing for younger children should use simpler vocabulary and sentence structure, as well as choose words that are more vivid and entertaining. They should treat their topics more lightly, and include humor when appropriate. Students who are writing for their classmates may use language that is more informal, as well as age-appropriate.

> **Review Video: <u>Writing Purpose and Audience</u>**
> Visit mometrix.com/academy and enter code: 146627

FORMALITY IN WRITING

LEVEL OF FORMALITY

The relationship between writer and reader is important in choosing a **level of formality** as most writing requires some degree of formality. **Formal writing** is for addressing a superior in a school or work environment. Business letters, textbooks, and newspapers use a moderate to high level of formality. **Informal writing** is appropriate for private letters, personal emails, and business correspondence between close associates.

For your exam, you will want to be aware of informal and formal writing. One way that this can be accomplished is to watch for shifts in point of view in the essay. For example, unless writers are using a personal example, they will rarely refer to themselves (e.g., "*I* think that *my* point is very clear.") to avoid being informal when they need to be formal.

Also, be mindful of an author who addresses his or her audience **directly** in their writing (e.g., "Readers, *like you*, will understand this argument.") as this can be a sign of informal writing. Good writers understand the need to be consistent with their level of formality. Shifts in levels of formality or point of view can confuse readers and cause them to discount the message.

Writing

141

CLICHÉS

Clichés are phrases that have been **overused** to the point that the phrase has no importance or has lost the original meaning. These phrases have no originality and add very little to a passage. Therefore, most writers will avoid the use of clichés. Another option is to make changes to a cliché so that it is not predictable and empty of meaning.

Examples:

When life gives you lemons, make lemonade.

Every cloud has a silver lining.

JARGON

Jargon is **specialized vocabulary** that is used among members of a certain trade or profession. Since jargon is understood by only a small audience, writers will use jargon in passages that will only be read by a specialized audience. For example, medical jargon should be used in a medical journal but not in a New York Times article. Jargon includes exaggerated language that tries to impress rather than inform. Sentences filled with jargon are not precise and are difficult to understand.

Examples:

"He is going to *toenail* these frames for us." (Toenail is construction jargon for nailing at an angle.)

"They brought in a *kip* of material today." (Kip refers to 1000 pounds in architecture and engineering.)

SLANG

Slang is an **informal** and sometimes private language that is understood by some individuals. Slang terms have some usefulness, but they can have a small audience. So, most formal writing will not include this kind of language.

Examples:

"Yes, the event was a blast!" (In this sentence, *blast* means that the event was a great experience.)

"That attempt was an epic fail." (By *epic fail*, the speaker means that his or her attempt was not a success.)

COLLOQUIALISM

A colloquialism is a word or phrase that is found in informal writing. Unlike slang, **colloquial language** will be familiar to a greater range of people. However, colloquialisms are still considered inappropriate for formal writing. Colloquial language can include some slang, but these are limited to contractions for the most part.

Examples:

"Can *y'all* come back another time?" (Y'all is a contraction of "you all.")

"Will you stop him from building this *castle in the air*?" (A "castle in the air" is an improbable or unlikely event.)

ACADEMIC LANGUAGE

In educational settings, students are often expected to use academic language in their schoolwork. Academic language is also commonly found in dissertations and theses, texts published by academic journals, and other forms of academic research. Academic language conventions may vary between fields, but general academic language is free of slang, regional terminology, and noticeable grammatical errors. Specific terms may also be used in academic language, and it is important to understand their proper usage. A writer's command of academic language impacts their ability to communicate in an academic or professional context. While it is acceptable to use colloquialisms, slang, improper grammar, or other forms of informal speech in social settings or at home, it is inappropriate to practice non-academic language in academic contexts.

COMMON TYPES OF WRITING

AUTOBIOGRAPHICAL NARRATIVES

Autobiographical narratives are narratives written by an author about an event or period in their life. Autobiographical narratives are written from one person's perspective, in first person, and often include the author's thoughts and feelings alongside their description of the event or period. Structure, style, or theme varies between different autobiographical narratives, since each narrative is personal and specific to its author and his or her experience.

REFLECTIVE ESSAY

A less common type of essay is the reflective essay. **Reflective essays** allow the author to reflect, or think back, on an experience and analyze what they recall. They should consider what they learned from the experience, what they could have done differently, what would have helped them during the experience, or anything else that they have realized from looking back on the experience. Reflection essays incorporate both objective reflection on one's own actions and subjective explanation of thoughts and feelings. These essays can be written for a number of experiences in a formal or informal context.

JOURNALS AND DIARIES

A **journal** is a personal account of events, experiences, feelings, and thoughts. Many people write journals to express their feelings and thoughts or to help them process experiences they have had. Since journals are **private documents** not meant to be shared with others, writers may not be concerned with grammar, spelling, or other mechanics. However, authors may write journals that they expect or hope to publish someday; in this case, they not only express their thoughts and feelings and process their experiences, but they also attend to their craft in writing them. Some authors compose journals to record a particular time period or a series of related events, such as a cancer diagnosis, treatment, surviving the disease, and how these experiences have changed or affected them. Other experiences someone might include in a journal are recovering from addiction, journeys of spiritual exploration and discovery, time spent in another country, or anything else someone wants to personally document. Journaling can also be therapeutic, as some people use journals to work through feelings of grief over loss or to wrestle with big decisions.

EXAMPLES OF DIARIES IN LITERATURE

The Diary of a Young Girl by Dutch Jew Anne Frank (1947) contains her life-affirming, nonfictional diary entries from 1942-1944 while her family hid in an attic from World War II's genocidal Nazis. *Go Ask Alice* (1971) by Beatrice Sparks is a cautionary, fictional novel in the form of diary entries by Alice, an unhappy, rebellious teen who takes LSD, runs away from home and lives with hippies, and eventually returns home. Frank's writing reveals an intelligent, sensitive, insightful girl, raised by intellectual European parents—a girl who believes in the goodness of human nature despite surrounding atrocities. Alice, influenced by early 1970s counterculture, becomes less optimistic.

Writing

However, similarities can be found between them: Frank dies in a Nazi concentration camp while the fictitious Alice dies from a drug overdose. Both young women are also unable to escape their surroundings. Additionally, adolescent searches for personal identity are evident in both books.

> **Review Video: Journals, Diaries, Letters, and Blogs**
> Visit mometrix.com/academy and enter code: 432845

LETTERS

Letters are messages written to other people. In addition to letters written between individuals, some writers compose letters to the editors of newspapers, magazines, and other publications, while some write "Open Letters" to be published and read by the general public. Open letters, while intended for everyone to read, may also identify a group of people or a single person whom the letter directly addresses. In everyday use, the most-used forms are business letters and personal or friendly letters. Both kinds share common elements: business or personal letterhead stationery; the writer's return address at the top; the addressee's address next; a salutation, such as "Dear [name]" or some similar opening greeting, followed by a colon in business letters or a comma in personal letters; the body of the letter, with paragraphs as indicated; and a closing, like "Sincerely/Cordially/Best regards/etc." or "Love," in intimate personal letters.

EARLY LETTERS

The Greek word for "letter" is *epistolē*, which became the English word "epistle." The earliest letters were called epistles, including the New Testament's epistles from the apostles to the Christians. In ancient Egypt, the writing curriculum in scribal schools included the epistolary genre. Epistolary novels frame a story in the form of letters. Examples of noteworthy epistolary novels include:

- *Pamela* (1740), by 18th-century English novelist Samuel Richardson
- *Shamela* (1741), Henry Fielding's satire of *Pamela* that mocked epistolary writing.
- *Lettres persanes* (1721) by French author Montesquieu
- *The Sorrows of Young Werther* (1774) by German author Johann Wolfgang von Goethe
- *The History of Emily Montague* (1769), the first Canadian novel, by Frances Brooke
- *Dracula* (1897) by Bram Stoker
- *Frankenstein* (1818) by Mary Shelley
- *The Color Purple* (1982) by Alice Walker

BLOGS

The word "blog" is derived from "weblog" and refers to writing done exclusively on the internet. Readers of reputable newspapers expect quality content and layouts that enable easy reading. These expectations also apply to blogs. For example, readers can easily move visually from line to line when columns are narrow, while overly wide columns cause readers to lose their places. Blogs must also be posted with layouts enabling online readers to follow them easily. However, because the way people read on computer, tablet, and smartphone screens differs from how they read print on paper, formatting and writing blog content is more complex than writing newspaper articles. Two major principles are the bases for blog-writing rules: The first is while readers of print articles skim to estimate their length, online they must scroll down to scan; therefore, blog layouts need more subheadings, graphics, and other indications of what information follows. The second is onscreen reading can be harder on the eyes than reading printed paper, so legibility is crucial in blogs.

144

RULES AND RATIONALES FOR WRITING BLOGS

1. Format all posts for smooth page layout and easy scanning.
2. Column width should not be too wide, as larger lines of text can be difficult to read
3. Headings and subheadings separate text visually, enable scanning or skimming, and encourage continued reading.
4. Bullet-pointed or numbered lists enable quick information location and scanning.
5. Punctuation is critical, so beginners should use shorter sentences until confident in their knowledge of punctuation rules.
6. Blog paragraphs should be far shorter—two to six sentences each—than paragraphs written on paper to enable "chunking" because reading onscreen is more difficult.
7. Sans-serif fonts are usually clearer than serif fonts, and larger font sizes are better.
8. Highlight important material and draw attention with **boldface**, but avoid overuse. Avoid hard-to-read *italics* and ALL CAPITALS.
9. Include enough blank spaces: overly busy blogs tire eyes and brains. Images not only break up text but also emphasize and enhance text and can attract initial reader attention.
10. Use background colors judiciously to avoid distracting the eye or making it difficult to read.
11. Be consistent throughout posts, since people read them in different orders.
12. Tell a story with a beginning, middle, and end.

SPECIALIZED TYPES OF WRITING

EDITORIALS

Editorials are articles in newspapers, magazines, and other serial publications. Editorials express an opinion or belief belonging to the majority of the publication's leadership. This opinion or belief generally refers to a specific issue, topic, or event. These articles are authored by a member, or a small number of members, of the publication's leadership and are often written to affect their readers, such as persuading them to adopt a stance or take a particular action.

RESUMES

Resumes are brief, but formal, documents that outline an individual's experience in a certain area. Resumes are most often used for job applications. Such resumes will list the applicant's work experience, certification, and achievements or qualifications related to the position. Resumes should only include the most pertinent information. They should also use strategic formatting to highlight the applicant's most impressive experiences and achievements, to ensure the document can be read quickly and easily, and to eliminate both visual clutter and excessive negative space.

REPORTS

Reports summarize the results of research, new methodology, or other developments in an academic or professional context. Reports often include details about methodology and outside influences and factors. However, a report should focus primarily on the results of the research or development. Reports are objective and deliver information efficiently, sacrificing style for clear and effective communication.

MEMORANDA

A memorandum, also called a memo, is a formal method of communication used in professional settings. Memoranda are printed documents that include a heading listing the sender and their job title, the recipient and their job title, the date, and a specific subject line. Memoranda often include an introductory section explaining the reason and context for the memorandum. Next, a memorandum includes a section with details relevant to the topic. Finally, the memorandum will conclude with a paragraph that politely and clearly defines the sender's expectations of the recipient.

Writing

TECHNOLOGY IN THE WRITING PROCESS

Modern technology has yielded several tools that can be used to make the writing process more convenient and organized. Word processors and online tools, such as databases and plagiarism detectors, allow much of the writing process to be completed in one place, using one device.

TECHNOLOGY FOR PLANNING AND DRAFTING

For the planning and drafting stages of the writing process, word processors are a helpful tool. These programs also feature formatting tools, allowing users to create their own planning tools or create digital outlines that can be easily converted into sentences, paragraphs, or an entire essay draft. Online databases and references also complement the planning process by providing convenient access to information and sources for research. Word processors also allow users to keep up with their work and update it more easily than if they wrote their work by hand. Online word processors often allow users to collaborate, making group assignments more convenient. These programs also allow users to include illustrations or other supplemental media in their compositions.

TECHNOLOGY FOR REVISING, EDITING, AND PROOFREADING

Word processors also benefit the revising, editing, and proofreading stages of the writing process. Most of these programs indicate errors in spelling and grammar, allowing users to catch minor errors and correct them quickly. There are also websites designed to help writers by analyzing text for deeper errors, such as poor sentence structure, inappropriate complexity, lack of sentence variety, and style issues. These websites can help users fix errors they may not know to look for or may have simply missed. As writers finish these steps, they may benefit from checking their work for any plagiarism. There are several websites and programs that compare text to other documents and publications across the internet and detect any similarities within the text. These websites show the source of the similar information, so users know whether or not they referenced the source and unintentionally plagiarized its contents.

TECHNOLOGY FOR PUBLISHING

Technology also makes managing written work more convenient. Digitally storing documents keeps everything in one place and is easy to reference. Digital storage also makes sharing work easier, as documents can be attached to an email or stored online. This also allows writers to publish their work easily, as they can electronically submit it to other publications or freely post it to a personal blog, profile, or website.

Research

SOURCES OF INFORMATION

PRIMARY SOURCES

In literature review, one may examine both primary and secondary sources. Primary sources contain original information that was witnessed, gathered, or otherwise produced by the source's author. **Primary sources** can include firsthand accounts, found in sources such as books, autobiographies, transcripts, speeches, videos, photos, and personal journals or diaries. Primary sources may also include records of information, such as government documents, or personally-conducted research in sources like reports and essays. They may be found in academic books, journals and other periodicals, and authoritative databases. Using primary sources allows researchers to develop their own conclusions about the subject. Primary sources are also reliable for finding information about a person or their personal accounts and experiences. Primary sources

146

such as photos, videos, audio recordings, transcripts, and government documents are often reliable, as they are usually objective and can be used to confirm information from other sources.

SECONDARY SOURCES

Secondary sources are sources that reference information originally provided by another source. The original source may be cited, quoted, paraphrased, or described in a secondary source. **Secondary sources** may be articles, essays, videos, or books found in periodicals, magazines, newspapers, films, databases, or websites. A secondary source can be used to reference another researcher's analysis or conclusion from a primary source. This information can inform the researcher of the existing discussions regarding their subject. These types of sources may also support the researcher's claims by providing a credible argument that contributes to the researcher's argument. Secondary sources may also highlight connections between primary sources or criticize both primary and other secondary sources. These types of secondary sources are valuable because they provide information and conclusions the researcher may not have considered or found, otherwise.

> **Review Video: Primary and Secondary Sources**
> Visit mometrix.com/academy and enter code: 383328

TYPES OF SOURCES

- **Textbooks** are specialized materials that are designed to thoroughly instruct readers on a particular topic. Textbooks often include features such as a table of contents, visuals, an index, a glossary, headings, and practice questions and exercises.
- **Newspapers** are collections of several written pieces and are primarily used to distribute news stories to their audience. In addition to news articles, newspapers may also include advertisements or pieces meant to entertain their audience, such as comic strips, columns, and letters from readers. Newspapers are written for a variety of audiences, as they are published on both the local and national levels.
- **Manuals** are instructional documents that accompany a product or explain an important procedure. Manuals include a table of contents, guidelines, and instructional content. Instructional manuals often include information about safe practices, risks, and product warranty. The instructions in manuals are often presented as step-by-step instructions, as they are meant to help users properly use a product or complete a task.
- **Electronic texts** are written documents that are read digitally and are primarily accessed online or through a network. Many electronic texts have characteristics similar to printed texts, such as a table of contents, publication information, a main text, and supplemental materials. However, electronic texts are more interactive and can be navigated more quickly. Electronic texts can also provide more accessibility, as they can be easily resized or narrated by text-to-speech software.

FINDING SOURCES

Finding sources for a research project may be intimidating or difficult. There are numerous sources available, and several research tools to help researchers find them. Starting with one of these tools can help narrow down the number of sources a researcher is working with at one time.

- **Libraries** house independent, printed publications that are organized by subject. This makes finding sources easy, since researchers can visit sections with sources relevant to their topic and immediately see what sources are available. Many libraries also offer printed journals and collections that include sources related to a common subject or written by the same author.

147

Writing

- **Databases** offer digital access to sources from a wide variety of libraries and online containers. To use a database, users search for keywords related to their topic or the type of source they want to use. The database then lists results related to or featuring those key words. Users can narrow their results using filters that will limit their results based on factors such as publication year, source type, or whether the sources are peer-reviewed. Database search results also list individual articles and methods of accessing the article directly. While databases help users find sources, they do not guarantee users access to each source.
- **Academic Journals** are collections of articles that cover a particular topic or fit within a certain category. These journals are often offered both online and in print. Academic journals typically contain peer-reviewed works or works that have undergone another type of reviewing process.

CREDIBILITY

There are innumerable primary and secondary sources available in print and online. However, not every published or posted source is appropriate for a research project. When finding sources, the researcher must know how to evaluate each source for credibility and relevance. Not only must the sources be reliable and relevant to the research subject, but they must also be appropriate and help form an answer to the research question. As researchers progress in their research and composition, the relevance of each source will become clear. Appropriate sources will contribute valuable information and arguments to the researcher's own thoughts and conclusions, providing useful evidence to bolster the researcher's claims. The researcher has the freedom to choose which sources they reference or even change their research topic and question in response to the sources they find. However, the researcher should not use unreliable sources, and determining a source's credibility is not always easy.

CONSIDERATIONS FOR EVALUATING THE CREDIBILITY OF A SOURCE
- The author and their purpose for writing the source
- The author's qualifications to write on the topic
- Whether the source is peer-reviewed or included in a scholarly publication
- The publisher
- The target audience
- The jargon or dialect the source is written in (e.g., academic, technical)
- The presence of bias or manipulation of information
- The date of publication
- The author's use of other sources to support their claims
- Whether any outside sources are cited appropriately in the source
- The accuracy of information presented

AUTHOR'S PURPOSE AND CREDIBILITY

Knowing who wrote a source and why they wrote it is important to determine whether a source is appropriate for a research project. The author should be qualified to write on the subject of the material. Their purpose may be to inform their audience of information, to present and defend an analysis, or even to criticize a work or other argument. The researcher must decide whether the author's purpose makes the source appropriate to use. The source's container and publisher are important to note because they indicate the source's reputability and whether other qualified individuals have reviewed the information in the source. Credible secondary sources should also reference other sources, primary or secondary, that support or inform the source's content. Evaluating the accuracy of the information or the presence of bias in a source will require careful

reading and critical thinking on the part of the researcher. However, a source with excellent credentials may still contain pieces of inaccurate information or bias, so it is the researcher's responsibility to be careful in their use of each source.

CITING SOURCES
INTEGRATING REFERENCES AND QUOTATIONS

In research papers, one can include studies whose conclusions agree with one's position (Reed 284; Becker and Fagen 93), as well as studies that disagree (Limbaugh 442, Beck 69) by including parenthetical citations as demonstrated in this sentence. Quotations should be selective: writers should compose an original sentence and incorporate only a few words from a research source. If students cannot use more original words than quotation, they are likely padding their compositions. However, including quotations appropriately increases the credibility of the writer and their argument.

PROPERLY INTEGRATING QUOTATIONS

When using sources in a research paper, it is important to integrate information so that the flow of the composition is not interrupted as the two compositions are combined. When quoting outside sources, it is necessary to lead into the quote and ensure that the whole sentence is logical, is grammatically correct, and flows well. Below is an example of an incorrectly integrated quote.

> During the Industrial Revolution, many unions organized labor strikes "child labor, unregulated working conditions, and excessive working hours" in America.

Below is the same sentence with a properly integrated quote.

> During the Industrial Revolution, many unions organized labor strikes to protest the presence of "child labor, unregulated working conditions, and excessive working hours" in America.

In the first example, the connection between "strikes" and the quoted list is unclear. In the second example, the phrase "to protest the presence of" link the ideas together and successfully creates a suitable place for the quotation.

When quoting sources, writers should work quotations and references seamlessly into their sentences instead of interrupting the flow of their own argument to summarize a source. Summarizing others' content is often a ploy to bolster word counts. Writing that analyzes the content, evaluates it, and synthesizes material from various sources demonstrates critical thinking skills and is thus more valuable.

PROPERLY INCORPORATING OUTSIDE SOURCES

Writers do better to include short quotations rather than long. For example, quoting six to eight long passages in a 10-page paper is excessive. It is also better to avoid wording like "This quotation shows," "As you can see from this quotation," or "It talks about." These are amateur, feeble efforts to interact with other authors' ideas. Also, writing about sources and quotations wastes words that should be used to develop one's own ideas. Quotations should be used to stimulate discussion rather than taking its place. Ending a paragraph, section, or paper with a quotation is not incorrect per se, but using it to prove a point, without including anything more in one's own words regarding the point or subject, suggests a lack of critical thinking about the topic and consideration of multiple alternatives. It can also be a tactic to dissuade readers from challenging one's propositions. Writers should include references and quotations that challenge as well as support their thesis statements.

Writing

Presenting evidence on both sides of an issue makes it easier for reasonably skeptical readers to agree with a writer's viewpoint.

TEXTUAL EVIDENCE

No analysis is complete without textual evidence. Summaries, paraphrases, and quotes are all forms of textual evidence, but direct quotes from the text are the most effective form of evidence. The best textual evidence is relevant, accurate, and clearly supports the writer's claim. This can include pieces of descriptions, dialogue, or exposition that shows the applicability of the analysis to the text. Analysis that is average, or sufficient, shows an understanding of the text; contains supporting textual evidence that is relevant and accurate, if not strong; and shows a specific and clear response. Analysis that partially meets criteria also shows understanding, but the textual evidence is generalized, incomplete, only partly relevant or accurate, or connected only weakly. Inadequate analysis is vague, too general, or incorrect. It may give irrelevant or incomplete textual evidence, or may simply summarize the plot rather than analyzing the work. It is important to incorporate textual evidence from the work being analyzed and any supplemental materials and to provide appropriate attribution for these sources.

CITING SOURCES

Formal research writers must **cite all sources used**—books, articles, interviews, conversations, and anything else that contributed to the research. One reason is to **avoid plagiarism** and give others credit for their ideas. Another reason is to help readers find the sources consulted in the research and access more information about the subject for further reading and research. Additionally, citing sources helps to make a paper academically authoritative. To prepare, research writers should keep a running list of sources consulted, in an electronic file or on file cards. For every source used, the writer needs specific information. For books, a writer needs to record the author's and editor's names, book title, publication date, city, and publisher name. For articles, one needs the author's name, article title, journal (or magazine or newspaper) name, volume and issue number, publication date, and page numbers. For electronic resources, a writer will need the author's name, article information plus the URL, database name, name of the database's publisher, and the date of access.

COMMON REFERENCE STYLES

Three common reference styles are **MLA** (Modern Language Association), **APA** (American Psychological Association), and **Turabian** (created by author Kate Turabian, also known as the Chicago Manual of Style). Each style formats citation information differently. Professors and instructors often specify that students use one of these. Generally, APA style is used in psychology and sociology papers, and MLA style is used in English literature papers and similar scholarly projects. To understand how these styles differ, consider an imaginary article cited in each of these styles. This article is titled "Ten Things You Won't Believe Dragons Do," written by author Andra Gaines, included in the journal *Studies in Fantasy Fiction*, and published by Quest for Knowledge Publishing.

MLA:

Gaines, Andra. "Ten Things You Won't Believe Dragons Do." Studies in Fantasy Fiction, vol. 3, no. 8, Quest for Knowledge Publishing, 21 Aug. 2019.

APA:

Gaines, A. (2019). Ten Things You Won't Believe Dragons Do. *Studies in Fantasy Fiction, 3(8)*, 42-65.

<u>CHICAGO</u>:

Gaines, Andra. "Ten Things You Won't Believe Dragons Do," *Studies in Fantasy Fiction* 3, no. 8 (2019): 42-65.

Within each of these styles, citations, though they vary according to the type of source and how its used, generally follow a structure and format similar to those above. For example, citations for whole books will probably not include a container title or a volume number, but will otherwise look very similar.

> **Review Video: <u>Citing Sources</u>**
> Visit mometrix.com/academy and enter code: 993637

Chapter Quiz

Ready to see how well you retained what you just read? Scan the QR code to go directly to the chapter quiz interface for this study guide. If you're using a computer, simply visit the bonus page at **<u>mometrix.com/bonus948/pert</u>** and click the Chapter Quizzes link.

PERT Practice Test #1

SCAN HERE

Want to take this practice test in an online interactive format?
Check out the bonus page, which includes interactive practice questions and
much more: **mometrix.com/bonus948/pert**

Mathematics

1. What is $(-11) + 27$?

    a. −37
    b. −16
    c. 16
    d. 37

2. Sean and Hillary are baking cookies for a bake sale. Sean baked 48 chocolate chip cookies, and Hillary baked 36 sugar cookies. If 50 cookies were sold altogether, how many were left over at the end of the bake sale?

    a. 43 cookies
    b. 33 cookies
    c. 34 cookies
    d. 44 cookies

3. Jamie has $\frac{1}{2}$ an acre of land. He wants to plant trees on $\frac{1}{4}$ of the land. How many acres of his land will Jamie use to plant trees?

    a. $\frac{1}{8}$
    b. $\frac{2}{8}$
    c. $\frac{1}{6}$
    d. $\frac{2}{6}$

4. What is the product of 1.67 and 4.09?

    a. 0.68303
    b. 6.8303
    c. 68.303
    d. 683.03

5. What is $0.924 - 0.439$?

    a. 0.485
    b. 0.595
    c. 4.850
    d. 5.950

6. What is $\frac{18}{24}$, in its most simplified form?

 a. $\frac{1}{4}$
 b. $\frac{1}{2}$
 c. $\frac{2}{4}$
 d. $\frac{3}{4}$

7. At noon, the temperature is 45 degrees Fahrenheit. The meteorologist predicts the temperature will drop 6 degrees per hour. Based on the meteorologist's prediction, what would the temperature be, in degrees Fahrenheit, at 8pm?

 a. −48° F
 b. −3° F
 c. 3° F
 d. 48° F

8. A boat rental company charges a $15 daily fee and $4 per hour for renting a boat. Which equation can be used to calculate the total rental fee for one day, y, for renting the boat for x number of hours?

 a. $y = 4x + 15$
 b. $y = 15x + 4$
 c. $x = 4y + 15$
 d. $x = 15y + 4$

9. The equation $x - 5 = 12$ is given. What is the value of x?

 a. $x = 6$
 b. $x = 7$
 c. $x = 17$
 d. $x = 60$

10. The equation $\frac{w}{92} = 5$ is given. What is the value of w?

 a. $w = 18$
 b. $w = 87$
 c. $w = 97$
 d. $w = 460$

153

PERT Practice Test #1

11. Graph the solution to the inequality: $7x - 8 > 2x + 17.$

a.

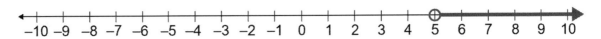

b.

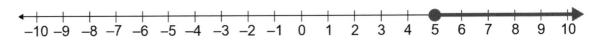

c.

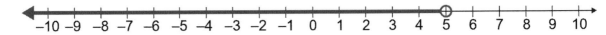

d.

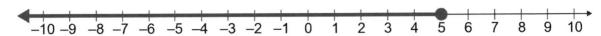

12. Which graph represents the linear equation $y = 2x - 3$?

a.

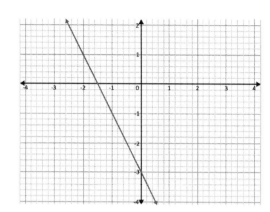

c.

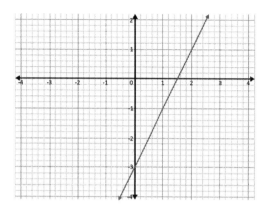

b.

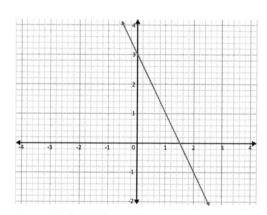

d.

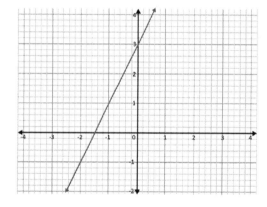

13. Which graph represents the linear equation $x = 4$?

a.

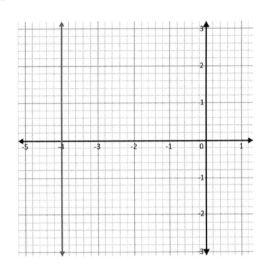

c.

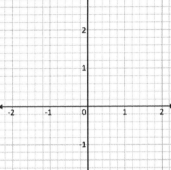

b.

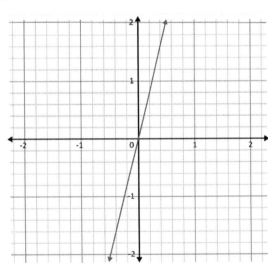

d.

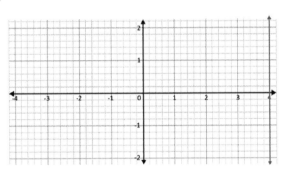

14. Evaluate the expression $4\sqrt{6} + 8\sqrt{6}$. Simplify your answer as much as possible.

a. $12\sqrt{12}$
b. 72
c. $12\sqrt{6}$
d. $24\sqrt{3}$

15. A dress is marked down by 20% and placed on a clearance rack, on which is posted a sign reading, "Take an extra 25% off already reduced merchandise." What fraction of the original price is the final sale price of the dress?

   a. $\frac{2}{5}$

   b. $\frac{9}{20}$

   c. $\frac{3}{5}$

   d. $\frac{11}{20}$

16. Which of the following expressions is equivalent to $-2x(x+6)^2$?

   a. $-2x^3 + 12x^2 - 36x$
   b. $-2x^3 - 24x^2 - 72x$
   c. $-2x^2 + 36x$
   d. $-2x^3 - 12x^2 - 72x$

17. Simplify the following expression: $2x + 5x^2 - 7x + 11 - 2x^2$.

   a. $7x^2 + 4x - 2$
   b. $3x^2 - 5x + 11$
   c. $4x^2 - 2x + 7$
   d. $11x^2 - 3x + 4$

18. Simplify the following expression: $\frac{4-(-12)}{-9+5}$.

   a. -8
   b. -4
   c. -2
   d. 4

19. Which of the following is equal to the difference between 4^3 and 3^4?

   a. 0
   b. 1
   c. 27
   d. 17

20. If $a = -6$ and $b = 7$, then what is $4a(3b + 5) + 2b$ equal to?

   a. -610
   b. -485
   c. 638
   d. 850

21. Let $y = \frac{x^4 - 2}{x^2 + 1}$. If $x = -2$, what is the value of y?

   a. $-3\frac{3}{5}$

   b. $2\frac{4}{5}$

   c. $-2\frac{4}{5}$

   d. $2\frac{2}{3}$

22. If $3(x + 14) = 4(x + 9)$, what does x equal?
    a. $x = 4$
    b. $x = 6$
    c. $x = 12$
    d. $x = 15$

23. Simplify the following expression: $\dfrac{16x^3 - 32x^2 + 8x}{4x}$
    a. $4x^3 - 8x^2 + 2x$
    b. $12x^2 - 28x^2 + 4$
    c. $4x^2 - 8x + 2$
    d. $4x^2 + 8x + 2$

24. Simplify the expression: $\left(y^2 + 9y - 2\right) + \left(4y^2 - y - 5\right)$
    a. $5y^2 + 8y - 7$
    b. $5y^2 + 8y + 10$
    c. $5y^2 + 10y - 7$
    d. $5y^2 + 10y + 10$

25. Use factoring to simplify the following:
$$x^2 + 7x + 12$$
    a. $(x + 6)(x + 2)$
    b. $(x + 4)(x + 3)$
    c. $(x + 6)(x + 1)$
    d. $(x + 5)(x + 2)$

26. Which of the following expressions is a factor of the polynomial $x^2 - 4x - 21$?
    a. $(x - 4)$
    b. $(x - 3)$
    c. $(x + 7)$
    d. $(x - 7)$

27. Solve the following for x:
$$x^2 + 8x + 16 = 0$$
    a. $x = -4, 4$
    b. $x = 4$
    c. $x = -4$
    d. $x = -2, 2$

28. If $x^2 + 5x = 6$, then what does x equal?
    a. −6 or −1
    b. −6 or 1
    c. −1 or 6
    d. 1 or 6

29. Simplify the expression $x^5 \times (2x)^3$.

    a. $2x^8$

    b. $2x^{15}$

    c. $8x^8$

    d. $8x^{15}$

30. Simplify the expression: $\left(a^{15} \times a^6\right)^2$.

    a. a^{18}

    b. a^{10}

    c. a^{36}

    d. a^{42}

Reading

Refer to the following for questions 1–5:

Cultivation of Tomato Plants

Tomato plants should be started in window boxes or greenhouses in late March so that they will be ready for the garden after the last frost. Use a soil of equal parts of sand, peat moss, and manure, and plant the seeds about a quarter of an inch deep. After covering, water them through a cloth to protect the soil and cover the box with a pane of glass. Keep the box in a warm place for a few days, then place it in a sunny window. After the second leaf makes its appearance on the seedling, transplant the plant to another box, placing the seedlings two inches apart. Another alternative is to put the sprouted seedlings in four-inch pots, setting them deeper in the soil than they stood in the seedbed. To make the stem stronger, pinch out the top bud when the seedlings are four or five inches in height.

Finally, place the plants in their permanent positions after they have grown to be twelve or fifteen inches high. When transplanting, parts of some of the longest leaves should be removed. Large plants may be set five or six inches deep.

The soil should be fertilized the previous season. Fresh, stable manure, used as fertilizer, would delay the time of fruiting. To improve the condition of the soil, work in a spade full of old manure to a depth of at least a foot. Nitrate of soda, applied at about two hundred pounds per acre, may be used to give the plant a good start.

Plants grown on supports may be set two feet apart in the row, with the rows three or four feet apart depending upon the variety. Plants not supported by stakes or other methods should be set four feet apart.

Unsupported vines give a lighter yield, and much of the fruit is likely to rot during the wet seasons. Use well-sharpened stakes about two inches in diameter and five feet long. Drive the stakes into the ground at least six inches from the plants so that the roots will not be injured. Tie the tomato vines to the stakes with strings made out of strips of cloth, as twine is likely to cut them. Care must be taken not to

159

wrap the limbs so tightly as to interfere with their growth. The training should start before the plants begin to trail on the ground.

1. What is the overall purpose of this passage?
   a. To describe how soil should be treated in order to plant tomatoes
   b. To give an overview of how tomato plants are cultured
   c. To teach the reader how to operate a farm
   d. To describe a method of supporting tomato vines

2. What does the passage imply as the reason that the seeds should not be planted outdoors immediately?
   a. A late freeze might kill the seedlings.
   b. The soil outdoors is too heavy for new seedlings.
   c. A heavy rain might wash away the seedlings.
   d. New seedlings need to be close to one another and then be moved apart later.

3. What would happen if the bud weren't pinched out of the seedlings when they are in individual pots?
   a. The plants would be weaker.
   b. The plants would freeze.
   c. The plants would need more water.
   d. The plants would not survive as long.

4. Why is old manure preferred to fresh manure?
   a. Fresh manure delays the plant's production of tomatoes.
   b. Fresh manure smells worse.
   c. Old manure is less expensive.
   d. Old manure mixes more readily with nitrate of soda.

5. What is the purpose of the last paragraph?
   a. To explain why unsupported plants give rotten fruit
   b. To explain why cloth is used rather than wire
   c. To describe in detail how tomato plants are cultured
   d. To instruct the reader in the method of supporting tomato vines for culture

Refer to the following for questions 6–10:

Garth

The next morning, she realized that she had slept. This surprised her—so long had sleep been denied her! She opened her eyes and saw the sun at the window. And then, beside it in the window, the deformed visage of Garth. Quickly, she shut her eyes again, feigning sleep. But he was not fooled. Presently, she heard his voice, soft and kind: "Don't be afraid. I'm your friend. I came to watch you sleep, is all. There now, I am behind the wall. You can open your eyes."

The voice seemed pained and plaintive. The Hungarian opened her eyes, and saw the window empty. Steeling herself, she arose, went to it, and looked out. She saw the man below, cowering by the wall, looking grief-stricken and resigned. Making an effort to overcome her revulsion, she spoke to him as kindly as she could.

"Come," she said, but Garth, seeing her lips move, thought she was sending him away. He rose and began to lumber off, his eyes lowered and filled with despair.

"Come!" she cried again, but he continued to move off. Then, she swept from the cell, ran to him, and took his arm. Feeling her touch, Garth trembled uncontrollably. Feeling that she drew him toward her, he lifted his supplicating eye, and his whole face lit up with joy.

She drew him into the garden, where she sat upon a wall, and for a while, they sat and contemplated one another. The more the Hungarian looked at Garth, the more deformities she discovered. The twisted spine, the lone eye, the huge torso over the tiny legs. She couldn't comprehend how a creature so awkwardly constructed could exist. And yet, from the air of sadness and gentleness that pervaded his figure, she began to reconcile herself to it.

"Did you call me back?" asked he.

"Yes," she replied, nodding. He recognized the gesture.

"Ah," he exclaimed. "Do you know that I am deaf?"

"Poor fellow," exclaimed the Hungarian, with an expression of pity.

"You'd think nothing more could be wrong with me," Garth put in, somewhat bitterly. But he was happier than he could remember having been.

6. During this passage, how do the girl's emotions toward Garth change?
a. They go from fear to loathing.
b. They go from anger to fear.
c. They go from fear to disdain.
d. They go from revulsion to pity.

7. What is a synonym for the word *supplicating*?
a. Castigating
b. Menacing
c. Repeating
d. Begging

8. Which of the following adjectives would you use to describe Garth's feelings toward himself?
a. Contemplative
b. Destitute
c. Resentment
d. Deflated

9. What two characteristics are contrasted in Garth?
a. Ugliness and gentleness
b. Fear and merriment
c. Happiness and sadness
d. Anger and fearfulness

PERT Practice Test #1

161

10. Why was the girl surprised that she had slept?

    a.   She usually tried to avoid sleeping.

    b.   It had been a long time since she had had the chance to sleep.

    c.   She hadn't intended to go to sleep.

    d.   Garth looked so frightening that she thought he would keep her awake.

Refer to the following for questions 11–15:

Leaving

(1) Even though Martin and Beth's steps were muffled by the falling snow, Beth could still hear the faint crunch of leaves underneath. (2) The hushed woods had often made Beth feel safe and at peace, but these days they just made her feel lonely.

(3) "I'm glad we decided to hike the trail, Martin. (4) It's so quiet and pretty."

(5) "Sure."

(6) Beth couldn't understand how it happened, but over the past few months this silence had grown between them, weighing down their relationship. (7) Of course, there was that thing with Mary, but Beth had forgiven Martin. (8) They moved on. (9) It was in the past.

(10) "Do you want to see a movie tonight?" asked Beth. (11) "There's a new one showing at the downtown theater."

(12) "Whatever you want."

(13) She wanted her husband back. (14) She wanted the laughter and games. (15) She wanted the late-night talks over coffee. (16) She wanted to forget Mary and Martin together. (17) She wanted to feel some sort of rapport again.

(18) "Is everything alright, Martin?"

(19) "I'm fine. (20) Just tired."

(21) "We didn't have to come; we could have stayed at home."

(22) "It's fine."

(23) Beth closed her eyes, tilted her head back, and breathed in the crisp air. (24) "Fine" once meant "very good," or "precious." (25) Now, it is a meaningless word, an excuse not to tell other people what's on your mind. (26) "Fine" had hung in the air between them for months now, a softly falling word that hid them from each other. (27) Beth wasn't even sure she knew Martin anymore, but she was confident that it was only a matter of time before everything was not "fine," only a matter of time before he told her...

(28) "I have to leave."

(29) "Huh? (30) What?"

(31) "I got a page. (32) My patient is going into cardiac arrest."

(33) "I wish you didn't have to leave."

(34) "I'm sorry, but I have to go."

(35) "I know."

11. It is reasonable to infer that Martin and Beth's relationship is strained because:
   a. Martin recently lost his job.
   b. Martin was unfaithful to Beth.
   c. Martin works too much.
   d. Martin does not want to go to the movies.

12. According to Beth, the word *fine* means:
   a. "Good"
   b. "Precious"
   c. "Very good"
   d. Nothing—it was a meaningless word

13. The best definition of the underlined word, *rapport*, is:
   a. A close relationship
   b. A sense of well-being
   c. A common goal
   d. Loneliness

14. Based on the passage, it is reasonable to infer that Martin is a:
   a. Mechanic
   b. Medical doctor
   c. Dentist
   d. Film director

15. Based on Beth's perception of her and Martin's relationship, it is reasonable to infer:
   a. Martin is dissatisfied with his job.
   b. Beth wants to have a baby.
   c. Martin is going to leave Beth.
   d. Martin and Beth have not known each other long.

Refer to the following for questions 16–22:

New Zealand Inhabitants

(1) The islands of New Zealand are among the most remote of all the Pacific islands. (2) New Zealand is an archipelago, with two large islands, and a number of smaller ones. (3) Its climate is far cooler than the rest of Polynesia. (4) Nevertheless, according to Maori legends, it was colonized in the early fifteenth century by a wave of Polynesian voyagers who traveled southward in their canoes and settled on North Island. (5) At this time, New Zealand will already be known to the Polynesians, who had probably first landed there some 400 years earlier.

(6) The Polynesian southward migration was limited by the availability of food. (7) Traditional Polynesian tropical crops such as taro and yams will grow on North Island, but the climate of the South Island is too cold for them. (8) The first settlers were forced to rely on hunting and gathering, and, of course, fishing. (9) Especially on the South Island, most settlements remained close to the sea. (10) At the time of the Polynesian incursion, enormous flocks of moa birds had their rookeries on the island shores. (11) These flightless birds were easy prey for the settlers, and within a few

centuries had been hunted to extinction. (12) Fish, shellfish and the roots of the fern were other important sources of food, but even these began to diminish in quantity as the human population increased. (13) The Maori had few other sources of meat: dogs, smaller birds, and rats. (14) Archaeological evidence shows that human flesh was also eaten, and that tribal warfare increased markedly after the moa disappeared.

(15) By far the most important farmed crop in prehistoric New Zealand was the sweet potato. (16) This tuber is hearty enough to grow throughout the islands, and could be stored to provide food during the winter months, when other food-gathering activities were difficult. (17) The availability of the sweet potato made possible a significant increase in the human population. (18) Thus, Maori tribes were often located near the most fertile farmlands in encampments called pa, which were fortified with earthen embankments.

16. A definition for the word *archipelago* as used in sentence 2 is:
   a. A country
   b. A place in the Southern Hemisphere
   c. A group of islands
   d. A roosting place for birds

17. This article is primarily about what?
   a. The geology of New Zealand
   b. New Zealand's early history
   c. The culture of New Zealand's first colonists
   d. Food sources used by New Zealand's first colonists

18. According to the passage, when was New Zealand first explored?
   a. In the 15th century
   b. Around the 11th century
   c. Thousands of years ago
   d. By flightless birds

19. What was a significant difference between the sweet potato and other crops known to the Polynesians?
   a. The sweet potato provided more protein.
   b. The sweet potato would grow on North Island.
   c. The sweet potato could be stored during the winter.
   d. The sweet potato could be cultured near their encampments.

20. Why was it important that sweet potatoes could be stored?
   a. They could be eaten in winter, when other foods were scarce.
   b. They could be traded for fish and other goods.
   c. They could be taken along by groups of warriors going to war.
   d. They tasted better after a few weeks of storage.

21. What was it about the moa that made them easy for the Māori to catch?
   a. They were fat.
   b. They roosted by the shore.
   c. They were not very smart.
   d. They were unable to fly.

22. Why did early settlements remain close to the sea?

a. The people liked to swim.
b. The people didn't want to get far from the boats they had come in.
c. Taro and yams grow only close to the beaches.
d. They were dependent upon sea creatures for their food.

Refer to the following for questions 23–30:

Daylight Saving Time

Daylight Saving Time (DST) is the practice of changing clocks so that afternoons have more daylight and mornings have less. Clocks are adjusted forward one hour in the spring and one hour backward in the fall. The main purpose of the change is to make better use of daylight.

DST began with the goal of conservation. Benjamin Franklin suggested it as a method of saving on candles. It was used during both World Wars to save energy for military needs. Although DST's potential to save energy was a primary reason behind its implementation, research into its effects on energy conservation is contradictory and unclear.

Beneficiaries of DST include all activities that can benefit from more sunlight after working hours, such as shopping and sports. A 1984 issue of *Fortune* magazine estimated that a seven-week extension of DST would yield an additional $30 million for 7-Eleven stores. Public safety may be increased by the use of DST: some research suggests that traffic fatalities may be reduced when there is additional afternoon sunlight.

On the other hand, DST complicates timekeeping and some computer systems. Tools with built-in timekeeping functions, such as medical devices, can be affected negatively. Agricultural and evening entertainment interests have historically opposed DST.

DST can affect health, both positively and negatively. It provides more afternoon sunlight in which to get exercise. It also impacts sunlight exposure; this is good for getting vitamin D, but bad in that it can increase skin cancer risk. DST may also disrupt sleep.

Today, daylight saving time has been adopted by more than one billion people in about 70 countries. DST is generally not observed in countries near the equator because sunrise times do not vary much there. Asia and Africa do not generally observe it. Some countries, such as Brazil, observe it only in some regions.

DST can lead to peculiar situations. One of these occurred in November 2007, when a woman in North Carolina gave birth to one twin at 1:32 a.m. and, 34 minutes later, to the second twin. Because of DST and the time change at 2:00 a.m., the second twin was officially born at 1:06, 26 minutes earlier than her brother.

23. According to the passage, what is the main purpose of DST?

    a. To increase public safety

    b. To benefit retail businesses

    c. To make better use of daylight

    d. To promote good health

24. Which of the following is NOT mentioned in the passage as a negative effect of DST?

    a. Energy conservation

    b. Complications with timekeeping

    c. Complications with computer systems

    d. Increased skin cancer risk

25. The passage states that DST involves:

    a. Adjusting clocks forward one hour in the spring and the fall

    b. Adjusting clocks backward one hour in the spring and the fall

    c. Adjusting clocks forward in the fall and backward in the spring

    d. Adjusting clocks forward in the spring and backward in the fall

26. Which interests have historically opposed DST, according to the passage?

    a. Retail businesses and sports

    b. Evening entertainment and agriculture

    c. 7-Eleven and health

    d. Medical devices and computing

27. According to the passage, increased sunlight exposure:

    a. Is only good for health

    b. Is only bad for health

    c. Has no effect on health

    d. Can be both good and bad for health

28. What is an example given in the passage of a peculiar situation that DST has caused?

    a. Sleep disruption

    b. Driving confusion

    c. Twin birth order complications

    d. Countries with DST only in certain regions

29. For what purpose did Benjamin Franklin first suggest DST?

    a. To save money for military needs

    b. To save candles

    c. To reduce traffic fatalities

    d. To promote reading

30. The article states that DST is observed only in some regions in which of the following?

    a. The equator

    b. Asia

    c. Africa

    d. Brazil

Writing

Refer to the following for questions 1–5:

(1) I had the same teacher for both third and 4th grades, which were difficult years for me. (2) My teacher and I did not get along, and I don't think she liked me. (3) Every day, I thought she was treating me unfairly and being mean. (4) Because I felt that way, I think I acted out and stopped doing my work. (5) In the middle of fourth grade, my family moved to a new town, and I had Mr. Shanbourne as my new teacher.

(6) From the very first day in Mr. Shanbourne's class, I was on guard. (7) I was expecting to hate my teacher and for him to hate me back when I started his class. (8) Mr. Shanbourne took me by surprise right away when he asked me if I wanted to stand up and introduce myself. (9) I said no, probably in a surly voice, and he just nodded and began teaching the first lesson of the day.

(10) I wasn't sure how to take this. (11) My old teacher forced me to do things and gave me detention if I didn't. (12) She loved detention and gave it to me for anything I did—talking back, working too loudly, forgetting an assignment. (13) He obviously didn't believe in detention, and I tried him! (14) During my first two weeks at my new school I did my best to get in trouble. (15) I zoned out in class, turned work in late, talked during lectures, and handed in assignments after the due date. (16) Mr. Shanbourne just nodded.

(17) Mr. Shanbourne asked me to stay in during recess. (18) *This is it*, I thought. I was going to get in trouble, get the detention my ten-year-old self had practically been begging for. (19) After all of the other kids ran outside, I walked up to Mr. Shanbourne's desk.

(20) "How are you doing, Alberto," he said.

(21) I mumbled something.

(22) He told me he was disappointed in my behavior over the last two weeks. (23) I had expected this and just took it. (24) The detention was coming any second. (25) Than Mr. Shanbourne took me by surprise. (26) He told me that even though he didn't know me very well, he believed I could be a hard worker and that I could be successful in his class. (27) He asked me how he could help listen better and turn my work in on time.

(28) I told him I had to think about it and rushed out to recess. (29) Even though my answer seemed rude, I was stunned. (30) I hadn't had a teacher in years who seemed to care about me, and said he believed in my abilities.

(31) To be honest, my behavior did not improve right away and I still turned in many of my assignments late. (32) But over the last few months of fourth grade, things changed. (33) Mr. Shanbourne continued to believe in me, encourage me and help me, and I responded by doing my best. (34) I had a different teacher for fifth grade, but whenever I was struggling I walked down to Mr. Shanbourne's classroom to get his advice. (35) I'll never forget how Mr. Shanbourne helped me, and I hope he'll never forget me either.

1. What correction should be made to sentence (1)?
a. Change *teacher* to *teachers*
b. Change *4ᵗʰ* to *fourth*
c. Delete the comma after *grades*
d. Change *years* to *year's*

2. Which is the best version of sentence (7)?
a. I started his class expecting my teacher to hate me back and for me to hate him.
b. Expecting to hate my teacher, I started his class expecting him to hate me back.
c. Starting his class expecting to hate my teacher, I also expected to hate him back.
d. I started his class expecting to hate my teacher and for him to hate me back.

3. Which is the best way to combine sentences (10) and (11)?
a. I wasn't sure how to take this, and my old teacher forced me to do things and gave me detention if I didn't.
b. I wasn't sure how to take this, although my old teacher forced me to do things and gave me detention if I didn't.
c. I wasn't sure how to take this because my old teacher forced me to do things and gave me detention if I didn't.
d. I wasn't sure how to take this as a result of my old teacher forced me to do things and gave me detention if I didn't.

4. Which phrase, if any, can be deleted from sentence (15) without changing the meaning of the sentence?
a. NO CHANGE
b. "...talked during lectures..."
c. "...handed in assignments after the due date."
d. "...zoned out in class..."

5. What transition should be added to the beginning of sentence (16)?
a. Surprisingly
b. Actually
c. Furthermore
d. Instead

6. Which of the following choices best completes the sentence?

When at last Amber was able to _____ the numerous difficulties associated with the task, she concluded the that wisdom of her grandfather was not only desirable, but absolutely necessary.

a. perceive
b. perception
c. perceptive
d. perceived

7. Which of the following words best completes the sentence?

The plan seemed flawless until its execution. The flames from the modified grill licked the bottom portion of the new wooden deck. Emil's elation warped into horror as he began to sweat. His grandparents had been extremely angry with the experiment on their car and his grandfather's red face hung before his eyes like a dark vision: "Before you _____ some other wild plan, talk to me first so we don't need to bring in the fire department."

a. concoct
b. invent
c. make
d. design

8. Which of the following sentences shows the correct usage of the hyphen?

a. Miriam was a real-estate-broker with Hendry and Henderson, so she understood the importance of a well-cared-for home.
b. Felipe dialed Joyce's number since it was easy-to-remember and listened with bated breath.
c. Although Biraju was not an accident-prone person, he knew his older brother did not share this trait.
d. James and Henry, both twenty-one year old students, had been able to pass the difficult test for medical school.

9. Which of the following choices is misspelled?

a. Conciliatory
b. Paroxism
c. Malevolence
d. Pernicious

10. Which of the following word choices best completes the sentence?

Matthew posted the notice in the main hall, and then proceeded to pass out the rest of the invitations to the _____ until his backpack was empty.

a. receive
b. reception
c. receivable
d. receiving

11. Which of the following would best support the idea that "fracking," shooting water and chemicals into the ground at a high pressure to gain access to underground gas stores, may be hazardous to the environment?

a. A letter in the science journal *Climatic Change* that includes results from research on fracking showing that it may be more damaging to the environment than burning coal
b. A letter to the editor of the *Chicago Tribune* from an activist who secretly taped what was going on at fracking locations throughout the US
c. A feature-length movie developed by a former politician that uses special effects to highlight the effects of fracking on climate change
d. An article in a newspaper discussing the impact of fracking on the local community, noting that all of the people interviewed were nervous about the issue

PERT Practice Test #1

12. Read the claim below. Which of the following supports a counterclaim?

Schools need to provide year-round education for students. Since the evolution of our society has moved us from an agrarian population to a largely urban one, there is no longer any need for the two-month break during the summer. It is, in fact, a waste of students'—and society's—precious time.

a. The prospect of a year-round education for students is akin to an endless prison sentence; however, the inmates, in this case, cannot speak for themselves. They are the most vulnerable among us, and there is no one who will be their voice in this debate. Let's face it. This debate isn't about longer school days to help children. It's about providing more funding to the school staff.

b. There's a reason teachers are fleeing the public school system. It's broken. Teachers often work long hours in difficult conditions—imagine having the occupant of your office throw a paper airplane at you while you are working—and get paid little. A longer school day punishes teachers who are already sweating blood over their occupation. Teachers not only work through the school day, but often spend hours at home, developing curricula, grading papers, and preparing for the following day.

c. The limitations of this view are clear: there are no scientifically backed works establishing that students perform better if they spend more time in school. However, there is significant research establishing the idea that learners do require time for creative pursuits and thinking. This supports the necessity of a summer break. In fact, it may be necessary to provide longer semester breaks so children have more time for their own creative pursuits.

d. In the interests of fairness, we must consider the possibility of a longer school day.

13. Which choice best completes the sentences below?

Our energy needs are not being adequately met, and in only a few short decades, we will be unable to satisfy the growing demand. _____, no one has developed a plan to address those needs. Both sides of the argument have facts, science, and history to back their claims. _____, fossil fuels are widely used and available. _____, there is a limited supply of them and they damage the environment.

a. So it seems, Similar to other claims, However
b. However, On one hand, On the other hand
c. On one hand, However, Similarly
d. Strangely, First of all, Second of all

14. Which of the following shows the correct punctuation for this quote from Richard Feynman?

a. If you thought that science was certain—well, that is just an error on your part.
b. If you thought that science was certain, well that is just an error on your part.
c. If you thought that, science was certain, well, that is just an error—on your part.
d. If you thought—that science was certain—well, that is just an error on your part.

15. Which of the following revisions would most improve the word choice in this sentence?

Employees are forced to check in at the main entrance if they arrive at the facility without their ID badge.

a. Change *forced* to *required*
b. Change *main* to *primary*
c. Change *if* to *whenever*
d. Change *facility* to *building*

16. Which of the following words is NOT spelled correctly?

    a. Complacency
    b. Indissoluble
    c. Indefategable
    d. Voracious

17. Which of the following is essential in the concluding statement of an argument?

    a. The introduction of new points that might lead to future arguments.
    b. A summary of the argument that clearly reinforces its main points.
    c. A contradiction of the argument's main points to provide fresh perspectives.
    d. An unrelated detail that might lighten the audience's mood after a heated debate.

18. Read the sentences, and then answer the question that follows.

I often have heard arguments claiming that complete freedom of speech could lead to dangerous situations. Without complete freedom of speech, we hardly are living in a free society.

Which word would best link these sentences?

    a. However
    b. Therefore
    c. So
    d. Supposedly

19. Which of the following statements would best conclude an essay about playwright William Shakespeare?

    a. William Shakespeare died of unknown causes on April 23, 1616.
    b. William Shakespeare wrote the most important plays ever written, and I think his best one is definitely *Romeo and Juliet*.
    c. William Shakespeare's plays have been staged in theaters throughout the world, yet he will always be most closely associated with the Globe Theater in London.
    d. Although William Shakespeare died in 1616, the artistry and eternal relevance of his work destined it to thrive for hundreds of years into the future.

20. Read the sentences, and then answer the question that follows.

In the past, television has been criticized as a medium without the complexity and artfulness of cinema. Contemporary programs, such as Mad Men, *are widely celebrated for their intricately structured narratives and beautifully realized design.*

Which of the following statements best links these sentences?

    a. Today's television shows prove that the medium has not changed much.
    b. *Mad Men* is a television show about the advertising business of the 1960s.
    c. This attitude has changed drastically over time.
    d. Television now offers a wide range of comedies, dramas, and reality shows.

21. Which version of the sentence is written correctly?

    a. A Los-Angeles-area homeowner decided to relocate to San Francisco.
    b. A Los Angeles area homeowner decided to relocate to San Francisco.
    c. A Los Angeles-area homeowner decided to relocate to San Francisco.
    d. A Los-Angeles-area-homeowner decided to relocate to San Francisco.

22. Which version of the sentence is written correctly?

    a.   Please lie the porcelain vase down gently to avoid chipping it.
    b.   Please lain the porcelain vase down gently to avoid chipping it.
    c.   Please lies the porcelain vase down gently to avoid chipping it.
    d.   Please lay the porcelain vase down gently to avoid chipping it.

23. As used in the sentence, "The beach is at its most placid at sunset, after most people have gone home," what does the word *placid* mean?

    a.   Peaceful
    b.   Pitiful
    c.   Pretty
    d.   Picturesque

24. Which version of the sentence does NOT contain any misspelled words?

    a.   The pompouse man thought he was better than everyone else.
    b.   The pompous man thought he was better than everyone else.
    c.   The pompus man thought he was better than everyone else.
    d.   The pompis man thought he was better than everyone else.

25. Which version of the sentence creates the best feeling of suspense?

    a.   The owl pounced on the rabbit suddenly when it spied the helpless animal emerging from the brush.
    b.   When the owl spied the rabbit emerging from the brush, it pounced on the helpless animal suddenly.
    c.   The owl pounced on the helpless animal suddenly when the owl spied the rabbit emerging from the brush.
    d.   Suddenly, the owl pounced on the rabbit when it spied the helpless animal emerging from the brush.

26. Which of the following choices is the best way to write the sentence?

    a.   There instantly is no way to learn a new language.
    b.   Instantly there is no way to learn a new language.
    c.   There is no instantly way to learn a new language.
    d.   There is no way to learn a new language instantly.

27. Which of the following choices best completes the passage?

    Standardized tests are becoming more important every year, and _____ these tests may seem like an easy way for educators to evaluate many students at once, there are considerable drawbacks. _____, teachers frequently teach to the test, which may raise scores but lowers the quality of education. _____: a recent survey showing that students know little information that is not tested on a standardized exam.

    a.   while, For example, Case in point
    b.   since, While, Interestingly
    c.   although, Consequently, Moreover
    d.   because, On the other hand, Yet

28. Which of the following choices best completes the passage?

Genetic engineering is not just a new way of approaching the same breeding methods used by farmers for centuries. _____, it is a completely new way of dealing with living things. _____ some scientists say that we are only working with what nature has given us, this is clearly not the case. We are not working with nature, we are creating it. We are making ourselves gods.

a. However, For example
b. On the contrary, While
c. Notably, Case in point
d. First, Second

29. Which of the following sentences best completes the selection?

The flu is a common disease that plagues millions of Americans every year. Symptoms include a runny nose, fever, coughing, and an overall feeling of achiness. While there is little that can be done once someone catches the flu, there is one important step most people fail to take to prevent themselves from getting it.

a. They don't wash their hands when they go to the bathroom.
b. They fail to do something that is vital to protecting their health.
c. They only wash their hands if someone is watching them.
d. They fail to wash their hands thoroughly and frequently.

30. Which of the following is correct?

a. Mary had said: "I believe in the rights of my fellow man."
b. Since Fred: Jerry: and Peter wanted to go, they drove the van.
c. The Constitution: it is one of the greatest documents of all time: it is vital to our freedom.
d. Scientists need to keep finding new sources: of money to support their research.

173

Answer Key and Explanations #1

Mathematics

1. C: Using the commutative property of addition, the expression can be rearranged as $27 + (-11)$. When adding a negative number, it is the same as subtracting, so subtract 11 from 27.

$$27 - 11 = 16$$

2. C: First, write an equation to represent the word problem. This scenario can be represented by the equation $48 + 36 - 50 = \_\_$. First, add the first two integers in the problem, 48 and 36. Write the problem vertically, making sure to line up the numbers according to place value. Start by adding the ones column to the right. Since $8 + 6 = 14$, write 4 in the ones place as part of the answer and carry the 1 over to the tens place column. Next, add the tens column. Since $1 + 4 + 3 = 8$, write 8 in the tens place as part of the answer. Therefore, $48 + 36 = 84$.

$$
\begin{array}{r} 48 \\ +36 \\ \hline \end{array}
\qquad
\begin{array}{r} {}^{1} \\ 48 \\ +36 \\ \hline 4 \end{array}
\qquad
\begin{array}{r} {}^{1} \\ 48 \\ +36 \\ \hline 84 \end{array}
$$

From here, subtract the next integer from the original problem, 50, from 84. Write the problem vertically, making sure to line up the numbers according to place value. Start by subtracting the ones column on the right. Since $4 - 0 = 4$, write 4 in the ones column as part of the answer. From here, move to the tens column and subtract. Since $8 - 5 = 3$, write 3 in the tens place as part of the answer. $48 + 36 - 50 = 34$. There were 34 cookies left over after the bake sale. Therefore, the correct answer is C.

$$
\begin{array}{r} 84 \\ -50 \\ \hline \end{array}
\qquad
\begin{array}{r} 84 \\ -50 \\ \hline 4 \end{array}
\qquad
\begin{array}{r} 84 \\ -50 \\ \hline 34 \end{array}
$$

3. A: To find the number of acres that Jamie will plant trees on, we need to find one-fourth of one-half, which we will do by multiplying $\frac{1}{4} \times \frac{1}{2}$. When multiplying two fractions, we multiply the numerator by one another and the denominators by one another. Therefore, Jamie will plant trees on $\frac{1}{8}$ of an acre of his land.

4. B: To find the product of two decimal numbers, we will multiply the two numbers as if they don't have a decimal. Then we can count the total number of decimal places in both numbers and then count that many decimal places from the right of the answer to find the placement of the decimal. In this problem, we will multiply 167 by 409 to get 68,303. Then, we count the decimal places in each number, which is 2, so a total of 4 decimal places. We start at the end of the answer and count four decimal places to the left, which will land us in between the 6 and the 8. Therefore, the product of 1.67 and 4.09 is 6.8303.

$$
\begin{array}{r}
\overset{2}{\cancel{6}}\,\overset{2}{\cancel{6}} \\
1.67 \\
\times 4.\cancel{0}\cancel{9} \\
\hline
1 \\
15\ 03 \\
00\ 00 \\
+6\ 68\ 00 \\
\hline
6.83\ 0^{3}
\end{array}
$$

5. A: To find the value of the expression $0.924 - 0.439$, we will line the two numbers at the decimal point vertically with 0.924 above 0.439. Since 4 is smaller than 9, we will borrow 1 from the hundredths column to make the 4 into 14, then we subtract 9 from 14 to get 5. Since we had to turn the 2 into a 1 to borrow, we now must subtract 3 from 1. Since 1 is smaller than 3, we will again borrow 1 from the tenths place to make the 1 into an 11 and subtract 3 from it to get 8. Since we had to borrow from the tenths place and changed the 9 into an 8, we will subtract 4 from 8 to get 4. Therefore, the value of the expression $0.924 - 0.439$ is 0.485.

$$
\begin{array}{r}
\overset{8}{\cancel{9}}\,\overset{\overset{11}{\cancel{1}}}{\cancel{2}}\,\overset{14}{\cancel{4}} \\
0\ .9\,2\,4 \\
-0\ .4\,3\,9 \\
\hline
0\ .4\,8^{5}
\end{array}
$$

6. D: To simplify the fraction, we start by finding the factors of the numerator and the denominator and canceling anything that is in both the numerator and denominator. Since any fraction where the numerator and denominator are the same is equivalent to 1, removing those numbers does not change the value of the fraction. The factors of 18 are $2 \times 3 \times 3$ and the factors of 24 are $2 \times 2 \times 2 \times 3$. Our fraction now looks like this: $\frac{2 \times 3 \times 3}{2 \times 2 \times 2 \times 3}$. We can cancel a 2 and a 3 from the numerator and denominator and what remains in the numerator is 3 and in the denominator is 2×2, which equals 4. Therefore, the fraction $\frac{18}{24}$ in its most simplified form is $\frac{3}{4}$.

7. B: Since the temperature is dropping, the 6-degree Fahrenheit temperature drop would be represented by –6. The temperature at 8pm would be 8 hours after the 45-degree temperature at noon. Therefore, the total temperature drop, from noon to 8pm, would be -6×8, which is –48. To find the temperature at 8pm we need to add 45 and –48, which is –3 degrees Fahrenheit.

8. A: To find the equation that can be used to calculate the total rental fee for one day, y, where the number of hours is modeled by x, we will set up the equation by multiplying the hourly rate by x and adding the flat daily fee, which will equal to the total rental fee for a day: $y = 4x + 15$.

9. C: To find the value of x, we will have to isolate x on one side of the equation. Since 5 is being subtracted from x, we will add 5 to both sides, which will cancel the 5 on the left side of the equation and leave us with x, and on the right side we will add 12 and 5 to get 17. Thus, $x = 17$.

10. D: To find the value of w, we will isolate the w on one side of the equation. In this problem, the w is being divided by 92, so we will multiply by 92 on both sides. On the left side we will be left with w. On the right side, we will multiply 92 by 5 to get 460, which is the value of w.

11. A: First, solve the inequality by isolating x on one side of the inequality.

$7x - 8 > 2x + 17$	Write down the inequality.
$7x - 8 - 2x > 2x + 17 - 2x$	Subtract $2x$ from both sides of the inequality to isolate x.
$5x - 8 > 17$	Simplify each side of the inequality.
$5x - 8 + 8 > 17 + 8$	Add 8 to both sides of the inequality.
$5x > 25$	Simplify each side of the inequality.
$\dfrac{5x}{5} > \dfrac{25}{5}$	Divide both sides of the inequality by 5.
$x > 5$	Simplify each side of the inequality.

The solution is the inequality stating all real numbers greater than 5. The graph of the solution on the number line shades all real numbers to the right of 5. Place an open circle at 5 to indicate the solution does not include 5.

12. C: Since the linear equation is given in slope-intercept form ($y = mx + b$), start by identifying the y-intercept, which is represented by the variable b. The y-intercept is –3, so the graph of the line will intersect the y-axis at –3, or $(0, -3)$.

Next, identify the slope, which is represented by the variable m in the equation. The slope is 2, or $\frac{2}{1}$.

Recall that slope is rise over run. Starting from the y-intercept at point $(0, -3)$, move 2 units up and 1 unit to the right to find the next point on the graph. The coordinate pair for this point is $(1, -1)$. The graph that represents the linear equation $y = 2x - 3$ must include points $(0, -3)$ and $(1, -1)$. Since the graph shown in answer C contains both points, the correct answer is C.

13. D: In the linear equation $x = 4$, the value of x is 4 for every value of y. The graph for $x = 4$ looks like a vertical line intersecting the x-axis at the point $(4,0)$. Therefore, the correct answer is D.

14. C: Because the radicals are the same, we can add the coefficients in front of the radicals and keep the radical the same.

$$4\sqrt{6} + 8\sqrt{6} = (4 + 8)\sqrt{6} = 12\sqrt{6}$$

Since the radicand, 6, has no perfect square factor, we cannot simplify this expression further.

15. C: When the dress is marked down by 20%, the cost of the dress is 80% of its original price. Since a percentage can be written as a fraction by placing the percentage over 100, the reduced price of the dress can be written as $\frac{80}{100}x$, or $\frac{4}{5}x$, where x is the original price. When discounted an extra 25%, the dress costs 75% of the reduced price. This results in the expression $\frac{75}{100}\left(\frac{4}{5}x\right)$, which can be simplified to $\frac{3}{4}\left(\frac{4}{5}x\right)$, or $\frac{3}{5}x$. So the final price of the dress is three-fifths of the original price.

16. B: The expression $(x + 6)^2$ may be expanded as $x^2 + 12x + 36$. Multiplication of $-2x$ by this expression gives $-2x^3 - 24x^2 - 72x$.

17. B: To simplify this expression, start by grouping like terms together and then combine them.

$$2x + 5x^2 - 7x + 11 - 2x^2$$

$$(5x^2 - 2x^2) + (2x - 7x) + 11$$

$$3x^2 - 5x + 11$$

18. B: First, simplify the numerator and the denominator of the expression, then perform the division.

$$\frac{4 - (-12)}{-9 + 5} = \frac{4 + 12}{-9 + 5} = \frac{16}{-4} = -4$$

19. D: Since $4^3 = 4 \times 4 \times 4 = 64$, and $3^4 = 3 \times 3 \times 3 \times 3 = 81$, the answer is $81 - 64 = 17$.

20. A: Start by substituting the given values into the expression.

$$4(-6)(3(7) + 5) + 2(7)$$

From here, simplify the expression using the order of operations. Start by simplifying the expression inside the parentheses.

$$4(-6)(21 + 5) + 2(7)$$
$$4(-6)(26) + 2(7)$$

From here, simplify the multiplication in order from left to right.

$$-24(26) + 2(7)$$
$$-624 + 14$$

Finally, add.

$$-624 + 14 = -610$$

21. B: The evaluation of the equation, for an x-value of -2, gives the following: $y = \frac{(-2)^4 - 2}{(-2)^2 + 1}$, which reduces to $y = \frac{16 - 2}{4 + 1}$, or $y = \frac{14}{5}$. The improper fraction $\frac{14}{5}$ can also be written as the mixed number $2\frac{4}{5}$. Thus, $y = 2\frac{4}{5}$.

22. B: To solve this equation, start by distributing on both sides of the equation.
$$3(x + 14) = 4(x + 9)$$
$$3x + 42 = 4x + 36$$

From here, isolate the variable using inverse operations. Start by subtracting **4x** from both sides.
$$3x + 42 - 4x = 4x + 36 - 4x$$
$$-x + 42 = 36$$

Then, subtract 42 from both sides.

$$-x + 42 - 42 = 36 - 42$$
$$-x = -6$$

Finally, divide both sides by –1.

$$\frac{-x}{-1} = \frac{-6}{-1}$$
$$x = 6$$

23. C: To simplify, each term in the numerator can be divided by $4x$ to eliminate the denominator. The law of exponents that indicates that $\frac{x^m}{x^n} = x^{m-n}$ must be observed.

$$\frac{16x^3 - 32x^2 + 8x}{4x} = \frac{16}{4}x^{3-1} - \frac{32}{4}x^{2-1} + \frac{8}{4}x^{1-1}$$
$$= 4x^2 - 8x^1 + 2x^0$$
$$= 4x^2 - 8x + 2$$

24. A: To add quadratic expressions, combine like terms. In this problem, there are three sets of like terms: the y^2-terms, the y-terms, and the constants. Set up the addition vertically, making sure to line up like terms, and then add them together:

$$
\begin{array}{rrrrrr}
 & y^2 & + & 9y & - & 2 \\
+ & 4y^2 & - & y & - & 5 \\
\hline
 & 5y^2 & + & 8y & - & 7
\end{array}
$$

25. B: The expression $x^2 + 7x + 12$ can be simplified by using the factors $(x + 4)(x + 3)$. To check the answer, multiply the first, outside, inside, and last terms (FOIL), then combine like terms to simplify.

$$x^2 + 3x + 4x + 12$$

$$x^2 + 7x + 12$$

26. D: The polynomial can be factored as $(x - 7)(x + 3)$. Thus, $(x - 7)$ is a factor of the given polynomial.

27. C: To solve for x, simplify this equation through factoring.

$$x^2 + 8x + 16 = 0$$
$$(x + 4)(x + 4) = 0$$
$$x + 4 = 0$$
$$x = -4$$

28. B: The given equation is a quadratic equation that can be solved by factorization. First, move everything to one side to get it in the correct form by subtracting 6 from both sides:

$$x^2 + 5x = 6$$
$$x^2 + 5x - 6 = 0$$

178

Then, factor the equation.

$$(x + 6)(x - 1) = 0$$

From here, set both factors equal to 0 and solve for the two solutions.

$$x + 6 = 0 \qquad\qquad x - 1 = 0$$
$$x = -6 \qquad\qquad x = 1$$

Thus, the two solutions to the equation are $x = -6$ and $x = 1$.

29. C: To simplify the expression, first simplify the expression with parentheses. To raise $2x$ to the third power, raise both 2 and x to the third power separately.

$$x^5 \times (2x)^3 = x^5 \times 2^3 \times x^3$$
$$= x^5 \times 8x^3$$

Next, multiply the terms. Since they have the same base and are being multiplied together, add the exponents to the like base.

$$x^5 \times 8x^3 = 8x^{5+3}$$
$$= 8x^8$$

30. D: Start by simplifying the expression inside the parentheses using the exponent property $x^m \times x^n = x^{m+n}$.

$$(a^{15} \times a^6)^2 = (a^{15+6})^2 = (a^{21})^2$$

Then, simplify further using the exponent property $(x^m)^n = x^{m \times n}$.

$$(a^{21})^2 = a^{21 \times 2} = a^{42}$$

Reading

1. B: The passage gives general instructions for tomato plant culture from seeding to providing support for the vines. Answers A and D are too specific, focusing on details of the text. Answer C is too general: the passage does not fully describe how to operate a farm.

2. A: The passage states that seeds germinated in late March will be ready for the garden after the last frost, implying that exposure to freezing temperatures would harm them.

3. A: The text states that pinching the bud is done to make the plants stronger.

4. A: The text states that use of fresh manure will delay fruiting.

5. D: Although all the other answers mention information contained in the paragraph, the overall purpose of this paragraph is, as stated, to describe the support procedure.

6. D: At first repelled by the sight of Garth in the window, the girl eventually expresses pity when she learns that he is deaf, too.

7. D: When the text states that "he lifted his supplicating eye," it is referring to the way that he is begging. He gives her a begging look and then stops.

8. C: The passage presents several pieces of evidence that Garth resents his life. He is presented as so deformed that other people are frequently repelled and try to avoid contact with him. The passage uses various words to indicate Garth's feelings, including the following: pained, grief-stricken, resigned, despairing, and bitter. Contemplative is another possible choice, but it does not do a good job of capturing Garth's sadness and bitterness at his condition. Despite being sad, Garth would not be considered destitute, as he is not starving or without his basic needs being met. The word "deflated" carries the impression that air has been let out of something that should be full of air. Think of a car tire or a balloon in which the air has been suddenly let out. Garth does not seem to be deflated, as he seems to be constantly sad and likely for a long time. In fact, the story indicates that he is the happiest that he can remember being.

9. A: Despite his ugliness and deformity, Garth is a gentle soul who wants to be accepted as a friend by the girl.

10. B: In the second sentence the phrase *so long had sleep been denied her* tells us she had been prevented from sleeping for some time.

11. B: This question is concerned with the main idea of the passage. Although the passage is not explicit about why Martin and Beth's relationship is strained, the right answer can be found by eliminating a number of answer choices. Choice A can be eliminated because Martin has not lost his job—he receives a page at the end of the passage concerning one of his patients. Choice B is not contradicted by the passage, and the reader is told that Martin and Mary were once together. Choices C and D can be eliminated because Beth expects Martin to leave her, which would not be explained by his workload or movie preferences. The best choice, then, is B.

12. D: This question asks for the definition of *fine* within the passage. *Fine* can mean "good," "precious," or "sharp," but this question asks for the meaning of *fine* within the passage itself. Choices A, B, and C are inappropriate because Beth says that fine used to mean these things but does not any longer. Choice D is the best answer because Beth says *fine* was "a meaningless word, an excuse not to tell other people what was on your mind."

13. A: A rapport is a relationship based on mutual understanding. With this in mind, choice A might be a good answer, even though it is not an exact match. Choice B can be eliminated because it does not describe a relationship. Choice C can be eliminated because individuals can have a relationship based on mutual understanding without sharing a common goal. Choice D can be eliminated because loneliness has nothing to do with the definition of *rapport*.

14. B: This question asks the reader to make a conclusion based on details from the passage. The reader knows that (1) Martin wears a pager for his job, (2) he has patients, and (3) one of his patients is going into cardiac arrest. Choices A and D can be eliminated because mechanics and film directors do not see patients. Choice C seems like a possibility. After all, dentists see patients. Choice B is the best choice because if a person goes into cardiac arrest, it is more likely a medical doctor rather than a dentist would be paged.

15. C: This question asks the reader to make an inference about what is going to happen based on the passage. Choice A is inappropriate because the passage says nothing about Martin's level of satisfaction with his job. Choice B can be eliminated for a similar reason—the passage says nothing about Beth's desire for children. Choice C seems like a good choice because while Martin tells Beth he has to leave to go to work, the structure of the sentence immediately preceding this makes it seem as if Beth knows Martin is going to leave her: "Beth wasn't even sure she knew Martin anymore, but she was confident that it was only a matter of time before everything was not 'fine,' only a matter of time before he told her..." Choice D is inappropriate because Beth and Martin have had problems "over the past few months," and enjoyed a happier period before that, suggesting they have been together for a while. The best choice, then, is C.

16. C: An archipelago is a large group or chain of islands.

17. D: The article deals primarily with the ways the colonists fed themselves: their crops and the foods they hunted. While the history and agriculture discussed are part of the Māori culture, that is not the focus of the passage.

18. B: The article states that the islands were colonized by Polynesians in the 15th century but that the first visitors had arrived some 400 years earlier than that.

19. C: The sweet potato could be stored, providing a source of food during the winter, when other food gathering activities were difficult.

20. A: The sweet potato provided a winter food source through storage, allowing the population to increase.

21. D: The moa were flightless birds, so they could not easily escape when humans came to hunt them.

22. D: The passage states that the first settlers were forced to rely on fishing for their food.

23. C: The first paragraph states that the main purpose of DST is to make better use of daylight.

24. A: Energy conservation is discussed as a possible benefit of DST, not a negative effect of it.

25. D: The first paragraph states that DST involves setting clocks forward one hour in the spring and one hour backward in the fall.

26. B: The last sentence in paragraph four notes that agricultural and evening entertainment interests have historically been opposed to DST.

27. D: The passage gives examples of both good and bad effects extra daylight can have on health.

28. C: The last paragraph of the passage notes that DST can lead to peculiar situations and relays an anecdote about the effect of DST on the birth order of twins.

29. B: In the second paragraph, the author asserts that Benjamin Franklin suggested DST as a way to save candles.

30. D: The sixth paragraph notes that DST is observed in only some regions of Brazil.

Writing

1. B: The word *fourth* should be written out to match the form of *third*. While the word *teacher* could become plural, choice A is incorrect because the second sentence of the passage shows that Alberto is talking about a single teacher. Choice C is incorrect because the comma correctly separates an independent clause from a phrase that gives extra detail. Choice D is incorrect because Alberto is talking about several years (plural) rather than something belonging to one year (possessive).

2. D: Answer choice D uses proper word order to get the point across. This sentence begins with a subject and verb and follows the verb with two objects. Choice A is incorrect because the phrases "my teacher to hate me back" and "for me to hate him" are written in reverse order. It is more logical for "for me to hate him" to be written first. Choice B is incorrect because the subject and verb separate Alberto's two emotions ("expecting to hate my teacher" and "expecting him to hate me back"). This separation makes the sentence more difficult to read and understand. Choice C is incorrect because it repeats that Alberto expected to hate Mr. Shanbourne.

3. C: The word *because* combines the sentence by showing that the second clause is an explanation for the first clause. Choice A is incorrect because the conjunction *and* doesn't show how the two clauses are connected. Choice B is incorrect because the word *although* implies contrast rather than explanation. While *as a result of* has a similar meaning to *because* and could be used to effectively combine the sentences, choice D is incorrect because the verbs *forced* and *gave* should be changed to *forcing* and *giving* in order for *as a result of* to be used correctly.

4. C: The phrase "handed in assignments after the due date" is redundant with the phrase "turned work in late"; only one of those phrases needs to be in the sentence. Choices B and D are incorrect because both phrases add unique information to the sentence. Choice A is incorrect because the sentence has two redundant phrases, and one of them should be deleted.

5. A: The word *surprisingly* correctly shows that the reaction was unexpected, given Alberto's behavior. Answers B and D are incorrect because *actually* and *instead* imply an alternative reaction was mentioned. Choice C does not work because the second sentence does not further support the first sentence; it is a new idea.

6. A: This is the correct form of the word for the sentence.

7. A: While the words are all very similar in meaning (denotation), *concoct* best matches the tone of the passage: Emil is prone to developing wild ideas that result in disaster. *Invent* (B) and *design* (D) have positive connotations, while *make* (C) has a neutral connotation.

8. C: One use of hyphens is to join up a descriptive phrase before a noun, as in choice C ("accident-prone person"). Choice A uses hyphens where none are necessary ("real estate broker" is correct), although it does use hyphens correctly in "well-cared-for home." Choice B also uses hyphens unnecessarily because the descriptive phrase, "easy to remember," comes after the noun, "number." Choice D needs additional hyphens because the entire phrase, "twenty-one-year-old," describes the noun "students."

9. B: A *paroxysm* is a fit or sudden attack of a disease or emotion.

10. B: The sentence requires a noun. In this case, *reception* is the only word that correctly completes the sentence.

11. A: Only choice A uses science-based research to back up an argument. All of the other choices involve emotional or inconclusive approaches to the issue.

12. C: Only choice C develops and supports a counterclaim. Choice A provides a counterclaim but does not give support. Choices B and D focus on related but separate issues (length of the school day, teacher salaries).

13. B: Choice B is the best choice because the first blank indicates a change in direction. The second blank indicates that an initial point will be made. The final blank indicates a counterargument.

Answer Key and Explanations #1

14. A: There are two types of punctuation in this sentence in addition to the period at the end: an em-dash and a comma. Both em-dashes and commas can serve multiple purposes.

Em-dashes can indicate a change in sentence structure or a pause or hesitation. They can also act similar to parentheses and set apart extraneous information from the rest of the sentence. In this quote, an em-dash is used to indicate a pause and a shift in focus and to emphasize the dramatic point that science is not certain.

After the em-dash, the word "well" serves as an interjection. An interjection is not an essential component of a sentence and is used to express a feeling rather than information. For example, "wow" is an interjection in the sentence "Wow, look at that!" An interjection should be followed by a comma.

In choice A, the em-dash is correctly placed at the point where the sentence structure changes and the sentence shifts meaning. Meanwhile, the comma is correctly placed after the interjection. Choice B is missing the em-dash and lacks the comma after the interjection, and choices C and D have em-dashes in inappropriate places.

15. A: Choice A is correct because it changes *forced*. The word *forced* is out of place here because it suggests that every employee without a badge is physically made to check in. The intended meaning of the sentence seems to be that there is a rule regarding badge-less employees: they must check in at the main entrance. Presumably, this rule could be broken, resulting not in the use of force but in a warning or reminder. This rule would be accurately indicated by *required*. The other choices are all plausible changes that would not introduce additional problems. However, none of them would address the issue that *forced* presents.

16. C: This word is spelled incorrectly; it should be *indefatigable*. The other words are all correct.

17. B: The key to an effective concluding statement is a concise summary of the argument's main points. Such a conclusion leaves the opponent and audience with a clear and organized understanding of the argument. The introduction of new points, or a detail added merely to lighten mood, would weaken the argument by straying off point at the last minute. Introducing contradictory perspectives would work against the argument's effectiveness.

18. A: The first sentence introduces an argument against complete freedom of speech. The second sentence makes an argument in favor of it. The second sentence opposes the first one, so the two sentences should be linked with the adverb *however*. *Therefore* and *so* would be used only if the sentences supported each other.

19. D: Choice D mentions the death of William Shakespeare, effectively indicating his end. It also refers to the importance and continued relevance of his work in the years to come, which is integral to any general essay about the playwright. This statement offers a stronger conclusion to an essay on William Shakespeare than stopping short with the cause and date of his death (A). In addition, this choice does not stray from an authoritative tone by presenting personal opinion about Shakespeare's best play (B) or a random detail about the theaters that staged his work (C).

20. C: The first sentence explains how television once was criticized. The second sentence shows how contemporary shows are now being praised. They require a linking sentence indicating that an attitude change toward television has occurred over time. Explaining the premise of *Mad Men* or the variety of shows on television is not the best way to link these sentences. Stating, "Today's television shows prove that the medium has not changed much," contradicts the second sentence.

21. C: A compound modifier consists of two or more words that must be linked with one or more hyphens. In this sentence, *Los Angeles-area* is a compound modifier. Although *Los Angeles* consists of two words, it is a single city name and does not require a hyphen between *Los* and *Angeles*.

22. D: The words *lie* and *lay* are often confused, but they are not used in the same way. *Lie* means to recline, as a person might lie on a bed. *Lay* means to place something or put it down. Since a person would put down a porcelain vase, the correct word in this sentence is *lay*.

23. A: Although the words *pretty* and *picturesque* make sense in the context of this sentence, *placid* means peaceful. A beach would be most peaceful when people have left it after sunset.

24. B: The word *pompous*, meaning arrogant or self-important, is spelled with an *ou*, creating an "uh" sound.

25. B: Although all of these sentences are technically correct, only choice B uses syntax to establish a feeling of suspense. It achieves this by saving the action—the owl pouncing on the rabbit—for the end of the sentence. The other answer choices give away the action right away.

26. D: In choices A, B, and C, the adverb *instantly* appears in places where it does not fit the sentence grammatically.

27. A: This is the best choice for this passage because an idea is introduced, and then there is a change in direction. The change in direction acknowledges another point of view. The next sentence illustrates part of the author's argument with a supporting idea (standardized tests lower the quality of education). The last sentence is talking about a specific example and using the colon to break up the sentence.

28. B: The transitions needed here must complete the sentences while preserving the direction of the passage. The first sentence gives us one direction, then the second sentence provides a contradiction. The third sentence is about what scientists are saying but includes a contrasting comment.

29. D: Choices A and C are too specific in stating the problem, which is with how people wash their hands in general. Choice B does not complete the passage.

30. A: This is the only choice that uses the colon correctly; it introduces a quotation. The other choices do not use the colon in the correct way to introduce something.

PERT Practice Test #2

Mathematics

1. $(-13) - 7 =$
    a. −20
    b. −6
    c. 6
    d. 20

2. Eli borrows $12 from his brother to buy a video game. Before Eli pays his brother back, another game he wants goes on sale, so he borrows an additional $20 from his brother to buy the game. How much money does Eli owe his brother?
    a. −$32
    b. −$8
    c. $8
    d. $32

3. What is $\frac{3}{7} \div \frac{2}{3}$?
    a. $\frac{11}{14}$
    b. $\frac{3}{7}$
    c. $\frac{8}{7}$
    d. $\frac{9}{14}$

4. The Smith family is taking a road trip. Along the way, they're stopping to visit their cousins who live 352.8 miles away. From there, the Smiths are driving another 76.5 miles to visit Grandma Smith. How many miles will the family travel altogether?
    a. 329.3 miles
    b. 324.3 miles
    c. 429.3 miles
    d. 276.3 miles

5. What is $0.164 + 0.972$?
    a. 0.808
    b. 1.136
    c. 8.080
    d. 11.36

185

6. Mike's movie streaming subscription costs him $16 each month. To figure out how much money he spends on four months of his subscription, he uses the following equation:

$$-16 \times 4 = \underline{}$$

Solve the equation to figure out how much Mike spends on four months of his movie streaming service.

    a. $-16 \times 4 = -64$, so Mike spends -$64.
    b. $-16 \times 4 = -64$, so Mike spends $64.
    c. $-16 \times 4 = 64$, so Mike spends $64.
    d. $-16 \times 4 = 0$, so Mike spends $0.

7. Lora has a savings account with $2,400. She wants to save money to buy a new car. She decides to put $300 from each paycheck into the savings account. Lora is paid once per month. Which equation can be used to model this situation, where x is the number of months that Lora has been saving money and y is the total amount of money in the savings account?

    a. $y = 300x + 2{,}400$
    b. $y = 2{,}400x + 300$
    c. $x = 300y + 2{,}400$
    d. $x = 2{,}400y + 300$

8. What is the value of x in the equation $\frac{x}{5} = -6$?

    a. $x = -30$
    b. $x = -11$
    c. $x = 11$
    d. $x = 30$

9. The equation $w - 57 = -279$ is given. Solve for w.

    a. $w = -336$
    b. $w = -222$
    c. $w = 222$
    d. $w = 336$

10. Given the formula $E = mc^2$, solve for m.

    a. $m = \dfrac{c^2}{E}$
    b. $m = \dfrac{E}{c^2}$
    c. $m = \dfrac{E}{c}$
    d. $m = Ec^2$

11. Marissa goes for a jog with her dog every morning. The distance jogged can be modeled by the equation $d = \frac{1}{10}m$, where d is the distance jogged in miles, and m is the number of minutes jogged. Which graph best represents the relationship between minutes and distance?

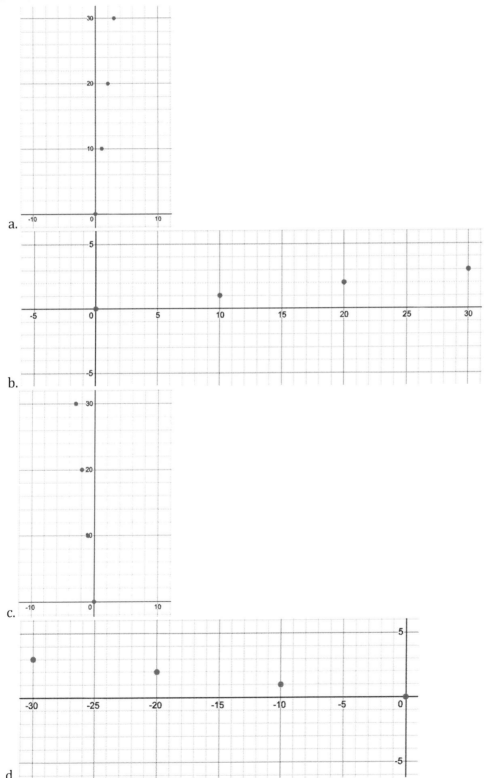

a.

b.

c.

d.

12. Which graph represents the linear equation $2x + 4y = 8$?

a.

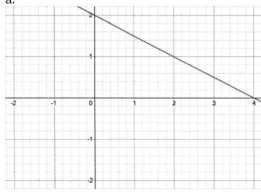

c.

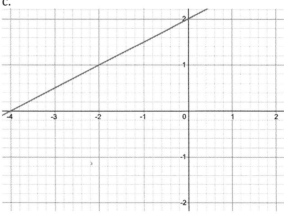

b.

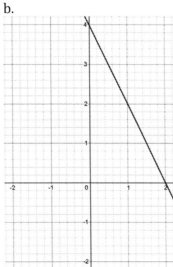

d.

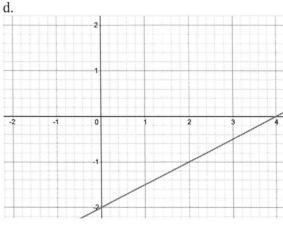

13. Simplify the radical expression $\sqrt{20}$ as much as possible.

    a. 10

    b. $4\sqrt{5}$

    c. $2\sqrt{10}$

    d. $2\sqrt{5}$

14. A plot of land has a width of w and a length of $2w + 3$. If the plot of land has an area of 90 square feet, what is the value of w, which is the width of the land?

    a. 5 feet

    b. 15 feet

    c. 6 feet

    d. $\frac{15}{2}$ feet

15. Solve this quadratic equation by factoring: $2x^2 - x - 6 = 0$.

   a. $x = -\frac{3}{2}$ and $x = -2$

   b. $x = -\frac{3}{2}$ and $x = 2$

   c. $x = \frac{2}{3}$ and $x = 1$

   d. $x = -\frac{2}{3}$ and $x = -2$

16. Elementary teachers in one school surveyed their students and discovered that 15% of their students have iPhones. Which of the following correctly states 15% in fraction, decimal, and ratio equivalents?

   a. $\frac{3}{20}$, 0.15, 3 : 20

   b. $\frac{3}{25}$, 0.15, 3 : 25

   c. $\frac{15}{10}$, 1.5%, 15 : 10

   d. $\frac{2}{1}$, 1.5%, 2 : 1

17. Simplify the following expression: $\frac{1}{4} \times \frac{3}{5} \div 1\frac{1}{8}$.

   a. $\frac{8}{15}$

   b. $\frac{27}{160}$

   c. $\frac{2}{15}$

   d. $\frac{27}{40}$

18. Which of the following expressions is equivalent to $-3x(x - 2)^2$?

   a. $-3x^3 + 6x^2 - 12x$

   b. $-3x^3 - 12x^2 + 12x$

   c. $-3x^2 + 6x$

   d. $-3x^3 + 12x^2 - 12x$

19. What is $3^3 - 2^5$?

   a. -9

   b. -5

   c.   5

   d.   9

20. Which of the following expressions is equivalent to $3\left(\frac{6x-3}{3}\right) - 3(9x + 9)$?

   a. $-3(7x + 10)$

   b. $-3x + 6$

   c. $(x + 3)(x - 3)$

   d. $3x^2 - 9$

21. Simplify the expression: $5(80 \div 8) + (7 - 2) - (9 \times 5)$

    a. −150

    b. 10

    c. 100

    d. 230

22. Evaluate the expression $(x - 2y)^2$**, where** $x = 3$ **and** $y = 2$.

    a. −2

    b. −1

    c. 1

    d. 4

23. Given the function $p(y) = \frac{4y}{2} + 5$**, what is the value of** $p(4)$**?**

    a. 9

    b. 7

    c. 13

    d. 37

24. Given the equation $\frac{3}{y-5} = \frac{15}{y+4}$**, what is the value of** y**?**

    a. $\frac{4}{29}$

    b. $\frac{29}{4}$

    c. 45

    d. 54

25. Which of the following expressions is equivalent to $\left(3x^{-2}\right)^3$**?**

    a. $9x^{-6}$

    b. $9x^6$

    c. $27x^{-4}$

    d. $27x^{-6}$

26. What is the simplified form of the expression $\left(b^3\right)^{-4} \times b^{15}$**?**

    a. b^{14}

    b. b^8

    c. b^{11}

    d. b^3

27. Which of the following expressions is equivalent to $(x - 3)^2$**?**

    a. $x^2 - 3x + 9$

    b. $x^2 - 6x - 9$

    c. $x^2 - 6x + 9$

    d. $x^2 + 3x - 9$

28. **Which of the following represents the difference of** $(3x^3 - 9x^2 + 6x) - (8x^3 + 4x^2 - 3x)$**?**
    a. $-5x^3 - 13x^2 + 9x$
    b. $11x^3 - 13x^2 + 3x$
    c. $-5x^3 - 5x^2 + 3x$
    d. $5x^3 + 13x^2 + 9x$

29. **Factor the equation** $12x^4 - 27x^3 + 6x^2$.
    a. $3x^2(4x - 1)(x - 2)$
    b. $3x^2(4x - 1)(x + 2)$
    c. $3x^2(4x + 1)(x - 2)$
    d. $3x^2(4x - 2)(x - 1)$

30. **Which of the following is the factored form of the expression** $x^2 + 3x - 28$**?**
    a. $(x - 14)(x + 2)$
    b. $(x + 6)(x - 3)$
    c. $(x + 4)(x - 1)$
    d. $(x - 4)(x + 7)$

Reading

Refer to the following for questions 1–6:

How to Choose and Purchase an Automobile

Choosing and purchasing an automobile in a volatile market is not simply a function of color or engine preference; on the contrary, consumers need to treat the purchase of an automobile as the investment that it is—they need to research the pros and cons of owning various automobiles, and they need to make an informed decision before arriving at the dealership. Failure to properly prepare for such an investment can result in an unnecessary economic loss for the consumer.

While there are many pros and cons associated with automobile ownership, many consumers do not adequately research the specific benefits and <u>detriments</u> associated with purchasing a particular vehicle. One of the most common concerns is economic: how much does it cost to own a particular vehicle over time? The cost of ownership is not limited to purchase price; it also includes things like insurance prices, repair costs, and gas consumption. While a given vehicle may have a higher sticker price, its low cost of ownership may, over time, offset this expense. Conversely, a vehicle may have a low sticker price but a high cost of ownership over time. Accordingly, consumers should thoroughly research vehicles before they visit an automobile dealership.

There are numerous ways for consumers to research the cost (defined broadly) of a vehicle before they ever step inside that vehicle. Most simply, there are a number of publications that list the relative depreciation of automobiles over time. Consumers can use these publications to track how a particular model tends to lose value over time and choose that vehicle that best retains its value. Consumers can also go directly to a manufacturer's website to compare gas mileage or the cost of replacement parts. Furthermore, insurance agents can provide insurance quotes for customers before a purchase is made. Awareness of factors such as these can also simplify the purchasing process.

When a consumer is finally ready to purchase a vehicle, he or she is less likely to be pressured by a salesperson if he or she is equipped with the relevant data for that purchase; if a consumer knows the long-term costs of a particular vehicle, he or she is less likely to be swayed by short-term or cosmetic benefits. Arriving at a dealership unprepared can result in an impulse purchase, which, in turn, may result in increased automotive expenditure over time. Conducting even a modicum of research, however, can potentially save the average automotive consumer thousands of dollars in the long run.

1. Why should consumers treat an automobile purchase as an investment?
- a. Automotive stock is traded on various stock exchanges.
- b. If consumers do not treat it as an investment, they may unnecessarily lose money.
- c. Vehicles may appreciate over time.
- d. Owning a vehicle has potential risks and rewards.

2. Based on the passage, which of the following is another word for the underlined word *detriments*?
- a. Purchases
- b. Cons
- c. Benefits
- d. Investments

3. According to the passage, which of the following is true?
- a. Vehicles with a higher sticker price always cost the most over time.
- b. SUVs are always expensive to own.
- c. Red automobiles are more expensive because their insurance rates are higher.
- d. Sticker price does not determine the overall cost of a vehicle.

4. What does the cost of ownership of a vehicle include?
- a. Purchase price
- b. Gas consumption
- c. Cost of repairs
- d. All of the above

5. If a consumer conducts research before going to an automobile dealership, he or she is:
- a. More likely to be swayed by high-pressure sales techniques
- b. Less likely to be swayed by the short-term benefits associated with a particular vehicle
- c. More likely to be dismissive with, or rude to, salespeople
- d. Less likely to be concerned with insurance rates associated with a particular vehicle

6. According to the passage, what information can consumers find on a manufacturer's website that can help them make a sound financial decision?
- a. The gas mileage of a particular vehicle
- b. The different colors offered for a particular vehicle
- c. The cost of replacement parts
- d. A and C

Refer to the following for questions 7–11:

School Days

As Bill lumbered up the stairs to Hendrickson Hall, he wondered if he was up to this—twenty years was a long time, and maybe he had forgotten the ropes. He wasn't even sure if this was the right building.

"Uh, hey, uh…is this where the Biology labs are?" stammered Bill to a young woman clad all in black. "She's probably an art student," thought Bill.

"No. This is, like, Hendrickson Hall. You know…the English building."

Bill appreciated neither the girl's eye-rolling nor the snooty way she emphasized "English." Nevertheless, he mumbled a thank-you and hurried towards the student center to check his schedule and the campus map.

"Martha, if you weren't gone, you'd be able to show me around this campus lickety-split. You'd probably say, 'Bill, you big dope, can't you find your way around a simple college? What would you do without me?'" Now that she was gone, Bill could answer such questions: without Martha, he made do. He neither succeeded nor failed; he simply made do.

As he approached the student center doors, a group of cheerleaders approached from inside the center. Without hesitation, Bill opened a door for them and stepped to the side. Ten young, attractive, laughing girls passed through the door without glancing at Bill. He felt like he should be angry or indignant, but instead, he was <u>dumbfounded</u>. He simply could not understand how one person would not think to thank, let alone acknowledge, another person who had done them a good turn. He stood there for about two minutes, silently holding the door, looking back and forth between the center and the direction of the parking lot. Bill gently closed the door, put his hands in his pockets, and began the long walk back to his car.

"I'm sorry Martha, but I can't do it. Things are just too different now. Don't be disappointed; I'll still find things to do. God, I miss you."

7. Based on the passage, exactly how old is Bill?
   a. Bill is twenty years old.
   b. Bill is forty years old.
   c. Bill is fifty years old.
   d. The passage does not state Bill's age.

8. Which of the following best describes Bill's state of mind in the passage?
   a. Apathetic
   b. Reflective
   c. Angry
   d. Confused

9. It is most reasonable to assume that Martha:

    a.   Left Bill for another man
    b.   Died suddenly
    c.   Is no longer in Bill's life
    d.   Is waiting at home for Bill

10. Which of the following is another word for the underlined word *dumbfounded*?

    a.   Perplexed
    b.   Rationalized
    c.   Dilapidated
    d.   Entreated

11. Based on the passage, it is reasonable to assume that:

    a.   Bill was once a car mechanic.
    b.   Bill is a retired college professor.
    c.   Bill will not return to college.
    d.   Bill never really loved Martha.

Refer to the following for questions 12–17:

Reduction

Reducing liquids is a fundamental culinary skill that any aspiring chef or cook must include in his or her repertoire. A reduction, in short, is a process whereby a given liquid is slowly simmered until its volume diminishes. This <u>diminution</u> causes the flavors of the reduced liquid to intensify and sometimes sweeten. The ability to perform effective reductions is integral because recipes ranging from simple sauces to desserts may call for reductions. Learning how to perform a reduction is perhaps best demonstrated through the classic reduction called for in the recipe for chicken marsala.

Prior to making the Marsala reduction in a chicken marsala dish, one should dredge thin chicken breasts in flour and fry the breasts over medium heat until browned. Once the chicken has been browned, remove the chicken and set it aside. Two tablespoons of butter should be melted over medium heat in the same pan in which the chicken was browned. When the butter is melted, one cup of Marsala wine should be added to the pan and heated until simmering (lightly boiling). The wine and butter should be allowed to boil down from approximately one cup to approximately one-half cup. When the sauce has reduced, one-half cup of chicken stock and the browned chicken breasts should be added to the mixture. The sauce should be brought back to a simmer and reduced by half (this should take approximately ten to fifteen minutes). When the sauce has reduced by half, it should be thick enough to adhere to the chicken. At this point, it is ready to serve.

The reduction that occurs in the above chicken marsala recipe is fairly typical of reductions. Whether one is reducing the volume of chicken stock for a soup or reducing balsamic vinegar or wine, the procedure is essentially the same: simmer the liquid until its volume reduces to the point where it changes the sauce's consistency. While reductions are fairly straightforward, there are some pitfalls in the process. One common mistake that people make is overboiling the sauce. If a sauce is boiled too vigorously, it may scorch, which will impart a burnt, acrid taste to the sauce. Another common mistake is adding thickening agents to the sauce because the reduction is not occurring fast enough. Adding starches to the sauce to force it to thicken will not bring out the same intensity of flavor that a reduction produces. It may also make the final sauce thick and lumpy. The process for making a reduction is simple, but it must be followed closely if one wants his or her sauce to be palatable.

12. The underlined word *diminution* most closely means:
a. Process
b. Liquid
c. Decrease
d. Skill

13. According to the passage, why is the ability to perform reductions important for chefs or cooks?
a. The ability to perform reductions demonstrates culinary skill.
b. Restaurant customers like reductions.
c. Reductions are popular in contemporary cuisine.
d. Many recipes call for reductions.

14. In the chicken marsala recipe, when should butter be added to the pan?
a. Before the chicken breasts are browned
b. After the chicken breasts are browned
c. After the wine has begun to simmer
d. While the chicken breasts are being browned

15. At what point does reduction occur in the chicken marsala recipe?
a. When the Marsala wine is reduced by half
b. When the butter is melted
c. When the wine/chicken stock mixture is reduced by half
d. At points A and C

16. Which of the following is a common mistake made when performing reductions?
a. Underboiling the sauce
b. Adding butter
c. Using starches to thicken the sauce
d. All of the above

17. What function does the chicken marsala recipe serve in the passage?
a. It illustrates the importance of reductions.
b. It is an example that demonstrates how to do a reduction.
c. It is an example that demonstrates how not to do a reduction.
d. It helps the reader relate his or her experience to the passage.

Refer to the following for questions 18–23:

The Grieving Process

Since its formulation, Dr. Kübler-Ross's model of the stages of grieving has been an invaluable tool in understanding how people cope with loss. Although individuals may experience the stages of grieving in varying degrees and in various progressions, the average person tends to go through the following stages when grieving: denial, anger, bargaining, depression, and acceptance. While most of these stages seem natural, many people do not understand the importance of the anger stage in the grieving process.

When a person experiences a significant loss in his or her life, experiencing anger as a result of this loss is both <u>cathartic</u> and therapeutic; in other words, anger at one's loss provides an emotional release and allows for the beginning of the healing process. By directing one's anger at a deity, fate, or even oneself, a grieving person can come to realize that tragedies are seldom the fault of an individual or a higher power; rather, loss is a natural part of living that each person must experience. Trying to assign blame can allow the grieving individual to abandon his or her anger by showing that there is no one to whom blame can be assigned. Having no one to blame allows the bereaved to begin to heal because he or she can begin to come to terms with the necessity of loss. If an individual cannot move beyond anger, however, he or she may exhibit destructive tendencies.

There are a number of ways that people can fail to properly go through the anger stage of the grieving process. Some individuals may never find an object for their anger. These people may feel a vague, continual irritability or may react unreasonably to circumstances. Other grieving individuals may assign blame to an object but not realize that a given person or entity is blameless. This may result in a loss of religious faith, an unreasonable hatred of an individual, or even self-destructive tendencies in those individuals who blame themselves. These and other destructive consequences may be avoided if the bereaved successfully negotiate the grieving process.

Anger is not generally approved of in contemporary society because it is associated with violence, hatred, and destruction. Anger does, however, have its place—it is a natural and healthy step in the grieving process. Without experiencing this vital stage, it is difficult, if not impossible, to begin to move past tragedy.

18. Which of the following is true according to the passage?
   a. Grieving individuals can be self-destructive.
   b. Grieving individuals need therapy.
   c. People who suffer tragedy never fully heal.
   d. Crying is a natural consequence of loss.

19. What is the main idea of the first paragraph?
   a. Depression is a normal and important part of the grieving process.
   b. No one grieves in the same way.
   c. Not moving through the anger stage of the grieving process can produce destructive consequences.
   d. Many people do not understand the importance of anger to the grieving process.

20. Based on the passage, the underlined word, *cathartic*, most likely means:

    a. Having to do with anger
    b. Unhealthy
    c. Healthy
    d. Related to emotional release

21. How does anger help individuals heal?

    a. It allows the bereaved to more quickly enter into the "bargaining" stage of the grieving process.
    b. It helps people understand that tragedy is usually blameless.
    c. It helps people to lash out at others.
    d. Anger raises immune responses to infection.

22. Why is anger not generally approved of in contemporary society?

    a. Anger does not serve any positive purpose.
    b. Anger makes people nervous.
    c. Angry people are unpleasant.
    d. Anger is associated with violence, hatred, and destruction.

23. Which of the following are possible consequences of failing to go through the anger stage of the grieving process?

    a. Vague, continued irritability
    b. The loss of religious faith
    c. Self-destructive tendencies
    d. All of the above

Refer to the following for questions 24–30:

The Coins of Ancient Greece

We don't usually think of coins as works of art, and most of them really do not invite us to do so. The study of coins, their development and history, is termed
5 *numismatics*. Numismatics is a topic of great interest to archeologists and anthropologists, but not usually from the perspective of visual delectation. The coin is intended, after all, to be a utilitarian object, not an artistic one.
10 Many early Greek coins are aesthetically pleasing as well as utilitarian, however, and not simply because they are the earliest examples of coin design. Rather, Greek civic individualism provides the reason. Every
15 Greek political entity expressed its identity through its coinage.

The idea of stamping metal pellets of a standard weight with an identifying design had its origin on the Ionian Peninsula around
20 600 B.C. Each of the Greek city-states produced its own coinage adorned with its particular symbols. The designs were changed frequently to commemorate battles, treaties, and other significant occasions. In
25 addition to their primary use as a pragmatic means of facilitating commerce, Greek coins were clearly an expression of civic pride. The popularity of early coinage led to a constant demand for new designs, such that there
30 arose a class of highly skilled artisans who took great pride in their work, so much so that they sometimes even signed it. As a result, Greek coins provide us not only with an invaluable source of historical knowledge,
35 but also with a genuine expression of the evolving Greek sense of form. These minuscule works reflect the development of Greek sculpture from the sixth to the second century B.C. as dependably as do larger works

197

40 made of marble. And since they are stamped with the place and date of their production, they provide an historic record of artistic

development that is remarkably dependable and complete.

24. What is the purpose of this passage?
   a. To attract new adherents to numismatics as a pastime.
   b. To show how ancient Greeks used coins in commerce.
   c. To teach the reader that money was invented in Greece.
   d. To describe ancient Greek coinage as an art form

25. What is a synonym for *delectation*, as used in the third sentence?
   a. Savoring
   b. Choosing
   c. Deciding
   d. Refusing

26. What is meant by the term *numismatics*?
   a. The study of numbers
   b. Egyptian history
   c. Greek history
   d. The study of coins

27. What is meant by the term *pragmatic*, as used in the fourth sentence of the second paragraph?
   a. Valuable
   b. Monetary
   c. Useful
   d. Practical

28. Why is it significant that new coin designs were required frequently?
   a. This indicates that there was a lot of commercial activity going on.
   b. This gave the designers a lot of practice.
   c. There were a lot of things to commemorate.
   d. The Greeks needed to find new sources of precious metals.

29. According to the text, how do ancient Greek coins differ from most other coinage?
   a. They are different simply because they were the first coins.
   b. Each political entity made its own coins.
   c. They were made of precious metals.
   d. They were designed with extraordinary care.

30. What is meant by the phrase "most of them really do not invite us to do so", as used in the first sentence?
   a. Money is not usually included when sending an invitation.
   b. Most coins are not particularly attractive.
   c. Invitations are not generally engraved onto coins.
   d. Coins do not speak.

Writing

Refer to the following for questions 1–5:

(1) The Freedom Trail is in Boston, Massachusetts and it's a two-and-a-half-mile path through the center of Boston that takes you past buildings and places that were important in Boston's history and in Revolutionary War history.

(2) The trail begins on the Boston Common, which is a big park with baseball fields and large grassy stretches. (3) Back in 1634 when it was first established, the Boston Common was usually used to keep livestock like cows. (4) Later, it was a place where soldiers camped out when they passed through the city.

(5) A bit down from there is the New State House, which was built in 1798, over 150 years after the Boston Common. (6) Paul Revere helped to decorate the State House by laying copper over the wood. (7) The Old State House, which gave its name to the new one, is located a few blocks away.

(8) The Granary Burying Ground, another spot on the Freedom Trail, is famous because many revolutionary figures are buried in it. (9) The Granary was first used as a cemetary in 1660 and got its name because it was next to a grain storage building. (10) The burying ground has 2,345 markers or gravestones, but some people think that up to 8,000 people are buried in it. (11) Some of the most famous people resting at the Granary are Benjamin Franklin's parents, John Hancock, Paul Revere, and victims of the Boston Massacre.

(12) The last stop on the Freedom Trail is the USS Constitution, which is a warship that was called Old Ironsides during the War of 1812. (13) Paul Revere had his hand in this ship as well because he created the copper fastenings on the ship. (14) These are just a few of the stops on the Freedom Trail, which is a great way for families to learn about the Revolutionary War and colonial times together. (15) Visit the Freedom Trail if you want to walk through history!

1. What correction should be made to sentence (1)?
- a. Add a comma after *Massachusetts*.
- b. Change *it's* to *its*.
- c. Add a comma after *buildings*.
- d. Add a comma after *Boston's history*.

2. What correction should be made to sentence (3)?
- a. Change *1634* to *sixteen thirty-four*.
- b. Add a comma after *1634*.
- c. Change *first* to *1st*.
- d. Change *usually* to *unusually*.

3. Which is the best version of sentence (7)?
- a. Because there is an Old State House a few blocks away, the New State House got its name.
- b. The Old State House, located a few blocks away, got its name from the New State House.
- c. A few blocks away from the New State House is the Old State House, which lent its name to the new State House.
- d. The New State House got its name because there is an Old State House a few blocks away.

4. What correction should be made to sentence (9)?

    a. Change *cemetary* to *cemetery*.
    b. Add a comma after *1660*.
    c. Change *its* to *it's*.
    d. Add a comma after *grain*.

5. Which is the best version of sentence (11)?

    a. NO CHANGE
    b. Benjamin Franklin's parents, John Hancock, Paul Revere, and victims of the Boston Massacre are resting at the Granary, which has some of the most famous people.
    c. Some of the most famous people, like Benjamin Franklin's parents, John Hancock, Paul Revere, and victims of the Boston Massacre are resting at the Granary.
    d. Resting at the Granary are some of the most famous people like Benjamin Franklin's parents, John Hancock, Paul Revere, and victims of the Boston Massacre.

6. Which of the following is the best way to write the sentence?

    a. Any person who uses a cell phone in a movie theater has little respect for the other audience members.
    b. Any people who use a cell phone in a movie theater has little respect for the other audience members.
    c. Any persons who uses a cell phone in a movie theater has little respect for the other audience members.
    d. Any person who use a cell phone in a movie theater has little respect for the other audience members.

7. Which of the following versions of the sentence is written correctly?

    a. To repeat ideas in an essay unnecessarily is to commit the mistake of redundant.
    b. To repeat ideas in an essay unnecessarily is to commit the mistake of redundantly.
    c. To repeat ideas in an essay unnecessarily is to commit the mistake of redundancy.
    d. To repeat ideas in an essay unnecessarily is to commit the mistake of redundance.

8. Which version of the sentence is written correctly?

    a. We stopped for extended visits in Indiana, Kansas, Nevada and California during our cross country trip.
    b. We stopped for extended visits, in Indiana, Kansas, Nevada and California during our cross-country trip.
    c. We stopped for extended visits in Indiana, Kansas, Nevada and California, during our cross-country trip.
    d. We stopped for extended visits in Indiana, Kansas, Nevada, and California during our cross-country trip.

9. Which version of the sentence does NOT contain any misspelled words?

    a. I gave my condolences to Juan, whose dog recently ran away from home.
    b. I gave my condolances to Juan, whose dog recently ran away from home.
    c. I gave my condolenses to Juan, whose dog recently ran away from home.
    d. I gave my condolanses to Juan, whose dog recently ran away from home.

10. Which version of the sentence does NOT contain any misspelled words?
   a. The suspect remained detained while the police conducted their inquisiton.
   b. The suspect remained detained while the police conducted their inquasition.
   c. The suspect remained detained while the police conducted their inquesition.
   d. The suspect remained detained while the police conducted their inquisition.

11. Which version of the sentence is written correctly?
   a. The two-year-old was just learning how to walk.
   b. The two-year old was just learning how to walk.
   c. The two year-old was just learning how to walk.
   d. The two year old was just learning how to walk.

12. Choose the word that correctly fills the blank in the following sentence:

   Joanne still needs to finish her homework: revise her essay, _____ the next chapter, and complete the math problems.

   a. reading
   b. to read
   c. read
   d. will read

13. Choose the correct spelling of the word that completes the following sentence:

   The black mangrove tree is native, or _____, to South Florida.

   a. indigenous
   b. endigenous
   c. indegenous
   d. endeginous

14. Choose the word that best fills the blank in the following sentence:

   Peter is so talented with horses that the skittish colt became _____ once Peter took over his training.

   a. frantic
   b. docile
   c. lucid
   d. prudent

15. Choose the words that best fill the blanks in the following sentence:

   King George III was _____ to have the American colonists _____ taxes to Britain on items such as tea and paper.

   a. devious, remand
   b. prudent, attribute
   c. detrimental, tribute
   d. determined, pay

16. Choose the words that best fill the blanks in the following sentence:

> Susan B. Anthony was _____ that women were _____ the same rights as men, such as equal pay and the right to vote.

a. glad, written
b. outraged, denied
c. determined, have
d. credulous, given

17. What does the word *cursory* mean in this sentence?

> The immigration officer gave Maria's passport a cursory examination before quickly moving on to the next person in line.

a. Lazy
b. Angry
c. Hasty
d. Careful

18. Choose the word set that best fills the blanks in the following sentence:

> As a student council _____, Travis endeavored to _____ his peers to the best of his ability.

a. represent, representational
b. representative, represent
c. representation, represent
d. represent, representative

19. Identify the literary device used in the following sentence:

> It was time to go home; the trees waved a fond farewell to speed us on our way.

a. Irony
b. Hyperbole
c. Personification
d. Euphemism

20. Choose the words that best fill the blanks in the following sentence:

> Harper Lee wrote *To Kill a Mockingbird* as an _____ of social _____.

a. argument, dance
b. incident, class
c. exposé, injustice
d. ulterior, inequalities

21. Which of the following versions of the sentence is best?

a. Because she wanted to reduce unnecessary waste, Cicily decided to have the television repaired instead of buying a new one.
b. Cicily decided to have the television repaired because she wanted to reduce unnecessary waste instead of buying a new one.
c. Cicily decided to have, because she wanted to reduce unnecessary waste, the television repaired instead of buying a new one.
d. Because Cicily decided to have the television repaired instead of buying a new one she wanted to reduce unnecessary waste.

22. **Based on how it is used in this sentence, what does the word _reminiscent_ mean?**

    The melody in that pop song is reminiscent of the one Beethoven used in the first movement of his ninth symphony.

    a. Superior
    b. Suggestive
    c. Situated
    d. Synonymous

23. **As used in the sentence, "Julie and I made tentative plans to go to the park because she might have to study that day," what does the word _tentative_ mean?**

    a. Specific
    b. Uncertain
    c. Absolute
    d. Unlikely

24. **Based on how it is used in this sentence, what does the word _translucent_ mean?**

    Although the street could not be seen through the translucent curtains, sunshine still flowed through them.

    a. Flimsy
    b. Transitory
    c. Semitransparent
    d. Opaque

25. **Which version of the sentence is written correctly?**

    a. Veronica was contemptible of the noisy construction workers who made it hard to concentrate on her work.
    b. Veronica was contemptuous of the noisy construction workers who made it hard to concentrate on her work.
    c. Veronica was contempt of the noisy construction workers who made it hard to concentrate on her work.
    d. Veronica was contemptful of the noisy construction workers who made it hard to concentrate on her work.

26. **According to Merriam-Webster's Dictionary, which word derives from the English word _fawney_, which referred to a gilded brass ring?**

    a. Fawning
    b. Phone
    c. Phony
    d. Fallen

27. **Choose the correct spelling of the word that fills the blank in the following sentence:**

    Plastic trash that ends up in the ocean can have a _____, or harmful, effect on marine life.

    a. diliterious
    b. deleterious
    c. delaterious
    d. dilaterious

PERT Practice Test #2

28. Which of the following sentences is correct?

    a.   Jason loves candy including: lollipops, chocolate bars, and gumdrops.

    b.   Jason loves candy except: lollipops, chocolate bars, and gumdrops.

    c.   Jason loves candy, for example: lollipops, chocolate bars, and gumdrops.

    d.   Jason loves candy: lollipops, chocolate bars, and gumdrops.

29. Choose the word that best fills the blank in the following sentence:

    The selection of the winning lottery numbers is entirely _____, with numbers being drawn at random out of a large ball.

    a.   diverse

    b.   arbitrary

    c.   deliberate

    d.   ubiquitous

30. Which of the following sentences is correct?

    a.   I am going to buy a new car it is a blue sedan.

    b.   I am going to buy a new car, it is a blue sedan.

    c.   I am going to buy a new car; it is a blue sedan.

    d.   I am going to buy a new car, therefore, it is a blue sedan.

Answer Key and Explanations #2

Mathematics

1. A: Subtracting a positive number from a negative number is making the negative number more negative, or smaller. In other words, you add the numbers and keep it negative. $13 + 7 = 20$, so the answer is –20.

$$(-13) - 7 = -20$$

2. D: Since the question asks how much money Eli owes his brother, the expression that would represent this scenario is $12 + 20$ because he borrowed $12 and then borrowed an additional $20. When adding two numbers with the same sign, we find the sum of the two numbers and the answer gets the sign of both numbers. Therefore, $12 + 20 = 32$. The amount of money Eli owes his brother is $32.

3. D: When dividing fractions, remember the phrase, "Keep, change, flip." *Keep* the first fraction the same. *Change* the division sign to a multiplication sign and *flip* the second fraction.

$$\frac{3}{7} \times \frac{3}{2}$$

Then, multiply across.

$$\frac{3}{7} \times \frac{3}{2} = \frac{9}{14}$$

Therefore, $\frac{3}{7} \div \frac{2}{3}$ is $\frac{9}{14}$.

4. C: To solve, write an equation that matches the scenario given in the word problem. Since the question asks how many miles the family travels altogether, find the total of both distances by adding. Write the problem vertically, making sure to line up the digits in each number according to place value. Start by adding the tenths column on the right. Since $8 + 5 = 13$, write 3 in the tenths place as part of the answer and carry the 1 over to the ones column. Next, add the ones column. Since $1 + 2 + 6 = 9$, write 9 in the ones place as part of the answer. From here, add the tens column. Since $5 + 7 = 12$, write 2 in the tens place as part of the answer and carry the 1 over to the hundreds column. Finally, add the hundreds column. Since $1 + 3 = 4$, write 4 in the hundreds place as part of the answer. $352.8 + 76.5 = 429.3$. The Smith family will travel 429.3 miles altogether. Therefore, the correct answer is C.

$$
\begin{array}{r}
352\;.8 \\
+\;\;76\;.5 \\
\hline
\end{array}
\qquad
\begin{array}{r}
\overset{1}{}\;\;\;\; \\
352\;.8 \\
+\;\;76\;.5 \\
\hline
.3
\end{array}
\qquad
\begin{array}{r}
\overset{1}{}\;\;\;\; \\
352\;.8 \\
+\;\;76\;.5 \\
\hline
9\;.3
\end{array}
\qquad
\begin{array}{r}
\overset{1}{}\overset{1}{}\;\;\; \\
352\;.8 \\
+\;\;76\;.5 \\
\hline
29\;.3
\end{array}
\qquad
\begin{array}{r}
\overset{1}{}\overset{1}{}\;\;\; \\
352\;.8 \\
+\;\;76\;.5 \\
\hline
429\;.\overset{3}{}
\end{array}
$$

5. B: To find the sum of 0.164 and 0.972, we will write the two numbers vertically with the decimals lined up. We will start by adding 4 and 2, which is 6. Then we add 6 and 7, which is 13. Write down 3 and carry over 1. Then we add 9, 1, and 1, which is 11. Write down 1 and carry over the second 1 to the next column, then add 1, 0, and 0. Therefore, the value of the expression $0.164 + 0.972$ is 1.136.

$$
\begin{array}{r}
\overset{1}{}\;\overset{1}{} \\
0\;.164 \\
+0\;.972 \\
\hline
1\;.13^{6}
\end{array}
$$

6. B: Set up the multiplication problem vertically, making sure to line up the numbers according to place value. Multiply 4 by the ones digit in –16. Since $4 \times 6 = 24$, write 4 in the ones place as part of the product and carry the 2 into the tens place. Next, multiply 4 by the tens digit in –16 and add the 2 that was carried over. $4 \times 1 = 4$ and $4 + 2 = 6$. Write 6 in the tens place as part of the product. Therefore, $-16 \times 4 = -64$ because a negative number times a positive number is a negative number. Since the word "spends" indicates that the integer is negative, there is no need to write a negative sign before the dollar sign. Mike spends $64, and this is represented by the integer –64. Therefore, the correct answer is B.

$$
\begin{array}{r}
-16 \\
\times\quad 4 \\
\hline
\end{array}
\qquad
\begin{array}{r}
\overset{2}{}\\
-16 \\
\times\quad 4 \\
\hline
4
\end{array}
\qquad
\begin{array}{r}
\overset{2}{}\\
-16 \\
\times\quad 4 \\
\hline
-64
\end{array}
$$

7. A: The equation that can model this situation would have to have the existing amount in Lora's savings as the constant, or y-intercept, and the slope would be 300, since she will be putting $300 in her savings each month. Therefore, the equation that best models this situation is $y = 300x + 2{,}400$.

8. A: To find the value of x, we will first ask ourselves, what is happening to x? In this problem, it is being divided by 5. Then we ask, what is the opposite of division? The answer is multiplication, so we will multiply both sides of the equation by 5 to isolate the x on one side. On the left side of the equation, we are left with x. On the right side of the equation, we will multiply 5 by –6 to get –30, which is the value of x.

9. B: To find the value of w, we will isolate the w on one side of the equation. Since 57 is being subtracted from w, to isolate w we will add 57 to both sides of the equation. On the left side of the equation, we will be left with w. On the right side, we will add 57 to –279, which is –222. Therefore, the value of w is –222.

10. B: To solve for m, c^2 must be moved to the other side of the equal sign. This can be done by dividing both sides of the equation by c^2.

$$
\frac{E}{c^2} = \frac{mc^2}{c^2}
$$

On the right side, the two c^2 terms cancel out, leaving $\frac{E}{c^2} = m$. So $m = \frac{E}{c^2}$.

11. B: Start by creating a table that shows the relationship between minutes jogged (m) and distance (d).

Minutes jogged (m)	Distance in miles (d)
0	0
10	1
20	2
30	3

As you can see, the table represents the equation $d = \frac{1}{10}m$. The independent variable is minutes (m), and the dependent variable is the distance (d). From here, we can use the data from the table to graph points on the coordinate plane. The x-axis represents the independent variable, which is minutes jogged, and the y-axis represents the dependent variable, which is distance run in miles.

Rewrite the data from the table as points on the coordinate plane, (x, y): $(0,0)$, $(10,1)$, $(20,2)$, $(30,3)$. Although all answer options contain the point $(0,0)$ on their coordinate planes, the only graph with all four coordinate pairs is answer B. Therefore, the correct answer is B.

12. A: Since $2x + 4y = 8$ is written in standard form, use the equation to find the x- and y-intercepts. Once we know where the line passes through each axis, we can match the graph to the equation. Start by finding the y-intercept. When using the standard form of an equation to find the y-intercept, make x equal to 0 and solve for y. Start by replacing x with 0 in the equation.

$$2x + 4y = 8$$
$$2(0) + 4y = 8$$

Next, simplify the equation and solve for y. Since $2 \times 0 = 0$, rewrite the equation as $0 + 4y = 8$, which is the same as $4y = 8$.

$$0 + 4y = 8$$
$$4y = 8$$

From here, isolate the variable y by doing inverse operations. Since the opposite of multiplying by 4 is dividing by 4, divide both sides of the equation by 4.

$$\frac{4y}{4} = \frac{8}{4}$$

$4y \div 4 = 1y$ (or y), and $8 \div 4 = 2$. Therefore, $y = 2$. The line intersects the y-axis at point $(0,2)$.

Now that we know the location of the y-intercept, find the x-intercept. When using the standard form of an equation to find the x-intercept, make y equal to 0 and solve for x. Start by replacing y with 0 in the equation.

$$2x + 4y = 8$$
$$2x + 4(0) = 8$$

Next, simplify the equation and solve for x. Since $4 \times 0 = 0$, rewrite the equation as $2x + 0 = 8$, which is the same as $2x = 8$.

$$2x + 0 = 8$$
$$2x = 8$$

From here, isolate the variable x by doing inverse operations. Since the opposite of multiplying by 2 is dividing by 2, divide both sides of the equation by 2.

$$\frac{2x}{2} = \frac{8}{2}$$

$2x \div 2 = 1x$ (or x), and $8 \div 2 = 4$. Therefore, $x = 4$. The line intersects the x-axis at point $(4,0)$.

Now that we know that the location of the x-intercept is $(4,0)$ and the location of the y-intercept is $(0,2)$, look for the graph that contains both coordinate pairs. Since the graph shown in answer A contains both points, the correct answer is A.

13. D: We try to factor the largest perfect-square factor out of the radicand (the expression under the square root symbol). Here, the radicand, 20, has the perfect-square factor 4. Since $\sqrt{ab} = \sqrt{a} \times \sqrt{b}$ whenever a and b are nonnegative numbers, we get the simplification $\sqrt{20} = \sqrt{4 \times 5} = \sqrt{4} \times \sqrt{5} = 2\sqrt{5}$.

14. C: First, write an equation that represents the scenario. Since area equals length times width, multiply w and $2w + 3$ to get a product of 90.

$$w(2w + 3) = 90$$

Next, convert the quadratic equation to standard form. To do so, distribute w to each term inside the parentheses. Move all the terms to the left side and set it equal to 0 by doing inverse operations. Subtract 90 from both sides of the equation.

$$2w^2 + 3w = 90$$
$$2w^2 + 3w - 90 = 90 - 90$$
$$2w^2 + 3w - 90 = 0$$

Next, factor the left side of the equation.

$$(2w + 15)(w - 6) = 0$$

From here, set each factor equal to 0 and solve for the variable, starting with $2w + 15 = 0$. Use inverse operations, and subtract 15 from both sides of the equation. Then, divide both sides by 2.

$$2w + 15 = 0$$
$$2w + 15 - 15 = 0 - 15$$
$$2w = -15$$
$$\frac{2w}{2} = \frac{-15}{2}$$
$$w = \frac{-15}{2}$$

208

Finally, solve $w - 6 = 0$. Use inverse operations, and add 6 to both sides of the equation.

$$w - 6 = 0$$
$$w - 6 + 6 = 0 + 6$$
$$w = 6$$

The solution set is $\left\{-\frac{15}{2}, 6\right\}$. Since measurements of length and width use positive numbers, omit $-\frac{15}{2}$ in this scenario. Therefore, the width of the plot of land is 6 feet.

15. B: Since the quadratic equation is already equal to zero, factor the quadratic expression on the left-hand side and solve both equations for x.

$$2x^2 - x - 6 = 0$$
$$(2x + 3)(x - 2) = 0$$

$2x + 3 = 0$	$x - 2 = 0$
$2x = -3$	$x = 2$
$x = -\frac{3}{2}$	

16. A: To convert a percentage to a fraction, remove the percent sign and place the number over 100. That means 15% can be written as $\frac{15}{100}$, which reduces to $\frac{3}{20}$. To convert a percentage to a decimal, remove the percent sign and move the decimal two places to the left. To convert a percentage to a ratio, first write the percentage as a fraction, and then rewrite the fraction as a ratio.

17. C: To multiply and divide fractions with mixed numbers, first convert the mixed number to an improper fraction. The mixed number $1\frac{1}{8}$ becomes the improper fraction $\frac{9}{8}$.

$$\frac{1}{4} \times \frac{3}{5} \div \frac{9}{8}$$

Simplify the expression by using the order of operations. Multiply and divide in order from left to right: $\frac{1}{4} \times \frac{3}{5} = \frac{3}{20}$.

$$\frac{3}{20} \div \frac{9}{8}$$

Then, simplify the division, which requires multiplying by the inverse of the second fraction.

$$\frac{3}{20} \div \frac{9}{8} = \frac{3}{20} \times \frac{8}{9} = \frac{24}{180}$$

This result simplifies to $\frac{2}{15}$.

18. D: The expression $(x - 2)^2$ may be expanded as $x^2 - 4x + 4$. Multiplication of $-3x$ by this expression gives $-3x^3 + 12x^2 - 12x$.

Answer Key and Explanations #2

19. B: Start by evaluating each exponent separately.

$$3^3 - 2^5$$
$$27 - 32$$

Then, subtract the two numbers.

$$27 - 32 = -5$$

20. A: To simplify the expression, start by distributing the 3s.

$$3\left(\frac{6x - 3}{3}\right) - 3(9x + 9)$$

$$6x - 3 - 27x - 27$$

Then, combine like terms.

$$(6x - 27x) + (-3 - 27)$$

$$-21x - 30$$

Since this isn't one of the answer choices, manipulate it to match one of the choices given. Factor out a –3 from each term.

$$-3(7x + 10)$$

Since this matches choice A, it is correct.

21. B: Remember the order of operations: parentheses, exponents, multiplication and division, addition and subtraction.

Perform the operations inside the parentheses first.

$$5(10) + (5) - (45)$$

Then, do any multiplication and division, working from left to right. Remember, a number next to parentheses tells you to multiply the two values.

$$50 + 5 - 45$$

Finally, do any adding or subtracting, working from left to right.

$$55 - 45 = 10$$

22. C: To evaluate the expression, start by substituting in the given values.

$$\left(3 - 2(2)\right)^2$$

Then, use the order of operations to simplify. Start by simplifying the expression inside the parentheses.

$$(3 - 4)^2 = (-1)^2 = 1$$

Therefore, the expression is equal to 1 when $x = 3$ and $y = 2$.

23. C: The equation describes a functional relationship between y and $p(y)$. To solve the equation, substitute 4 as the value of y.

$$p(4) = \frac{4(4)}{2} + 5 = \frac{16}{2} + 5 = 8 + 5 = 13$$

24. B: Solve this equation by first using cross multiplication.

$$3(y + 4) = 15(y - 5)$$

From here, distribute on both sides.

$$3y + 12 = 15y - 75$$

Subtract $3y$ from both sides.

$$12 = 12y - 75$$

Add 75 to both sides of the equation.

$$87 = 12y$$

Finally, divide both sides by 12 and simplify the fraction.

$$\frac{87}{12} = \frac{29}{4} = y$$

25. D: To simplify the expression, use the exponent rule $(x^m)^n = x^{m \times n}$.

$$(3x^{-2})^3 = (3)^3 (x^{-2})^3 = 27x^{-6}$$

26. D: To simplify the expression, start by using the exponent rule $(x^m)^n = x^{m \times n}$.

$$(b^3)^{-4} \times b^{15} = b^{3 \times -4} \times b^{15} = b^{-12} \times b^{15}$$

Then, use the exponent rule $x^m \times x^n = x^{m+n}$.

$$b^{-12} \times b^{15} = b^{-12+15} = b^3$$

27. C: The expression $(x - 3)^2$ can be rewritten as $(x - 3)(x - 3)$. Use the FOIL method to multiply the first terms, outer terms, inner terms, and last terms. Then, add these four terms together to get $x^2 - 3x - 3x + 9$. Combining like terms gives $x^2 - 6x + 9$.

28. A: After distributing the minus sign across the second trinomial, the expression can be rewritten as $3x^3 - 9x^2 + 6x - 8x^3 - 4x^2 + 3x$. Combining like terms gives $-5x^3 - 13x^2 + 9x$.

29. A: First, notice that each of the coefficients is divisible by 3 and that each of the x terms has a power of 2 or more. Factor out a 3 from each term and you have $3(4x^4 - 9x^3 + 2x^2)$. Next, factor out x^2 from each term and you are left with $3x^2(4x^2 - 9x + 2)$. The portion inside the parentheses can be further factored as follows: $3x^2(4x^2 - 9x + 2) = 3x^2(4x - 1)(x - 2)$. This step may take a bit of trial and error. Look at the answer choices to get a hint. If a combination you are considering is not a choice, then it is not the correct answer.

If you are having trouble factoring the problem, you can always work backward. Look at the answer choices and multiply them out to see which one gives the original problem as its answer. This method is more time-consuming, but it will yield a correct answer if you get stumped.

30. D: To factor the expression, start by determining what two things multiply to make x^2. We will use $x \cdot x$.

$$(x + \_)(x + \_)$$

To figure out what goes on the right sides of the expressions, find two numbers whose product is −28 and whose sum is 3. These two numbers must be 7 and −4 because $7 \times (-4) = -28$ and $7 + (-4) = 3$. Therefore, the factored form of this expression is:

$$(x - 4)(x + 7)$$

Reading

1. B: This question basically asks for the main idea of the passage as a whole. Choice A is inappropriate because the passage does not discuss automotive stock. Choice B is a good choice because the final sentence of the first paragraph says exactly the same thing. Choice C is not only inappropriate, it is also only true for a very limited number of vehicles. Choice D is so general that it does not really say anything at all. The best choice is, therefore, Choice B.

2. B: Even if the meaning of "detriments" is unclear, the sentence it is used in provides some clues: "While there are many pros and cons associated with automobile ownership, many consumers do not adequately research the specific benefits and <u>detriments</u> associated with purchasing a particular vehicle." The sentence's structure makes it probable that there is an identification of "pros and cons" with "benefits and detriments." Leaving this aside, if it is clear that "pros" and "benefits" are the same thing, then it is likely that "cons" and "detriments" are the same thing. The best answer, then, is B, "Cons."

3. D: This is a detail question with tricky wording in the answer choices. The use of the term "always" should make the reader suspicious. In the real world, things are almost never "always" x or y. For example, choice A is explicitly contradicted in the second paragraph. Choice B is doubly inappropriate because of its use of "always" and its irrelevance to the passage (SUVs are not discussed in the passage). While choice C does not use "always," it is not a good choice because the relationship between color and cost is not discussed in the passage. Choice D is supported by the second paragraph and is the best overall choice.

4. D: Because this is an "all of the above question," if the reader can confirm two of the answer choices, he or she need not examine the third. Choice A is a good one because the second paragraph says that the cost of a vehicle is not limited to purchase price alone. Choices B and C are included in the passage as additional costs of ownership Since A has already been confirmed, confirming either B or C means that the correct answer is D.

5. B: According to the passage, choice A is inappropriate because if the consumer has done research, he or she will be less likely to be swayed by less important concerns. Choice B is explicitly stated in the final paragraph. Choice C is inappropriate because the passage says nothing about the consumer's attitude towards salespeople. Choice D is directly contradicted in the third paragraph. Thus, choice B is the best answer.

6. D: This is a difficult question because it is easy to make a simple mistake. The passage explicitly says that choices A and C can be explored on a manufacturer's website. While it seems likely that one could visit a manufacturer's website and find information on a vehicle's color, two things should be noted. First, the passage does not discuss a vehicle's color with reference to a manufacturer's website. Second, the passage does not discuss the relationship between a vehicle's color and its cost. For both of these reasons, choice B is a poor choice; thus, the best answer is choice D.

7. D: Although the passage implies that Bill has not been in school for twenty years, the passage does not say how old Bill is. It might be tempting to try to extrapolate Bill's age from the passage, but this is impossible; in other words, Bill could be forty, fifty, or seventy-five years old (he must be older than twenty because he has not been at school for twenty years), but the passage gives no indication of exactly how old he is. Accordingly, D is the best answer.

8. D: In Bill's exchange with the girl in black, the passage shows that Bill is confused. It is also clear that Bill is sad—he misses Martha. The best answer, then, should mention Bill's confusion, his sadness, or both. Choice A mentions neither—this choice says that Bill is bored, or does not care about what is going on. Although Bill is somewhat reflective in the passage, B is not the best choice because it does not capture Bill's general state of mind. Choice C is not appropriate because even though Bill gets offended, he does not really get angry. Choice D is the best answer because it is directly supported by the passage: Bill cannot find the Biology labs, and he cannot understand why the cheerleaders do not thank him for holding the door open.

9. C: It is tempting to tell a story to answer this question, but the only information that is provided about Martha in the passage is that she is no longer with Bill. Since the passage says nothing about Martha leaving Bill for another man, choice A is unacceptable. Likewise, choice B may be eliminated because the passage remains noncommittal as to Martha's death. Choice C is a good choice because it succinctly describes Martha's relationship with Bill: she is somehow absent. Choice D is not supported by the passage. The best choice is C.

10. A: From the structure of the sentence, it seems likely that *dumbfounded* means unable to understand. Choice A is a good choice because *perplexed* is a synonym of *confused*. Choice B is inappropriate because if something is *rationalized*, it is explained or justified. Choice C is inappropriate because *dilapidated* means run-down. To *entreat* means to beg or ask for something, so choice D is inappropriate. Thus, A is the best choice.

11. C: The passage says nothing about Bill's past profession, so any inferences drawn about his work are in error. Choices A and B are therefore unacceptable. C is a good choice because the final paragraph has a sense of finality about it—Bill is leaving the school, and it is unlikely that he will return. Choice D is not supported by the passage. If Bill misses Martha as much as he says, then it is likely that he really does love her. The best answer is choice C.

12. C: The sentence preceding *diminution* describes "a process whereby a given liquid is slowly simmered until its volume diminishes." The word *diminishes* means *lessens* or *decreases*, so it is reasonable to guess that *diminution* means *decrease*, choice C.

13. D: This question is tricky because a number of the answer choices seem correct but are not supported by the passage. Choice A seems reasonable, but the passage does not focus on how

213

performing reductions demonstrates skill. Choices B and C also seem reasonable—if reductions are in many dishes, then restaurant customers probably like them, which means that they are popular in contemporary cuisine. However, the passage does not say these things. The passage does explicitly say that many recipes call for reductions, so choice D is a good answer.

14. B: This question asks for a specific detail from the passage. Rereading the relevant portion of the passage is thus a wise strategy. Rereading the passage reveals that the chicken is browned and removed, then the butter is added, followed by the wine. So, choice B is the best option.

15. D: According to the passage, the wine-and-butter mixture should be reduced by half. After this, chicken stock and chicken breasts should be added. The sauce in this new mixture should be reduced by half. This results in two reductions (A and C in the answer choices). Choice B is not a reduction, according to the passage. The best answer choice is D because it includes the two reductions but not the melting of the butter.

16. C: Choice A is inappropriate because it contradicts the passage. A common mistake is overboiling, not underboiling. Choice B is likewise contradicted by the passage. Adding butter is part of the chicken Marsala recipe. Since two of the choices have thus far been eliminated, choice D can be eliminated. Choice C is a good answer because the passage describes how adding starches can diminish a sauce's flavor and make it too thick.

17. B: Choice A seems like a possibility, but the importance of reductions is really given in the first paragraph: reductions are important because they are present in many recipes. Choice B makes sense because the chicken marsala recipe is, indeed, an example of a reduction. Choices C and D are not supported by the passage.

18. A: This question asks for a detail from the passage. Choice A is the only choice that the passage states to be true —in the third paragraph it explicitly says that grieving individuals can be self-destructive. Choice B is not appropriate because the passage does not mention therapy. Choice C is not appropriate because the passage does not discuss complete, or full, healing; it says that the bereaved can begin to heal when they move beyond anger. Choice D is not appropriate because the passage does not mention crying.

19. D: This question is difficult because the first paragraph of the passage is largely introductory. While the paragraph seems to be concerned with the different stages of the grieving process, these stages serve as context for the main idea of the paragraph: the anger stage of the grieving process is both natural and misunderstood. Choice D is the best choice. Choice A is not appropriate because depression is mentioned only briefly in the first paragraph. Choice B is partially contradicted by the first paragraph. Choice C is a detail from paragraph three.

20. D: Even if one does not know the meaning of *cathartic*, closely examining the sentence's structure can help determine what the word means. The phrase "in other words" alerts the reader that what follows is a restatement of what comes before; thus, *cathartic* and *therapeutic* are related to the phrase "emotional release and allows for the beginning of the healing process." Since something therapeutic "allows for the beginning of the healing process," it stands to reason that something cathartic is related to "emotional release," which is exactly what answer choice D says.

21. B: Although this question seems to ask for a detail, it actually asks for a larger point from the passage. Choice B is the only good choice because paragraph three discusses how individuals can come to understand how tragedy is generally blameless. Choices A, C, and D are all inappropriate because the passage does not address them.

22. D: This question asks for a detail from the passage. Choice A is not a good answer because it is directly contradicted by the passage—anger helps with the grieving process. Choices B and C, while probably true, are not discussed in the passage and so are inappropriate answers. The only remaining choice is D, which is explicitly stated in the fourth paragraph of the passage.

23. D: This is a detail question that lists "all of the above" as a possible answer choice. The passage tells the reader that people who fail to go through the grieving process may experience vague, continued irritability, so answer choice A seems good. Choice B also looks good because the third paragraph explicitly states that such individuals may lose religious faith. Because two answer choices are correct, choice C does not even have to be examined—the correct answer choice must be D, all of the above.

24. D: The passage describes the artistry of ancient Greek coins and gives the reasons why so much effort went into designing them.

25. A: *Delectation* means to savor or to enjoy the flavor or beauty of something, in this case the design of the coins.

26. D: The word is defined in the second sentence of the passage.

27. D: The sentence contrasts the artistic content of the coins with their use as a practical means of commercial exchange.

28. B: The frequent need for new designs meant that the artisans who did the work had ample opportunity to perfect their skills.

29. D: The passage describes the coins as artistic objects, not simply because they were the first coins, but also because of the historical situation which is described, and which led to their being designed with great care and pride.

30. B: The first sentence indicates that coins are utilitarian objects, and few are designed well enough to be worth considering them as anything more.

Writing

1. A: When a state name follows a city name, it should be set off by commas. Choice B is incorrect because *it's* is a contraction for *it is*, while *its* (without the apostrophe) is the possessive form of the word *it*. Choice C is incorrect because *buildings and places* is a two-item series connected by *and*; a comma should not be used in a two-item series written in this format. Choice D is incorrect for the same reason; the phrase is a two-item series connected by *and*.

2. B: *Back in 1634* is an adverbial phrase beginning the sentence and should be separated from the rest of the sentence by a comma. Choice A is incorrect because years should be written using Arabic numerals; they should not be written out. Choice C is incorrect for the opposite reason; in an essay, small numbers should be written out rather than using Arabic numerals. Choice D is incorrect because *unusually* changes the meaning of the sentence. Using the word *usually* helps indicate that the Boston Common was most often used for livestock but also had other uses.

3. D: This choice most effectively explains how the New State House got its name. Choice A is incorrect because the word order of the sentence makes it difficult to understand why the New State House got its name; the dependent clause is not adequately supported. Choice B is incorrect because it changes the meaning of the sentence; the new building got its name from the old, not the other way around. Choice C is incorrect because it is wordier than the correct answer.

4. A: The correct spelling of the word *cemetery* ends with *-ery*. Choice B is incorrect because a comma should only be used before a conjunction if the conjunction precedes an independent clause. Choice C is incorrect because *its* without an apostrophe is the possessive form of *it*. Choice D is incorrect because *grain storage* is a single phrase that describes building; grain and storage do not describe building independently.

5. A: The original version of the sentence is the most succinct and clear. Also, only the original version explains that the people listed are some of the most famous people buried at the Granary, not merely that they are "some of the most famous people" and happen to be buried at the Granary.

6. A: The subject *person* is singular and must use the singular verbs *uses* and *has*. The subjects *people* and *persons* are both plural and must be paired with the plural verbs *use* and *have*. Only choice A correctly matches the subject with both verbs.

7. C: In the context of this sentence, the word *redundant* should appear in its noun form, which is *redundancy* (meaning "unnecessary repetition"). *Redundant* is an adjective, and *redundantly* is an adverb. *Redundance* is a nonstandard variant of *redundancy* and is not widely accepted.

8. D: The comma that comes after the next-to-last item in a list (in this case, Nevada) is called the serial comma. It is okay to include it (choice D) or not (the other three choices). But choices B and C each include an extra comma where it does not belong. Choice A misses the essential hyphen that should join the adjective phrase *cross-country*.

9. A: The word *condolences* means an expression of sympathy, and only choice A spells it correctly.

10. D: Although the word *inquisition* means "a prolonged process of questioning," it is not spelled with an *e*, as is the word *question*. The correct spelling uses an *i*, as in *inquire*.

11. A: Adjective phrases consisting of more than one word (compound modifiers) should be hyphenated, even if the person, place, or thing they're describing is only implied. The word *child* is only implied in this sentence, but the adjective phrase describing it ("two-year-old") still needs to be fully hyphenated in order for it to be correct.

12. C: *Read* (present tense form of the verb) maintains the parallel structure of the sentence and matches the verb tense for *revise* and *complete*. The other answer choices represent the present participle (*reading*), infinitive (*to read*), and future tense (*will read*) of the word.

13. A: The correct spelling of the word is *indigenous*.

14. B: The word *docile* means "easily taught" or "ready to be taught." The sentence should read: Peter is so talented with horses that the skittish colt became docile once Peter took over his training.

15. D: The sentence should read: King George III was determined to have the American colonists pay taxes to Britain on items such as tea and paper.

16. B: The sentence should read: Susan B. Anthony was outraged that women were denied the same rights as men, such as equal pay and the right to vote.

17. C: The context of the sentence and use of the phrase "quickly moving on" indicate that the immigration officer is in a hurry and does not spend a lot of time examining Maria's passport.

18. B: *Representative* acts as a noun, and *represent* acts as a verb. The sentence should read: As a student council representative, Travis endeavored to represent his peers to the best of his ability.

19. C: Personification is an expression in which animals or objects are given human characteristics. In this sentence, the trees are given the human ability to wave a fond farewell.

20. C: The sentence should read: Harper Lee wrote *To Kill a Mockingbird* as an exposé of social injustice.

21. A: The syntax of this sentence is correct. It uses a comma to offset the subordinate clause ("Because she wanted to reduce unnecessary waste") from the independent clause ("Cicily decided to have the television repaired instead of buying a new one"). Placing the independent clause, which is the most important idea in the sentence, at the end for emphasis also makes the sentence stronger.

22. B: The sentence compares the melody of a pop song to that of the first movement in Beethoven's ninth symphony. Therefore, concluding that they probably are similar is logical. The pop song reminds the speaker of the Beethoven piece, which means the pop song suggests the melody of the Beethoven piece. *Reminiscent* and *suggestive* are synonyms in this context.

23. B: Julie may have to study on the day she and the speaker consider going to the park, which means their plans are uncertain. The plans might happen, but they also might not happen. Based on this context, you can conclude that the word *tentative* means "uncertain." Because the speaker does not indicate that either the plan to go to the park or the possibility Julie may have to study is more likely, *unlikely* is not the best answer choice.

24. C: According to the sentence, while certain things could not be seen through the curtains, light could. The curtains are not transparent enough to show the street, yet they are transparent enough to show sunshine. The prefix *semi-* means "partially." Based on this context, you can conclude that *translucent* and *semitransparent* share the same meaning. Although something that is flimsy may be transparent, this is not always the case, so the words are not synonyms. *Transitory* shares the root *trans-*, meaning "through," but *transitory* means "not lasting." Something that is opaque does not allow light to pass through it at all.

25. B: *Contempt* is a feeling of scorn or disdain, and to be *contemptuous* is to experience or express that feeling. *Contemptible* refers to something that inspires contempt, which in Veronica's case, would be the noisy construction workers. *Contemptful* is not a word in standard English.

26. C: A word's origin, or etymology, can give you a clue to its meaning. A brass ring merely gilded with gold, a fawney, is hardly the same thing as a solid gold ring. Attempting to pass off such a ring as pure gold would be untruthful, and the ring would only be a fake gold ring. The words *phony* and *fake* share the same meaning. Although *fawning* sounds and looks similar to *fawney*, the former means "flattering" or "submissive," which provides no indication of the real meaning of *fawney*.

27. B: The correct spelling of the word is *deleterious*.

28. D: It is appropriate to use a colon to introduce a list. It is not appropriate to use a colon following a preposition (choice B), or after the phrases "including" and "for example" as used in choices A and C, which make the use of a colon redundant.

29. B: The word *arbitrary* means that an outcome is not determined by predictable rules, so a random drawing fits this meaning. The sentence should read: The selection of the winning lottery numbers is entirely arbitrary, with numbers being drawn at random out of a large ball.

30. C: "I am going to buy a new car" and "it is a blue sedan" are independent clauses (they each contain a subject and a verb and express a complete thought). It is appropriate to join two independent clauses in a single sentence with a semicolon. Choice A is a run-on sentence. Choice B is a comma splice. Choice D uses a comma to precede the conjunctive adverb *therefore*, which is incorrect.

PERT Practice Test #3

Mathematics

1. What is 783 − 124?

    a. 559
    b. 584
    c. 619
    d. 659

2. What is 19 + 23 + 81 + 4?

    a. 104
    b. 113
    c. 123
    d. 127

3. Maria buys $\frac{1}{5}$ of a pound of grapes and $\frac{3}{4}$ of a pound of berries. How many total pounds of fruit did Maria buy?

    a. $\frac{4}{20}$
    b. $\frac{4}{9}$
    c. $\frac{5}{8}$
    d. $\frac{19}{20}$

4. Solve: $\$8.45 − \$0.56 =$

    a. $7.45
    b. $7.99
    c. $7.89
    d. $8.11

5. What is the sum of 0.77 and 0.54?

    a. 0.131
    b. 0.20
    c. 1.31
    d. 2.00

6. What is 156 ÷ 4?

    a. 13
    b. 27
    c. 35
    d. 39

7. Lex charges $25 to mow a lawn. He spends $80 a week on fuel for his lawn mower. Which equation can be used to model this situation, where x is the number of lawns Lex mows in one week and y is the total amount of money that he makes in one week?

   a. $x = 25y - 80$
   b. $x = 80y - 25$
   c. $y = 25x - 80$
   d. $y = 80x - 25$

8. The equation $y - 14 = 63$ is given. What is the value of y?

   a. $y = 49$
   b. $y = 57$
   c. $y = 71$
   d. $y = 77$

9. The equation $\frac{y}{17} = 22$ is given. What is the value of y?

   a. $y = 5$
   b. $y = 39$
   c. $y = 110$
   d. $y = 374$

10. Which graph represents the linear equation $y = -6$?

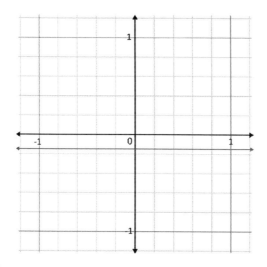

a.

c.

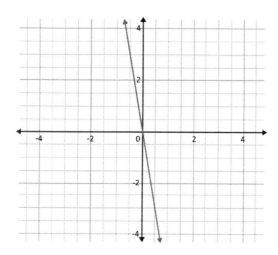

b.

d.

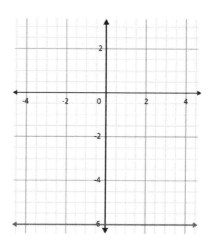

PERT Practice Test #3

11. Which graph represents the linear equation $-6x + 3y = 15$?

a.

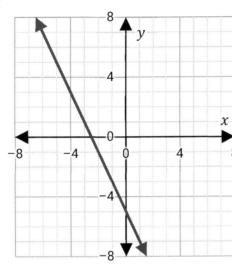

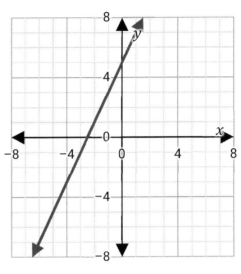

c.

b.

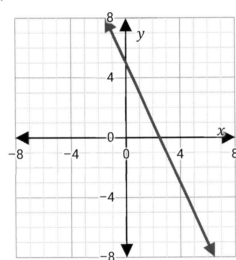

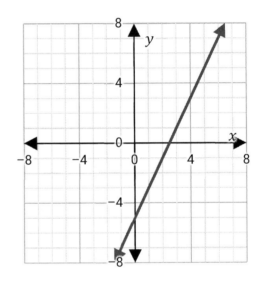

d.

12. Evaluate the product $3\sqrt{11} \times 4\sqrt{14}$. Simplify your answer as much as possible.

  a. $24\sqrt{38}$
  b. $12\sqrt{154}$
  c. $24\sqrt{39}$
  d. 60

13. Maddie is creating a garden in her backyard. The area of her garden is 15 square meters. The length of the garden is 2 meters more than its width. Using this information, write a quadratic equation that represents this scenario, and solve to identify the length and width of the garden.

  a.   The length is 15 meters, and the width is 0 meters.
  b.   The length is -3 meters, and the width is -5 meters.
  c.   The length is 5 meters, and the width is 3 meters.
  d.   The length is 3 meters, and the width is 5 meters.

222

Mometrix

14. Solve this quadratic equation by factoring: $x^2 + 5x = -6$.
    a. $x = -3$ and $x = -2$
    b. $x = 2$ and $x = 3$
    c. $x = -1$ and $x = 6$
    d. $x = -6$ and $x = 1$

15. Which of the following is the percentage equivalent of 0.0016?
    a. 16%
    b. 160%
    c. 1.6%
    d. 0.16%

16. Simplify the following expression: $3\frac{1}{6} - 1\frac{5}{6}$.
    a. $2\frac{1}{3}$
    b. $1\frac{1}{3}$
    c. $2\frac{1}{9}$
    d. $\frac{5}{6}$

17. Which of the following expressions is equivalent to $-5x(x-1)^2$?
    a. $-5x^3 + 10x^2 - 5x$
    b. $-5x^3 - 10x^2 - 5x$
    c. $-5x^2 + 5x$
    d. $-5x^3 + 10x^2 + 5x$

18. What is the simplest form of the following polynomial:
$$4x^3 + 5x - x^3 + 2x^2 + 17 - 3x^3 + 5x - 2x^2 + 3$$
    a. $10x + 20$
    b. $x + 2$
    c. $10(x + 2)$
    d. $x^3 + 2$

19. Given the equation $2^x = 64$, what is the value of x?
    a. 4
    b. 5
    c. 6
    d. 7

20. Evaluate $x^2 - (2y - 3)$ if $x = 4$ and $y = 3$.
    a. 12
    b. 13
    c. 10
    d. 8

21. Which of the following graphs best represents the number of questions Joshua must answer correctly?

a. number line from 0 to 30, open circles at 0 and 30

b. number line from 0 to 30, closed circles at 0 and 30

c. number line from 0 to 30, circle at ~22 and closed at 30

d. number line from 0 to 30, closed circles near 22 and 30

22. Simplify the expression $(3x)^3 \times (5x^2)$.

   a. $27x^6$
   b. $8x^5$
   c. $135x^5$
   d. $15x^5$

23. Simplify the expression: $2x^5 \times 7x^{18}$.

   a. $14x^{23}$
   b. $14x^{13}$
   c. $9x^{23}$
   d. $9x^{13}$

24. What are the factors of the following polynomial: $2x^2 + 7x - 15$?

   a. $(2x + 5)(x - 3)$
   b. $(x + 5)(2x - 3)$
   c. $(2x - 5)(x + 3)$
   d. $(x - 5)(2x + 3)$

25. What are the factors of the following polynomial: $x^2 - x - 56$?

   a. $(x - 7)(x + 8)$
   b. $(x + 7)(x - 8)$
   c. $(x - 7)(x - 8)$
   d. $(x + 7)(x + 8)$

26. What is the value of the expression $-3 \times 5^2 + 2(4 - 18) + 33$?

   a. -130
   b. -70
   c. -20
   d. 74

27. If $f(x) = \dfrac{x^3 + 3x + 2}{2x}$, what is $f(-1)$?

   a. -2
   b. $\dfrac{1}{2}$
   c. 1
   d. -1

28. Solve for x in the following equation: $4(2x - 6) = 10x - 6$.

    a. $x = 5$
    b. $x = -7$
    c. $x = -9$
    d. $x = 10$

29. Which of the following expressions is equivalent to $-2x(x + 6)^2$?

    a. $-2x^3 + 12x^2 - 36x$
    b. $-2x^3 - 24x^2 - 72x$
    c. $-2x^2 + 36x$
    d. $-2x^3 - 12x^2 - 72x$

30. Find the difference: $(-8x^2 + 5xy - 4y - 10) - (-8x^2 + 12y^2 + 5x - 6y - 10)$.

    a. $5xy + 12y^2 + 5x - 10y - 20$
    b. $5xy - 12y^2 - 5x + 2y - 20$
    c. $5xy - 12y^2 - 5x + 2y$
    d. $-16x^2 + 5xy - 12y^2 - 5x + 2y$

Reading

Refer to the following for questions 1–5:

Chang-rae Lee's debut and award-winning novel *Native Speaker* is about Henry Park, a Korean American individual who struggles to find his place as an immigrant in a suburb of New York City. This novel addresses the notion that, as the people who know us best, our family, peers, and lovers are the individuals who direct our lives and end up defining us. Henry Park is confronted with this reality at the very start of the novel, which begins:

The day my wife left she gave me a list of who I was.

Upon separating from his wife, Park struggles with racial and ethnic identity issues due to his loneliness. Through Park's work as an undercover operative for a private intelligence agency, the author presents the theme of espionage as a metaphor for the internal divide that Park experiences as an immigrant. This dual reality creates two worlds for Park and increases his sense of uncertainty with regard to his place in society. While he constantly feels like an outsider looking in, he also feels like he belongs to neither world.

Chang-rae Lee is also a first-generation Korean American immigrant. He immigrated to America at the early age of three. Themes of identity, race, and cultural alienation pervade his works. His interest in these themes no doubt stems from his firsthand experience as a kid growing up in a Korean household while going to an American school. Lee is also the author of *A Gesture Life* and *Aloft*. The protagonists of these novels are similar in that they deal with labels placed on them based on race, color, and language. Consequently, all of these characters struggle to belong in America.

Lee's novels address differences within a nation's mix of race, religion, and history, and the necessity of assimilation between cultures. In his works and through his characters, Lee shows us both the difficulties and the subtleties of the immigrant experience in America. He urges us to consider the role of borders and to think about why the idea of opening up one's borders is so frightening. In an ever-changing world in which cultures are becoming more intermingled, the meaning of identity must be constantly redefined, especially when the security of belonging to a place is becoming increasingly elusive. As our world grows smaller with increasing technological advances, these themes in Lee's novels become even more pertinent.

1. Which of the following best describes the purpose of this passage?
   a. To criticize
   b. To analyze
   c. To entertain
   d. To inform

2. Why does the author of the passage quote the first line of the novel *Native Speaker*?
   a. To illustrate one of the themes in the novel
   b. To show how the book is semi-autobiographical
   c. It is the main idea of the novel
   d. To create interest in the novel

3. According to the passage, which of the following is NOT a main theme of Lee's novels?
   a. Identity
   b. Culture
   c. Immigration
   d. Espionage

4. According to the passage, why do Lee's novels focus on race and cultural identity?
   a. Because Lee was born in Korea
   b. Because Lee's ancestors are Korean
   c. Because Lee immigrated to America at a young age
   d. Because Lee feels racial and cultural issues are the biggest problem facing America

5. How does the author of the passage feel about the ideas presented in Lee's novels?
   a. Concerned about the disappearance of cultures in a rapidly expanding and mixed world
   b. Excited that immigrants are easily able to redefine and establish themselves in new cultures
   c. Certain that all borders will eventually be eliminated so world cultures will commingle and fully assimilate
   d. Critical regarding the role technology has played in society and how it destroys the immigrant experience

Refer to the following for questions 6–10:

The following passage is an excerpt from Emma *by Jane Austen, originally published in 1815.*

Emma Woodhouse, handsome, clever, and rich, with a comfortable home and happy disposition, seemed to unite some of the best blessings of existence; and had lived nearly twenty-one years in the world with very little to distress or vex her.

She was the youngest of the two daughters of a most affectionate, indulgent father; and had, in consequence of her sister's marriage, been mistress of his house from a very early period. Her mother had died too long ago for her to have more than an indistinct

226

remembrance of her caresses; and her place had been supplied by an excellent woman as governess, who had fallen little short of a mother in affection.

Sixteen years had Miss Taylor been in Mr. Woodhouse's family, less as a governess than a friend, very fond of both daughters, but particularly of Emma. Between them it was more the intimacy of sisters. Even before Miss Taylor had ceased to hold the nominal office of governess, the mildness of her temper had hardly allowed her to impose any restraint; and the shadow of authority being now long passed away, they had been living together as friend and friend very mutually attached, and Emma doing just what she liked; highly esteeming Miss Taylor's judgment, but directed chiefly by her own.

The real evils, indeed, of Emma's situation were the power of having rather too much her own way, and a disposition to think a little too well of herself; these were the disadvantages which threatened her many enjoyments. The danger, however, was at present so unperceived, that they did not by any means rank as misfortunes with her.

Sorrow came—a gentle sorrow—but not at all in the shape of any disagreeable consciousness—Miss Taylor married. It was Miss Taylor's loss which first brought grief. It was on the wedding-day of this beloved friend that Emma first sat in mournful thought of any continuance. The wedding over, and the bride-people gone, her father and herself were left to dine together, with no prospect of a third to cheer a long evening. Her father composed himself to sleep after dinner, as usual, and she had then only to sit and think of what she had lost.

The event had every promise of happiness for her friend. Mr. Weston was a man of unexceptionable character, easy fortune, suitable age, and pleasant manners; and there was some satisfaction in considering with what self-denying, generous friendship she had always wished and promoted the match; but it was a black morning's work for her. The want of Miss Taylor would be felt every hour of every day. She recalled her past kindness—the kindness, the affection of sixteen years—how she had taught and how she had played with her from five years old—how she had devoted all her powers to attach and amuse her in health—and how nursed her through the various illnesses of childhood. A large debt of gratitude was owing here...the equal footing and perfect unreserve which had soon followed Isabella's marriage, on their being left to each other, was yet a dearer, tenderer recollection. She had been a friend and companion such as few possessed: intelligent, well-informed, useful, gentle, knowing all the ways of the family, interested in all its concerns, and peculiarly interested in herself, in every pleasure, every scheme of hers—one to whom she could speak every thought as it arose, and who had such an affection for her as could never find fault.

How was she to bear the change?—It was true that her friend was going only half a mile from them; but Emma was aware that great must be the difference between a Mrs. Weston, only half a mile from them, and a Miss Taylor in the house; and with all her advantages, natural and domestic, she was now in great danger of suffering from intellectual solitude. She dearly loved her father, but he was no companion for her. He could not meet her in conversation, rational or playful.

The evil of the actual disparity in their ages (and Mr. Woodhouse had not married early) was much increased by his constitution and habits; for having been a valetudinarian all his life, without activity of mind or body, he was a much older man in ways than in years; and though everywhere beloved for the friendliness of his heart and his amiable temper, his talents could not have recommended him at any time.

Her sister, though comparatively but little removed by matrimony, being settled in London, only sixteen miles off, was much beyond her daily reach; and many a long October and November evening must be struggled through at Hartfield, before Christmas brought the next visit from Isabella and her husband, and their little children, to fill the house, and give her pleasant society again.

6. How does Miss Taylor's marriage affect Emma?

    a. Miss Taylor's marriage disrupts the comfort Emma had enjoyed all her life.
    b. Emma is happy her friend is marrying a wonderful man.
    c. Emma regards the change as a challenge and opportunity for intellectual growth.
    d. Miss Taylor's marriage makes Emma think about getting married herself.

7. As used in the first paragraph, what does the word *vex* mean?

    a. Interest
    b. Fulfill
    c. Support
    d. Displease

8. Based on this excerpt, Emma can be described as:

    a. Unfortunate
    b. Devious
    c. Selfish
    d. Studious

9. How do themes of class and maturity interact in this excerpt?

    a. Emma's upper-class background gives her greater access to education, thereby making her more interested in intellectual stimulation than a less mature person might be.
    b. The privilege that comes with an upper-class background can prevent a person from having the necessary skills for dealing with change in a mature way.
    c. Emma's first 21 years were so happy because she enjoyed a privileged, upper-class lifestyle, and that happiness made her a more mature person.
    d. Having people constantly take care of her has prevented Emma from developing feelings of kindness and love for others.

10. Why does the author describe Miss Taylor's wedding as a "black morning's work"?

    a. Emma has to work to pretend she is happy about the wedding.
    b. The day of Miss Taylor's wedding is a bad day for Emma.
    c. Emma worked hard to organize the wedding.
    d. The wedding party dresses in black.

Refer to the following for questions 11–15:

Excerpt from The Federalist No. 1

By Alexander Hamilton

To the People of the State of New York:

AFTER an unequivocal experience of the inefficacy of the subsisting federal government, you are called upon to deliberate on a new Constitution for the United States of America. The subject speaks its own importance; comprehending in its consequences nothing less than the existence of the UNION, the safety and welfare of the parts of which it is composed, the fate of an empire in many respects the most interesting in the world. It has been frequently remarked that it seems to have been reserved to the people of this country, by their conduct and example, to decide the important question, whether societies of men are really capable or not of establishing good government from reflection and choice, or whether they are forever destined to depend for their political constitutions on accident and force. If there be any truth in the remark, the crisis at which we are arrived may with propriety be regarded as the era in which that decision is to be made; and a wrong election of the part we shall act may, in this view, deserve to be considered as the general misfortune of mankind.

This idea will add the inducements of philanthropy to those of patriotism, to heighten the solicitude which all considerate and good men must feel for the event. Happy will it be if our choice should be directed by a judicious estimate of our true interests, unperplexed and unbiased by considerations not connected with the public good. But this is a thing more ardently to be wished than seriously to be expected. The plan offered to our deliberations affects too many particular interests, innovates upon too many local institutions, not to involve in its discussion a variety of objects foreign to its merits, and of views, passions and prejudices little favorable to the discovery of truth.

Among the most formidable of the obstacles which the new Constitution will have to encounter may readily be distinguished the obvious interest of a certain class of men in every State to resist all changes which may hazard a diminution of the power, emolument, and consequence of the offices they hold under the State establishments; and the perverted ambition of another class of men, who will either hope to aggrandize themselves by the confusions of their country, or will flatter themselves with fairer prospects of elevation from the subdivision of the empire into several partial confederacies than from its union under one government.

It is not, however, my design to dwell upon observations of this nature. I am well aware that it would be disingenuous to resolve indiscriminately the opposition of any set of men (merely because their situations might subject them to suspicion) into interested or ambitious views. Candor will oblige us to admit that even such men may be actuated by upright intentions; and it cannot be doubted that much of the opposition which has made its appearance, or may hereafter make its appearance, will spring from sources, blameless at least, if not respectable—the honest errors of minds led astray by preconceived jealousies and fears. So numerous indeed and so powerful are the causes which serve to give a false bias to the judgment, that we, upon many occasions, see wise and good men on the wrong as well as on the right side of questions of the first magnitude to society. This circumstance, if duly attended to, would furnish a lesson of moderation to those who are ever so much persuaded of their being in the right in any controversy. And a further reason for caution, in this respect, might be drawn from the reflection that we are not always sure that those who advocate the truth are influenced by purer principles than their antagonists. Ambition, avarice, personal animosity, party opposition, and many other motives not more laudable than these, are apt to operate as well upon those who support as those who oppose the right side of a question. Were there not even these inducements to moderation, nothing could be

229

more ill-judged than that intolerant spirit which has, at all times, characterized political parties. For in politics, as in religion, it is equally absurd to aim at making proselytes by fire and sword. Heresies in either can rarely be cured by persecution.

And yet, however just these sentiments will be allowed to be, we have already sufficient indications that it will happen in this as in all former cases of great national discussion. A torrent of angry and malignant passions will be let loose. To judge from the conduct of the opposite parties, we shall be led to conclude that they will mutually hope to evince the justness of their opinions, and to increase the number of their converts by the loudness of their declamations and the bitterness of their invectives. An enlightened zeal for the energy and efficiency of government will be stigmatized as the offspring of a temper fond of despotic power and hostile to the principles of liberty. An over-scrupulous jealousy of danger to the rights of the people, which is more commonly the fault of the head than of the heart, will be represented as mere pretense and artifice, the stale bait for popularity at the expense of the public good. It will be forgotten, on the one hand, that jealousy is the usual concomitant of love, and that the noble enthusiasm of liberty is apt to be infected with a spirit of narrow and illiberal distrust. On the other hand, it will be equally forgotten that the vigor of government is essential to the security of liberty; that, in the contemplation of a sound and well-informed judgment, their interest can never be separated; and that a dangerous ambition more often lurks behind the specious mask of zeal for the rights of the people than under the forbidden appearance of zeal for the firmness and efficiency of government. History will teach us that the former has been found a much more certain road to the introduction of despotism than the latter, and that of those men who have overturned the liberties of republics, the greatest number have begun their career by paying an <u>obsequious</u> court to the people; commencing demagogues, and ending tyrants.

11. How does the opening of this excerpt affect the writer's argument?

a. By criticizing the United States Constitution explicitly, he is challenging readers to look at old institutions in new ways that may have positive effects on the federal government.

b. By portraying the subsisting federal government as suffering from inefficacy, he is seeking to alienate overly patriotic readers.

c. By saying that it is up to "the people of this country" to establish a "good government," he is suggesting that he expects input from his fellow Americans regarding how to improve the United States Constitution.

d. By drawing attention to the "unequivocal" "inefficacy" of the subsisting federal government, Alexander Hamilton immediately explains why the federal government is in need of change.

12. What effect does the author's use of first-person point of view have on his argument?

a. It attempts to establish an agreement between the reader and himself.

b. It establishes an informal tone that makes him seem friendlier and more approachable.

c. It forces the reader to feel responsibility for the federal government's problems.

d. It implies the reader also needs to suggest methods for improving the federal government.

13. Which of the following sentences from the excerpt exemplifies an attempt to sway the reader's opinion of the writer's opponents?

a. And yet, however just these sentiments will be allowed to be, we have already sufficient indications that it will happen in this as in all former cases of great national discussion.

b. For in politics, as in religion, it is equally absurd to aim at making proselytes by fire and sword.

c. To judge from the conduct of the opposite parties, we shall be led to conclude that they will mutually hope to evince the justness of their opinions, and to increase the number of their converts by the loudness of their declamations and the bitterness of their invectives.

d. This idea will add the inducements of philanthropy to those of patriotism, to heighten the solicitude which all considerate and good men must feel for the event.

14. Why does the writer follow paragraph 3 by stating, "It is not, however, my design to dwell upon observations of this nature"?

a. He regrets criticizing politicians currently holding office and wants the reader to focus on the less inflammatory details in his argument.

b. He wants to give the impression that the purpose of his argument is not merely to criticize politicians who are currently holding office.

c. He realizes he lacks the information to continue criticizing politicians currently holding office and cannot continue his argument.

d. He believes that criticizing politicians currently holding office is a weak way to present his argument and will stop doing so.

15. As used in the final sentence of the excerpt, what does the word *obsequious* mean?

a. Submissive

b. Free

c. Revolutionary

d. Dominant

Refer to the following for questions 16–23:

Excerpt from Anna Karenina

By Leo Tolstoy

The young Princess Kitty Shtcherbatskaya was eighteen. It was the first winter that she had been out in the world. Her success in society had been greater than that of either of her elder sisters, and greater even than her mother had anticipated. To say nothing of the young men who danced at the Moscow balls being almost all in love with Kitty, two serious suitors had already this first winter made their appearance: Levin, and immediately after his departure, Count Vronsky.

Levin's appearance at the beginning of the winter, his frequent visits, and evident love for Kitty, had led to the first serious conversations between Kitty's parents as to her future, and to disputes between them. The prince was on Levin's side; he said he wished for nothing better for Kitty. The princess for her part, going round the question in the manner peculiar to women, maintained that Kitty was too young, that Levin had done nothing to prove that he had serious intentions, that Kitty felt no great attraction to him, and other side issues; but she did not state the principal point, which was that she looked for a better match for her daughter, and that Levin was not to her liking, and she did not understand him. When Levin had abruptly departed, the princess was delighted, and said to her husband triumphantly: "You see I was right." When Vronsky appeared on the scene, she was still more delighted, confirmed in her opinion that Kitty was to make not simply a good, but a brilliant match.

In the mother's eyes there could be no comparison between Vronsky and Levin. She disliked in Levin his strange and uncompromising opinions and his shyness in society, founded, as she supposed, on his pride and his queer sort of life, as she considered it, absorbed in cattle and peasants. She did not very much like it that he, who was in love with her daughter, had kept coming to the house for six weeks, as though he were waiting for something, inspecting, as though he were afraid he might be doing them too great an honor by making an offer, and did not realize that a man, who continually visits at a house where there is a young unmarried girl, is bound to make his intentions clear. And suddenly, without doing so, he disappeared. "It's as well he's not attractive enough for Kitty to have fallen in love with him," thought the mother.

Vronsky satisfied all the mother's desires. Very wealthy, clever, of aristocratic family, on the highroad to a brilliant career in the army and at court, and a fascinating man. Nothing better could be wished for.

Vronsky openly flirted with Kitty at balls, danced with her, and came continually to the house, consequently there could be no doubt of the seriousness of his intentions. But, in spite of that, the mother had spent the whole of that winter in a state of terrible anxiety and agitation.

Princess Shtcherbatskaya had herself been married thirty years ago, her aunt arranging the match. Her husband, about whom everything was well known before hand, had come, looked at his future bride, and been looked at. The match-making aunt had ascertained and communicated their mutual impression. That impression had been favorable. Afterwards, on a day fixed beforehand, the expected offer was made to her parents, and accepted. All had passed very simply and easily. So it seemed, at least, to the princess. But over her own daughters she had felt how far from simple and easy is the business, apparently so commonplace, of marrying off one's daughters. The panics that had been lived through, the thoughts that had been brooded over, the money that had been wasted, and the disputes with her husband over marrying the two elder girls, Darya and Natalia! Now, since the youngest had come out, she was going through the same terrors, the same doubts, and still more violent quarrels with her husband than she had over the elder girls. The old prince, like all fathers indeed, was exceedingly punctilious on the score of the honor and reputation of his daughters. He was irrationally jealous over his daughters, especially over Kitty, who was his favorite. At every turn he had scenes with the princess for compromising her daughter. The princess had grown accustomed to this already with her other daughters, but now she felt that there was more ground for the prince's touchiness. She saw that of late years much was changed in the manners of society, that a mother's duties had become still more difficult. She saw that girls of Kitty's age formed some sort of clubs, went to some sort of lectures, mixed freely in men's society; drove about the streets alone, many of them did not curtsey, and, what was the most important thing, all the girls were firmly convinced that to choose their husbands was their own affair, and not their parents'. "Marriages aren't made nowadays as they used to be," was thought and said by all these young girls, and even by their elders. But how marriages were made now, the princess could not learn from any one. The French fashion—of the parents arranging their children's future—was not accepted; it was condemned. The English fashion of the complete independence of girls was also not accepted, and not possible in Russian society. The Russian fashion of match-making by the offices of intermediate persons was for some reason considered unseemly; it was ridiculed by everyone, and by the princess herself. But how girls were to be married, and how parents were to marry them, no one knew. Everyone with whom the princess had chanced to discuss the matter said the same thing: "Mercy on us, it's high time in our day to cast off all that old-fashioned business. It's the young people have to marry; and not their parents; and so we ought to leave the young people to arrange it as they choose." It was very easy for anyone to say that who had no daughters, but the princess realized that in the process of getting to know each other, her daughter might fall in love, and fall in love with someone who did not care to marry her or who was quite unfit to be her husband. And, however much it was instilled into the princess that in our times young people ought to arrange their lives for themselves, she was unable to believe it, just as she would have been unable to believe that, at any time whatever, the most suitable playthings for children five years old ought to be loaded pistols. And so the princess was more uneasy over Kitty than she had been over her elder sisters.

Now she was afraid that Vronsky might confine himself to simply flirting with her daughter. She saw that her daughter was in love with him, but tried to comfort herself with the thought that he was an honorable man, and would not do this. But at the same time she knew how easy it is, with the freedom of manners of today, to turn a girl's head, and how lightly men generally regard such a crime. The week before, Kitty had told her mother of a conversation she had with Vronsky during a mazurka. This conversation had partly reassured the princess; but perfectly at ease she could not be. Vronsky had told Kitty that both he and his brother were so used to obeying their mother that they never made up their minds to any important undertaking without consulting her. "And just now, I am impatiently awaiting my mother's arrival from Petersburg, as peculiarly fortunate," he told her.

Kitty had repeated this without attaching any significance to the words. But her mother saw them in a different light. She knew that the old lady was expected from day to day, that she would be pleased at her son's choice, and she felt it strange that he should not make his offer through fear of vexing his mother. However, she was so anxious for the marriage itself, and still more for relief from her fears, that she believed it was so. Bitter as it was for the princess to see the unhappiness of her eldest daughter, Dolly, on the point of leaving her husband, her anxiety over the decision of her youngest daughter's fate engrossed all her feelings. Today, with Levin's reappearance, a fresh source of anxiety arose. She was afraid that her daughter, who had at one time, as she fancied, a feeling for Levin, might, from extreme sense of honor, refuse Vronsky, and that Levin's arrival might generally complicate and delay the affair so near being concluded.

"Why, has he been here long?" the princess asked about Levin, as they returned home.

"He came today, mamma."

"There's one thing I want to say…" began the princess, and from her serious and alert face, Kitty guessed what it would be.

"Mamma," she said, flushing hotly and turning quickly to her, "please, please don't say anything about that. I know, I know all about it."

She wished for what her mother wished for, but the motives of her mother's wishes wounded her.

"I only want to say that to raise hopes…"

"Mamma, darling, for goodness' sake, don't talk about it. It's so horrible to talk about it."

"I won't," said her mother, seeing the tears in her daughter's eyes; "but one thing, my love; you promised me you would have no secrets from me. You won't?"

"Never, mamma, none," answered Kitty, flushing a little, and looking her mother straight in the face, "but there's no use in my telling you anything, and I…I…if I wanted to, I don't know what to say or how…I don't know…"

"No, she could not tell an untruth with those eyes," thought the mother, smiling at her agitation and happiness. The princess smiled that what was taking place just now in her soul seemed to the poor child so immense and so important.

16. What is one difference between Levin and Count Vronsky?
a. Levin is shy, and Count Vronsky has uncompromising opinions.
b. Levin is focused on life in the countryside, while Count Vronsky has an aristocratic background.
c. Levin has uncompromising opinions, while Count Vronsky is absorbed by cattle and peasants.
d. Levin is wealthy, while Count Vronsky comes from an aristocratic family.

17. Read the following dictionary entry.

Fancy v. 1. To be interested in 2. To imagine something 3. To believe something that may or may not be true 4. To interpret something

Which definition best matches the way the word *fancied* is used in paragraph 8?
a. Definition 1
b. Definition 2
c. Definition 3
d. Definition 4

18. This story is set in Russia. Why is the location important to the story?
a. Princess Kitty is only interested in marrying a Russian.
b. Princess Kitty will be matched according to the Russian style of using a matchmaker.
c. The characters are, in part, shaped by their national heritage.
d. Princess Kitty ultimately rebels against Russian society by choosing a husband using the English method.

19. What is the likely importance of Vronsky's mother's arrival?
   a. Vronsky is going to introduce his mother to Princess Kitty.
   b. Vronsky is going to take his mother to a Moscow ball.
   c. Vronsky is going to ask his mother if he should marry Kitty.
   d. Vronsky is going to show his mother around Moscow.

20. In paragraph 6, what does the word *punctilious* most likely mean?
   a. Careful
   b. Punctual
   c. On time
   d. Boisterous

21. Which sentence or phrase best demonstrates that customs in Moscow have changed?
   a. The panics that had been lived through, the thoughts that had been brooded over, the money that had been wasted, and the disputes with her husband over marrying the two elder girls, Darya and Natalia!
   b. She saw that girls of Kitty's age formed some sort of clubs, went to some sort of lectures, mixed freely in men's society
   c. The French fashion—of the parents arranging their children's future—was not accepted
   d. And so the princess was more uneasy over Kitty than she had been over her elder sisters.

22. In paragraph 6, Kitty's mother is concerned that Kitty might marry someone who is "unfit to be her husband." What characteristic is Kitty's mother mostly like to think makes a suitor unfit?
   a. Shyness
   b. Being a member of the aristocracy
   c. Cleverness
   d. Obedience

23. The author uses paragraph 1 to:
   a. Introduce Princess Kitty's mother
   b. Introduce the central conflict of the passage
   c. Describe the Moscow balls
   d. Describe Levin and Count Vronsky

Refer to the following for questions 24–30:

Excerpt from Great Britain and Her Queen

By Anne E. Keeling

Chapter I

The Girl-Queen and Her Kingdom

Rather more than one mortal lifetime, as we average life in these later days, has elapsed since that June morning of 1837, when Victoria of England, then a fair young princess of eighteen, was roused from her tranquil sleep in the old palace at Kensington, and bidden to rise and meet the Primate, and his dignified associates the Lord Chamberlain and the royal physician, who "were come on business of state to the Queen"—words of startling import, for they meant that, while the royal

235

maiden lay sleeping, the aged King, whose heiress she was, had passed into the deeper sleep of death. It is already an often-told story how promptly, on receiving that summons, the young Queen rose and came to meet her first homagers, standing before them in hastily assumed wrappings, her hair hanging loosely, her feet in slippers, but in all her hearing such royally firm composure as deeply impressed those heralds of her greatness, who noticed at the same moment that her eyes were full of tears. This little scene is not only charming and touching, it is very significant, suggesting a combination of such qualities as are not always found united: sovereign good sense and readiness, blending with quick, artless feeling that sought no disguise—such feeling as again betrayed itself when on her ensuing proclamation the new Sovereign had to meet her people face to face, and stood before them at her palace window, composed but sad, the tears running unchecked down her fair pale face.

That rare spectacle of simple human emotion, at a time when a selfish or thoughtless spirit would have leaped in exultation, touched the heart of England deeply, and was rightly held of happy omen. The nation's feeling is aptly expressed in the glowing verse of Mrs. Browning, praying Heaven's blessing on the "weeping Queen," and prophesying for her the love, happiness, and honour which have been hers in no stinted measure. "Thou shalt be well beloved," said the poetess; there are very few sovereigns of whom it could be so truly said that they *have* been well beloved, for not many have so well deserved it. The faith of the singer has been amply justified, as time has made manifest the rarer qualities joyfully divined in those early days in the royal child, the single darling hope of the nation.

Once before in the recent annals of our land had expectations and desires equally ardent centred themselves on one young head. Much of the loyal devotion which had been alienated from the immediate family of George III had transferred itself to his grandchild, the Princess Charlotte, sole offspring of the unhappy marriage between George, Prince of Wales, and Caroline of Brunswick. The people had watched with vivid interest the young romance of Princess Charlotte's happy marriage, and had bitterly lamented her too early death—an event which had overshadowed all English hearts with forebodings of disaster. Since that dark day a little of the old attachment of England to its sovereigns had revived for the frank-mannered sailor and "patriot king," William IV; but the hopes crushed by the death of the much-regretted Charlotte had renewed themselves with even better warrant for Victoria. She was the child of no ill-omened, miserable marriage, but of a fitting union; her parents had been sundered only by death, not by wretched domestic dissensions. People heard that the mortal malady which deprived her of a father had been brought about by the Duke of Kent's simple delight in his baby princess, which kept him playing with the child when he should have been changing his wet outdoor garb; and they found something touching and tender in the tragic little circumstance. And everything that could be noticed of the manner in which the bereaved duchess was training up her precious charge spoke well for the mother's wisdom and affection, and for the future of the daughter.

It was indeed a happy day for England when Edward, Duke of Kent, the fourth son of George III, was wedded to Victoria of Saxe-Coburg, the widowed Princess of Leiningen—happy, not only because of the admirable skill with which that lady conducted her illustrious child's education, and because of the pure, upright principles, the frank, noble character, which she transmitted to that child, but because the family connection established through that marriage was to be yet further serviceable to the interests of our realm. Prince Albert of Saxe-Coburg was second son of the Duchess of Kent's eldest brother, and thus first cousin of the Princess Victoria—"the Mayflower," as, in fond allusion to the month of her birth, her mother's kinsfolk loved to call her: and it has been made plain that dreams of a possible union between the two young cousins, very nearly of an age, were early cherished by the elders who loved and admired both.

The Princess's life, however, was sedulously guarded from all disturbing influences. She grew up in healthy simplicity and seclusion; she was not apprised of her nearness to the throne till she was twelve years old; she had been little at Court, little in sight, but had been made familiar with her own land and its history, having received the higher education so essential to her great position; while simple truth and rigid honesty were the very atmosphere of her existence. From such a training much might be hoped; but even those who knew most and hoped most were not quite prepared for the strong individual character and power of self-determination that revealed themselves in the girlish being so suddenly transferred "from the nursery to the throne." It was quickly noticed that the part of Queen and mistress seemed native to her, and that she filled it with not more grace than propriety. "She always strikes me as possessed of singular penetration, firmness, and independence," wrote Dr. Norman Macleod in 1860; acute observers in 1837 took note of the same traits, rarer far in youth than in full maturity, and closely connected with the "reasoning, searching" quality of her mind, "anxious to get at the root and reality of things, and abhorring all shams, whether in word or deed."

It was well for England that its young Sovereign could exemplify virile strength as well as womanly sweetness; for it was indeed a cloudy and dark day when she was called to her post of lonely grandeur and hard responsibility; and to fill that post rightly would have overtasked and overwhelmed a feebler nature. It is true that the peace of Europe, won at Waterloo, was still unbroken. But already, within our borders and without them, there were the signs of coming storm. The condition of Ireland was chronically bad; the condition of England was full of danger; on the Continent a new period of earth-shaking revolution announced itself not doubtfully.

It would be hardly possible to exaggerate the wretched state of the sister isle, where fires of recent hate were still smouldering, and where the poor inhabitants, guilty and guiltless, were daily living on the verge of famine, over which they were soon to be driven. Their ill condition much aggravated by the intemperate habits to which despairing men so easily fall a prey. The expenditure of Ireland on proof spirits alone had in the year 1829 attained the sum of £6,000,000.

In England many agricultural labourers were earning starvation wages, were living on bad and scanty food, and were housed so wretchedly that they might envy the hounds their dry and clean kennels. A dark symptom of their hungry discontent had shown itself in the strange crime of rick-burning, which went on under cloud of night season after season, despite the utmost precautions which the luckless farmers could adopt. The perpetrators were not dimly guessed to be half-famished creatures, taking a mad revenge for their wretchedness by destroying the tantalising stores of grain, too costly for their consumption; the price of wheat in the early years of Her Majesty's reign and for some time previously being very high, and

237

reaching at one moment (1847) the extraordinary figure of a hundred and two shillings per quarter.

There was threatening distress, too, in some parts of the manufacturing districts; in others a tolerably high level of wages indicated prosperity. But even in the more favoured districts there was needless suffering. The hours of work, unrestricted by law, were cruelly long; nor did there exist any restriction as to the employment of operatives of very tender years. "The cry of the children" was rising up to heaven, not from the factory only, but from the underground darkness of the mine, where a system of pitiless infant slavery prevailed, side by side with the employment of women as beasts of burden, "in an atmosphere of filth and profligacy." The condition of too many toilers was rendered more hopeless by the thriftless follies born of ignorance. The educational provision made by the piety of former ages was no longer adequate to the needs of the ever-growing nation; and all the voluntary efforts made by clergy and laity, by Churchmen and Dissenters, did not fill up the deficiency—a fact which had only just begun to meet with State recognition. It was in 1834 that Government first obtained from Parliament the grant of a small sum in aid of education. Under a defective system of poor-relief, recently reformed, an immense mass of idle pauperism had come into being; it still remained to be seen if a new Poor Law could do away with the mischief created by the old one.

Looking at the earliest years of Her Majesty's rule, the first impulse is to exclaim:

"And all this trouble did not pass, but grew."

24. Which of these is NOT one of the immediate problems that faced the nation at the time that Victoria was crowned?
   a. Europe was at war.
   b. The people in Ireland were suffering.
   c. Agricultural laborers were not earning enough money.
   d. There wasn't enough money for education.

25. What is Paragraph 3 mainly about?
   a. Victoria's childhood
   b. The royal family
   c. Victoria's cousin
   d. Victoria's father, the Duke of Kent

26. In paragraph 2, the author uses a quote from Mrs. Browning to show which of the following?
   a. Queen Victoria was not beloved.
   b. Queen Victoria inspired the work of many poets.
   c. Mrs. Browning accurately predicted the people's opinion about Queen Victoria.
   d. Queen Victoria had a selfish and thoughtless spirit.

27. What is the primary purpose of paragraphs 7-9?
   a. To illustrate Queen Victoria's first acts as queen
   b. To show the poor conditions for workers in manufacturing districts
   c. To show the problems faced by the people of Ireland
   d. To describe the challenges faced by Victoria when she became queen

28. According to the author, what was one specific problem that resulted from the government's efforts to aid the poor?

    a. Poverty increased.
    b. There wasn't enough money for education.
    c. The trouble grew.
    d. The system was reformed.

29. What is one reason why Victoria's childhood was relatively simple?

    a. She spent much of her childhood with her cousin.
    b. She didn't know she had a possibility of being queen until she was twelve.
    c. She was very independent.
    d. She received a lot of education.

30. Which word or phrase best helps the reader understand the meaning of *tender years* in paragraph 9?

    a. Needless suffering
    b. Cruelly long
    c. Pitiless infant slavery
    d. Beasts of burden

Writing

Refer to the following for questions 1–5:

(1) In the early 1760s, Paul Revere, ran a busy metalworking shop. (2) People from all over Boston came to buy the silver and gold cups, medals, and cutlery he made. (3) Everything changed in 1765. (4) Many colonists ran low on money and stopped shopping at Paul's shop.

(5) Things got worse when the british passed the Stamp Act. (6) The Stamp Act created a tax to help the British earn money. (7) Colonists like Paul Revere hated the Stamp Act because it would make things more expensive.

(8) Under the Stamp Act, colonists needed to pay for everything that was printed, such as newspapers, magazines, and business contracts. (9) After a colonist paid the tax, the tax collector put a stamp on the paper to show that the tax had been paid. (10) The Stamp Act made it very expensive for Paul to run his business. (11) For example, if he wanted a new apprentice for his silver shop, he needed to buy a Stamp for the signed contract.

(12) Paul wasn't just angry about buying stamps. (13) He also felt that the British shouldn't be allowed to tax the colonies. (14) There was no American colonists in the British parliament, which passed the tax. (15) Paul and the other colonists didn't want taxation without representation. (16) They wanted to be able to choose their own taxes.

(17) The colonists refused to buy stamps. (18) They were determined to get the Stamp Act repealed.

(19) Paul joined a group called the Sons of Liberty. (20) They wore silver medals on their coats that said "Sons of Liberty." (21) Paul may have helped make the medals in his silver shop.

(22) The Sons of Liberty staged demonstrations at the Liberty Tree, a huge elm tree, that stood in Boston. (23) Paul drew cartoons and wrote poems about liberty. (24) He published them in the local newspaper, *The Boston Gazette*.

(25) After a year of hard work fighting the Stamp Act Paul and the Sons of Liberty received the happy news. (26) The Stamp Act had been repealed!

(27) People celebrated all over Boston; they lit bonfires, set off fireworks, and decorated houses and ships with flags and streamers. (28) Paul attended the biggest celebration, which took place at the Liberty Tree. (29) The people hung 280 lanterns on the tree's branches lighting up the night sky.

(30) Some members of the Sons of Liberty constructed a paper obelisk. (31) An obelisk is the same shape as the Washington Monument. (32) They decorated the obelisk with pictures and verses about the struggle to repeal the Stamp Act and hung it from the Liberty Tree.

(33) Paul may have helped construct the obelisk, even if he wasn't involved in the direct construction, he probably knew about and supported it. (34) After the celebration, he made a copper engraving showing the pictures and verses on the obelisk's four sides. (35) His engraving records the celebration under the Liberty Tree. (36) Even though Paul Revere may be better known for his silver work and famous ride, his engravings, like the engraving of the obelisk, help us see the American Revolution through his eyes.

1. What correction should be made to sentence (1)?
   a. Change *1760s* to *1760's*.
   b. Delete the comma after *1760s*.
   c. Delete the comma after *Revere*.
   d. Add a comma after *busy*.

2. What correction should be made to sentence (5)?
   a. Change *got* to *get*.
   b. Change *worse* to *worst*.
   c. Change *british* to *British*.
   d. Change *Stamp Act* to *stamp act*.

3. Which is the best way to combine sentences (30) and (31)?
   a. Some members of the Sons of Liberty constructed a paper obelisk, which is the same shape as the Washington Monument.
   b. Some members of the Sons of Liberty constructed a paper obelisk which is the same shape as the Washington Monument.
   c. Some members of the Sons of Liberty constructed a paper obelisk, that is the same shape as the Washington Monument.
   d. Some members of the Sons of Liberty constructed a paper obelisk; which is the same shape as the Washington Monument.

4. What correction should be made to sentence (14)?
    a. Change *was* to *were*.
    b. Change *parliament* to *parlament*.
    c. Delete the comma after *parliament*.
    d. Change *which* to *that*.

5. Which is the best way to combine sentences (17) and (18)?
    a. The colonists refused to buy stamps and they were determined to get the Stamp Act repealed.
    b. The colonists refused to buy stamps, and they were determined to get the Stamp Act repealed.
    c. The colonists refused to buy stamps, and were determined to get the Stamp Act repealed.
    d. The colonists refused to buy stamps, were determined to get the Stamp Act repealed.

6. Which of the following sentences is correct?
    a. Sonja works very hard, she is tired all the time.
    b. Sonja works very hard she is tired all the time.
    c. Sonja works very hard, however, she is tired all the time.
    d. Sonja works very hard; she is tired all the time.

7. Choose the word that correctly fills the blank in the following sentence:

Mrs. Simmons asked her students to get their books, read the first chapter, and _____ the questions at the end.

    a. answer
    b. to answer
    c. answering
    d. will answer

8. Choose the correct spelling of the word that fills the blank in the following sentence:

Plastic trash that ends up in the ocean can have a _____, or harmful, effect on marine life.

    a. diliterious
    b. deleterious
    c. delaterious
    d. dilaterious

9. Which of the following choices best defines the underlined word?

The impoverished shepherds stumbled upon the <u>stele</u> while desperately searching for some lost sheep; they were surprised and puzzled by the bizarre lines and squiggles that covered its face.

    a. An item that has been looted from a tomb
    b. A sign that indicates direction
    c. The side of a cliff
    d. A large, inscribed stone

10. Which of the following words is NOT spelled correctly?

a. Aggregate
b. Mischevious
c. Subservient
d. Ought

11. Which of the following choices best completes the selection below?

The letter _____ explained all his hopes and dreams for my success; _____ outpouring of his love for me.

a. my grandfather, it contained an
b. from my grandfather, which containing
c. grandfather, since it contained
d. from my grandfather, it contained an

12. Which of the following choices is correct?

a. Whether the unexamined life is worth living or not; there is little doubt that people who do not carefully consider their actions often fall into difficulties.
b. There are basically two ways to live: with your conscience or moral code, which can be a difficult and painful road; or against your conscience, which may seem easy and attractive until you discover how much pain and suffering you've caused others.
c. Folding the paper over carefully so the contents were in full view; Caroline, fearful of what was coming next in the article, leaned closer to the printed page in order to more fully absorb the awful truths contained there.
d. It is unnecessary to become a philosopher to take a careful look at your existence to understand the nature of it; its application; its fundamental principles, and its future.

13. Which of the following words is NOT spelled correctly?

a. Onomatopoeia
b. Fastidious
c. Meticulus
d. Minutiae

14. What is the meaning of the underlined word?

The girls sat at the table, comforting each other and sobbing through lachrymose stories about their own struggles with bad haircuts.

a. Consolatory
b. Blithe
c. Mournful
d. Lethargic

15. Which of the following choices best completes the sentence?

_____, there's no way you can be a part of the swimming relay competition.

a. Unless you find a new partner
b. You have a new partner
c. This is your partner
d. As you can find a partner

16. Which of the following choices shows the best way to punctuate the sentence?

   a. I packed a picnic to take to the park with my friends; I made sure that I brought all of the plates and cups, too.

   b. I packed a picnic to take to the park with my friends, I made sure that I brought all of the plates and cups, too.

   c. I packed a picnic to take to the park with my friends I made sure that I brought all of the plates and cups, too.

   d. I packed a picnic to take to the park with my friends: I made sure that I brought all of the plates and cups, too.

17. Which of the following words is spelled incorrectly?

   a. Salubrious

   b. Sureptitious

   c. Artifice

   d. Requisition

18. Which of the following best approximates the meaning of the underlined word?

The discussion over the new park had begun well, but it soon descended into an <u>acrimonious</u> debate over misuse of tax revenues.

   a. Shocking

   b. Childish

   c. Rancorous

   d. Revealing

19. To temporarily postpone repayment of a loan is to:

   a. Decry

   b. Defer

   c. Differ

   d. Debtor

20. Which of the following choices best completes the sentence?

Natalie reviewed the notes carefully, with one eye on the judge's _____ and another eye on the _____ of the decision. There was certainly more than one way to _____ the case.

   a. interpretation, evolve, interpret

   b. interpretation, evolution, interpret

   c. interpret, evolution, interpretation

   d. interpretation, evolution, interpretation

21. Based on how it is used in this sentence, what does the word *omniscient* mean?

The floor supervisor seemed to be omniscient; always intervening just in time to prevent a problem.

   a. Cautious

   b. All-knowing

   c. Micromanaging

   d. Eager

22. Read the following introduction from an essay about Mary Shelley.

> Mary Shelley conceived of Dr. Frankenstein and the hideous monster he created, which helped the English novelist to make an immeasurable impact on literature and popular culture.

Which of the following statements most effectively revises this introduction?

    a. English novelist Mary Shelley had an immeasurable impact on literature and popular culture when she conceived of Dr. Frankenstein and the hideous monster he created.

    b. Dr. Frankenstein created a hideous monster, and they were conceived by English novelist Mary Shelley, who had an immeasurable impact on literature and popular culture.

    c. English novelist Mary Shelley conceived of Dr. Frankenstein and the hideous monster he created and had an immeasurable impact on literature and popular culture.

    d. Novelist Mary Shelley from England had an immeasurable impact on literature and popular culture when she conceived of Dr. Frankenstein and the hideous monster he created.

23. According to Merriam-Webster's Dictionary, what is the correct pronunciation of the word *impromptu*?

    a. \im-promp-too

    b. \imp-römp-tu

    c. \im-'präm(p)-(,)tü

    d. \im-prömpt-ü

24. Read the following introduction from an essay about automobiles.

> A valuable tool for crossing long distances the automobile is a friend, and perpetrator of toxic pollution, the automobile is a foe.

What is the MOST effective revision of this introduction?

    a. The automobile crosses long distances, which is a good thing, but it is also a perpetrator of toxic pollution, which is bad.

    b. Both a valuable tool for crossing long distances and a perpetrator of toxic pollution, the automobile is both friend and foe.

    c. Automobiles are good because they help us cross long distances, but they are bad because they create a lot of pollution.

    d. Both a valuable tool for crossing long distances— the automobile is both friend and foe— and perpetrator of toxic pollution.

25. Read the following line from a speech arguing in favor of a road repair.

> Repairing Route 211 will save members of this community a lot of money.

Which of the following is the BEST follow-up statement?

    a. Also, the potholes that run the entire length of Route 211 are unpleasant to look at.

    b. Another road that requires a great deal of attention in this community is Central Highway.

    c. Last year, local drivers spent over $16,000 to repair damages caused by potholes in the road.

    d. During economically uncertain times, financial matters are at the forefront of all Americans' concerns.

26. According to Merriam-Webster's Dictionary, which word derives from an old Italian phrase meaning "bad air"?

a. Noxious
b. Odiferous
c. Malaria
d. Consumption

27. What does the word *felicity* mean in this sentence?

Mara enjoyed great felicity when her missing dog found his way home.

a. Discomfort
b. Anxiety
c. Disbelief
d. Happiness

28. Choose the word that best fills the blank in the following sentence:

Stanley had never liked Nathan, but he grudgingly _____ Nathan for his idea of holding a car wash for the school fundraiser.

a. exalted
b. glorified
c. honored
d. commended

29. What does "hunting down the truth" mean in this sentence?

The detective dedicated his life to hunting down the truth.

a. The detective preferred to work with a gun.
b. The detective was determined to tell the truth.
c. The detective wanted to eradicate the truth.
d. The detective was determined to learn the truth.

30. Choose the sentence that most effectively follows the conventions of standard written English:

a. Betty MacDonald became famous for her first novel, *The Egg and I*, which chronicles her adventures in chicken farming.
b. *The Egg and I*, a book written by Betty MacDonald, made the book's author famous and chronicled her adventures in chicken farming.
c. Betty MacDonald wrote *The Egg and I*, and became famous chronicling her adventures in chicken farming.
d. *The Egg and I* chronicles the author's adventures in chicken farming, and made Betty MacDonald famous.

Answer Key and Explanations #3

Mathematics

1. D: First, place 783 on top of 124 to subtract vertically. Then, subtract from right to left. $3 - 4$ is negative, so borrow from the 8 to make 3 become 13 and 8 is reduced to 7. $13 - 4 = 9$, so write a 9 under the 4. $7 - 2 = 5$, so write a 5 under the 2. $7 - 1 = 6$, so write a 6 under the 1. This gives a final answer of 659.

$$
\begin{array}{r} 783 \\ -124 \\ \hline \end{array}
\qquad
\begin{array}{r} ^{7\ 13}\!\!\!7\cancel{8}\cancel{3} \\ -124 \\ \hline 9 \end{array}
\qquad
\begin{array}{r} ^{7\ 13}\!\!\!7\cancel{8}\cancel{3} \\ -124 \\ \hline 59 \end{array}
\qquad
\begin{array}{r} ^{7\ 13}\!\!\!7\cancel{8}\cancel{3} \\ -124 \\ \hline 659 \end{array}
$$

2. D: Add from left to right. $19 + 23 = 42$, then $42 + 81 = 123$, and finally, $123 + 4 = 127$.

3. D: Since we are finding the total pounds of fruit, we will add $\frac{1}{5}$ and $\frac{3}{4}$. To add the two fractions, we must first find the common denominator, which we will do by multiplying the first fraction by $\frac{4}{4}$ and the second fraction by $\frac{5}{5}$. We will then evaluate the expression $\frac{4}{20} + \frac{15}{20}$, by keeping the denominator and adding the numerators to get $\frac{19}{20}$. Therefore, the total amount of fruit that Maria bought is $\frac{19}{20}$ of a pound.

4. C: Start by writing the problem vertically, making sure to line up the digits in each number according to place value. To subtract, begin with the hundredths column on the right. Since $5 - 6$ results in a negative number, we need to borrow from the tenths place. Cross out 4 in the tenths place and replace it with 3 since we are taking 1 away. Next, write the borrowed 1 in front of the 5 in the hundredths place to get 15. Since $15 - 6 = 9$, write 9 in the hundredths place as part of the answer. From here, move to the tenths column and subtract. Since $3 - 5$ results in a negative number, we need to borrow from the ones place. Cross out the 8 in the ones place and replace it with 7 since we are taking 1 away. Next, write the borrowed 1 in front of the 3 in the tenths place to get 13. Since $13 - 5 = 8$, write 8 in the tenths place as part of the answer. Finally, move to the ones column and subtract. Since $7 - 0 = 7$, write 7 in the ones place as part of the answer. Therefore, $\$8.45 - \$0.56 = \$7.89$, so the correct answer is C.

$$
\begin{array}{r} 8.45 \\ -0.56 \\ \hline \end{array}
\qquad
\begin{array}{r} ^{\ \ \ 3\ 15}8.\cancel{4}\cancel{5} \\ -0.56 \\ \hline 9 \end{array}
\qquad
\begin{array}{r} ^{7\ \ \ \ \cancel{3}\ 15}\!\!\cancel{8}.\cancel{4}\cancel{5} \\ -0.56 \\ \hline .89 \end{array}
\qquad
\begin{array}{r} ^{7\ \ \ 3\ 15}\!\!\cancel{8}/.\cancel{4}\cancel{5} \\ -0.56 \\ \hline 7.8^{9} \end{array}
$$

5. C: To find the sum of two numbers with decimals, we will line the numbers vertically with the decimal and add. We will bring the decimal down into the answer where it is lined up. For this problem, when we line the numbers vertically with the decimal and add, we start by adding 7 and 4, which is 11, 1 gets carried over to the next column. Then we add 7, 5 and 1, which is 13, the 1 gets

246

carried over again. Lastly, we add 1, 0 and 0, which is 1. Then we will bring the decimal down where it lines up with the answer, and we find that the sum of 0.77 and 0.54 is 1.31.

$$
\begin{array}{r}
\overset{1}{}\overset{1}{}\\
0\,.77\\
+\,0\,.54\\
\hline
1\,.3\,{}^{1}
\end{array}
$$

6. D: The correct answer is 39. This can be found by using long division.

$$
\begin{array}{r}
39\\
4\overline{)\,156}\\
-12\\
\hline
36\\
-36\\
\hline
0
\end{array}
$$

7. C: The equation that can model this situation would have to have the amount of money Lex spends each week as the constant, or y-intercept, and the rate, or the slope, would be the amount of money he charges for each lawn he mows. Therefore, the best equation to model this situation is $y = 25x - 80$.

8. D: To find the value of y, we ask the question, what is happening to y? The answer is that 14 is being subtracted from y, so we do the opposite operation, which is addition. We will add 14 to both sides of the equation. On the left side we will be left with y, and on the right side we will add 63 and 14 to get 77, which is the value of y.

9. D: To find the value of y, we will start by isolating the y on one side of the equation. Since y is being divided by 17, we will multiply both sides of the equation by 17. On the left side of the equation, we will be left with y. On the right side of the equation, we will multiply 22 by 17 to get 374, which is the value of y.

10. D: In the linear equation $y = -6$, the value of y is –6 for every value of x. The graph for $y = -6$ looks like a horizontal line intersecting the y-axis at point $(0, -6)$. Therefore, the correct answer is D.

11. C: Since $-6x + 3y = 15$ is written in standard form, use the equation to find the x- and y-intercepts. Once we know where the line passes through each axis, we can match the graph to the equation. Start by finding the y-intercept by setting x equal to 0 and solve for y.

$$
\begin{aligned}
-6x + 3y &= 15\\
-6(0) + 3y &= 15\\
0 + 3y &= 15\\
3y &= 15\\
y &= 5
\end{aligned}
$$

The line intersects the y-axis at point (0,5).

247

Now that we know the location of the y-intercept, find the x-intercept. When using the standard form of an equation to find the x-intercept, make y equal to 0 and solve for x.

$$-6x + 3y = 15$$
$$-6x + 3(0) = 15$$
$$-6x + 0 = 15$$
$$-6x = 15$$
$$x = -2.5$$

The line intersects the x–axis at point $(-2.5,0)$.

Now that we know that the location of the x-intercept is $(-2.5,0)$ and the location of the y-intercept is $(0,5)$, look for the graph that contains both coordinate pairs. Since the graph shown in choice C contains both points, the correct answer is C.

12. B: Applying the rule that $\sqrt{a}\sqrt{b} = \sqrt{ab}$ when $a, b \geq 0$, we get $3\sqrt{11} \times 4\sqrt{14} = 3 \times 4 \times \sqrt{11} \times \sqrt{14} = 12\sqrt{154}$. Since the radicand, 154, has no perfect square factors, we cannot further simplify this answer.

13. C: First, write an equation that represents the scenario. Use n to represent the width. Since the length is 2 meters more than the width, use $n + 2$ to represent the length. Since $A = lw$, multiply n and $n + 2$ to get a product of 15.

$$n(n + 2) = 15$$

Next, convert the quadratic equation to standard form. To do so, distribute n to each term inside the parentheses. Move all the terms to the left side and set it equal to 0 by doing inverse operations. Subtract 15 from both sides of the equation.

$$n^2 + 2n = 15$$
$$n^2 + 2n - 15 = 15 - 15$$
$$n^2 + 2n - 15 = 0$$

Next, factor the left side of the equation.

$$(n + 5)(n - 3) = 0$$

From here, set each factor to 0 and solve for the variable, starting with $n + 5 = 0$. Use inverse operations, and subtract 5 from both sides of the equation.

$$n + 5 = 0$$
$$n + 5 - 5 = 0 - 5$$
$$n = -5$$

Finally, solve $n - 3 = 0$. Use inverse operations, and add 3 to both sides of the equation.

$$n - 3 = 0$$
$$n - 3 + 3 = 0 + 3$$
$$n = 3$$

The solution set is {−5,3}. Since measurements of length and width use positive integers, omit −5 in this scenario. Therefore, the width of the garden is 3 meters, and the length is 5 meters.

$$\text{width} = n = 3$$

$$\text{length} = n + 2 = (3) + 2 = 5$$

14. A: Since we need to factor to solve the quadratic equation, first set the equation equal to zero.

$$x^2 + 5x = -6$$
$$x^2 + 5x + 6 = -6 + 6$$
$$x^2 + 5x + 6 = 0$$

Factor the quadratic on the left hand-side and solve both equations for x.

$$x^2 + 5x + 6 = 0$$
$$(x + 3)(x + 2) = 0$$

$$x + 3 = 0 \qquad\qquad x + 2 = 0$$
$$x = -3 \qquad\qquad\qquad x = -2$$

15. D: To find a percentage from a decimal, multiply by 100: $0.0016(100) = 0.16\%$.

16. B: Since the denominator is the same for both fractions, this is simple subtraction. Start by subtracting the fractions. Since 1 is less than 5, borrow from the 3. The expression is now: $2\frac{7}{6} - 1\frac{5}{6}$. Now the fractions can be subtracted: $\frac{7}{6} - \frac{5}{6} = \frac{2}{6}$, which simplifies to $\frac{1}{3}$. Then, subtract the whole numbers: $2 - 1 = 1$. Putting these two parts together gives the final answer: $3\frac{1}{6} - 1\frac{5}{6} = 1\frac{1}{3}$.

17. A: The expression $(x - 1)^2$ may be expanded as $x^2 - 2x + 1$. Multiplication of $-5x$ by this expression gives $-5x^3 + 10x^2 - 5x$.

18. C: To simplify the polynomial, group and combine all terms of the same order.

$$= 4x^3 + 5x - x^3 + 2x^2 + 17 - 3x^3 + 5x - 2x^2 + 3$$
$$= (4x^3 - x^3 - 3x^3) + (2x^2 - 2x^2) + (5x + 5x) + (17 + 3)$$
$$= 0 + 0 + 10x + 20$$
$$= 10(x + 2)$$

19. C: The power to which 2 is raised to give 64 is 6: $2^6 = 64$. Thus, $x = 6$.

20. B: Substitute each of the given values for x and y into the equation, and simplify using the order of operations.

$$(4)^2 - (2(3) - 3)$$
$$= 16 - (6 - 3)$$
$$= 16 - 3$$
$$= 13$$

21. C: Since Joshua has to earn more than 92 points to qualify and each question is worth 4 points, the inequality $4x > 92$, where x is the number of questions he gets correct, best represents this situation. To solve for x, the number of questions Joshua needs to answer correctly, divide both sides of the inequality by 4. This results in the inequality $x > 23$. Since there are only 30 questions, the inequality becomes $23 < x \leq 30$.

To graph this inequality, put an open dot at 23 because there is a greater than sign and not a greater than or equal to sign. This shows that 23 is not included in the solution set. Put a closed dot at 30 to show that it is included in the solution set. Then, connect the two dots with a line.

22. C: To simplify the expression, first simplify the expression raised to an exponent. To raise $2x$ to the third power, raise both 2 and x to the third power separately.

$$(3x)^3 \times (5x^2) = 3^3 \times x^3 \times 5x^2$$
$$= 27 \times 5 \times x^3 \times x^2$$

Next, multiply the terms. Since they have the same base and are being multiplied together, add the exponents for the terms with like bases.

$$27 \times 5 \times x^3 \times x^2 = 135x^{3+2} = 135x^5$$

23. A: To simplify the expression, start by multiplying the coefficients by one another. Then, apply the exponent rule $x^m \times x^n = x^{m+n}$.

$$2x^5 \times 7x^{18} = 14(x^{5+18}) = 14x^{23}$$

24. B: To factor the polynomial, start by finding two factors that multiply to $2x^2$ that will make up the first parts of the binomials. The two factors must be $2x$ and x.

$$(2x+?)(x+?)$$

From here, find two numbers that multiply to –15 and will give you a middle coefficient of 7 when the two binomials are multiplied together. These numbers must be –3 and 5, which will create this polynomial in factored form:

$$(2x - 3)(x + 5)$$

Pay close attention to the placement and signs of the numbers. This method may take a little guessing and checking, especially when you are trying to figure out how to get the middle term. Once you have your polynomial factored, multiply it out to make sure that it matches the original polynomial.

$$2x^2 + 10x - 3x - 15 = 2x^2 + 7x - 15$$

25. B: To factor the polynomial, find factors of the first and third term whose product can be added to get the middle term. Here, the factors 7 and –8 have a product of –56, and when added together, yield –1. Another way to find the correct answer is to multiply the answer choices and select the choice that yields the original equation. In this case:

$$(x + 7)(x - 8) = (x)(x) + (x)(-8) + (7)(x) + (7)(-8)$$
$$= x^2 - 8x + 7x - 56$$
$$= x^2 - x - 56$$

26. B: Use the order of operations to find the value for this expression. The order of operations is: parentheses, exponents, multiplication and division, addition and subtraction.

$$-3 \times 5^2 + 2(4 - 18) + 33$$
$$= -3 \times 5^2 + 2(-14) + 33$$
$$= -3 \times 25 + 2(-14) + 33$$
$$= -75 + (-28) + 33$$
$$= -70$$

The value of the expression is –70.

27. C: Substituting –1 for each x-value gives:

$$f(-1) = \frac{(-1)^3 + 3(-1) + 2}{2(-1)} = \frac{-1 - 3 + 2}{-2} = 1$$

28. C: Start by distributing the 4, and then use inverse operations to solve for x.

$$8x - 24 = 10x - 6$$
$$-24 = 2x - 6$$
$$-18 = 2x$$
$$-9 = x$$

29. B: To simplify this expression, start by expanding the squared term using the FOIL method.

$$(x + 6)^2 = (x + 6)(x + 6) = x^2 + 6x + 6x + 36 = x^2 + 12x + 36$$

The expression now becomes $-2x(x^2 + 12x + 36)$. From here, distribute the $-2x$ to each term in the set of parentheses.

$$-2x \cdot x^2 - 2x \cdot 12x - 2x \cdot 36$$
$$-2x^3 - 24x - 72$$

30. C: One way to find this is to align like terms and subtract them vertically, remembering that subtraction of a term is equivalent to adding its opposite. This gives us:

	$-8x^2$	$+5xy$			$-4y$	-10
$-$	$(-8x^2$		$+12y^2$	$+5x$	$-6y$	$-10)$
	$0x^2$	$+5xy$	$-12y^2$	$-5x$	$+2y$	$+0$

This result simplifies to $5xy - 12y^2 - 5x + 2y$.

251

Reading

1. B: The passage was written to analyze the works by Chang-rae Lee and the themes presented in his most famous novels.

2. A: The author of this passage uses the first line of the novel to provide an example of one of the themes of the novel.

3. D: Espionage is part of the plot of the novel *Native Speaker*, but it is not a theme that recurs in Lee's works.

4. C: The passage states that Lee's interests in cultural identity and race emerge from his own experiences with these subjects as a young immigrant to America.

5. A: The tone of the last paragraph suggests concern over the preservation of cultural identities in an increasingly mixed and expanding world.

6. A: Emma's life had been marked by the comfort of consistency, a close relationship with Miss Taylor, and the knowledge that she tended to get her own way. Miss Taylor's marriage upsets that comfort and consistency because a major aspect of Emma's life will change. Emma is afraid her intellect will be stifled without Miss Taylor, so she does not approach the change as an opportunity for possible intellectual growth.

7. D: The author uses words such as *comfortable* and *happy* to describe Emma's first 21 years. During this time, little vexed her. Based on this context, you can conclude that *vex* has the opposite meaning of words such as *comfortable* and *happy*. The answer choice most different from these positive words is *displease*.

8. C: The author states that Emma possessed the "power of having rather too much her own way," and instead of feeling happy for her recently married friend, she feels sorry for herself. These descriptions characterize Emma as selfish. Emma may consider herself unfortunate following Miss Taylor's marriage, but a lifetime of privilege and having her own way hardly makes her an unfortunate character. While Emma may indeed prove to be devious, this excerpt offers no evidence of deviousness. Although Emma seems to value intellectual interaction, nothing in the excerpt implies that she is particularly studious.

9. B: A product of upper-class privilege, Emma has grown accustomed to always getting her way. When Miss Taylor's marriage disrupts this aspect of her life, Emma cannot deal with the situation in a mature fashion and instead sinks into self-pity and sorrow. Although Emma cannot enjoy Miss Taylor's happiness at her wedding because Emma is so wrapped up in her own feelings, this does not mean she feels neither kindness nor love for her friend.

10. B: The color black is often used figuratively to suggest badness. Emma is sad about Miss Taylor's wedding, and enduring the event has become nothing more than "black work" to her. Perhaps she pretends she is happy about the wedding, but no evidence in this excerpt suggests this conclusion. In addition, no evidence in the excerpt suggests that Emma organized the wedding. The author does not use *black* as a literal color in this excerpt, and no evidence in the excerpt suggests the wedding party wears black clothing.

11. D: By beginning his argument with a criticism of the existing federal government, he immediately portrays it as a system in need of improvement. By presenting the government's inefficacy in no uncertain terms, Hamilton assumes the reader will take his claim at face value and be convinced of his subsequent argument for improvements. Hamilton only criticizes the federal government explicitly; he does not criticize the Constitution.

12. A: By addressing the reader directly and uniting himself with the reader by using words such as *we*, Hamilton is establishing a sense of agreement between himself and the reader. By doing so, he tries to convince the reader that he and the reader share the same desires for and concerns about America. The first-person point of view does not necessarily establish a friendly or informal tone.

13. C: Alexander Hamilton describes his opponents as loud and bitter in this sentence. Such words suggest a lack of rationality, self-control, and kindness. This word usage almost represents an attempt to portray his political opponents as less than human. Hamilton is seeking to strengthen his argument by suggesting those who oppose his argument are angry and irrational.

14. B: In paragraph 3, Alexander Hamilton attacks politicians who fear any change resulting from the Constitution that might diminish their power. Although this attack may be central to his argument, Hamilton does not want to leave the reader with the bitter feeling that Hamilton's sole reason for writing is to attack his opponents. Ironically, he then continues his attacks for the remainder of the excerpt.

15. A: According to the writer, a tyrant would start by pretending to be submissive to the will of the people (that is, paying court to the people) to gain popularity, then abuse his or her newfound power. Based on this context, you can conclude that *obsequious* and *submissive* share the same meaning.

16. B: The passage says in paragraph 3 that Levin is absorbed in cattle and peasants, which can be found in the countryside. Paragraph 4 states that Vronsky comes from an aristocratic background, or family. While it's true that Levin is shy, choice A is incorrect because Levin is the character who has uncompromising opinions, not Vronsky. Choice C is incorrect because it is Levin who is absorbed by cattle and peasants, not Vronsky. Choice D is incorrect because paragraph 4 states that Vronsky is wealthy, not Levin.

17. C: The context of the sentence shows that Kitty's mother believed, or fancied, that Kitty had feelings for Levin. While it might also be true that Kitty fancies (or is interested in) Levin, choice A is incorrect because the structure of the sentence shows that *fancied* is used to show the mother's opinion. Choice B is incorrect because Kitty's mother is not imagining Kitty's feelings; based on Kitty's behavior earlier, she believes that Kitty was in love with Levin. Choice D is incorrect because Kitty's mother is not interpreting current events; instead, she fancies that Kitty had feelings for Levin based on her observations of Kitty's past behavior.

18. C: Kitty's mother is torn by the changes that are reshaping her society. The reader can best understand the impact of these changes by understanding original Russian society, which is partly explained in paragraphs 1 and 6. Choice A is incorrect because the passage does not present evidence that Kitty is only interested in marrying a Russian; while this may be true, the passage does not indicate Kitty's feelings. Choice B is incorrect because paragraph 6 states that the Russian style of matchmaking was unseemly and no longer used. Choice D is incorrect because the reader does not yet know whom Kitty will marry or whether Kitty will use the English method by choosing her husband herself.

19. C: Paragraph 7 says that Vronsky never makes important decisions without consulting his mother, and her visit will be an opportunity for him to ask her important questions. Choice A is incorrect because the passage doesn't indicate that Kitty might meet Vronsky's mother. Choice B is incorrect because Vronsky attends balls to dance with Kitty, not his mother. While Vronsky might show his mother around Moscow, choice D is incorrect because the passage does not imply that this will happen.

20. A: The rest of the sentence explains that Kitty's father is punctilious about his daughters' honor and reputation, which means that he's careful to guard them. Choice B is incorrect because *punctual* means "on time," and the passage doesn't show Kitty's father attempting to arrive anywhere promptly. Choice C is incorrect because it has the same meaning as *punctual*. Choice D is incorrect because *boisterous* means energetic, loud, or intense and, while that may be true of "scenes" described in the following sentences, it does not match the meaning of *punctilious*.

21. B: Choice B gives specific details about new behaviors, such as forming clubs and going to lectures. Choice A is incorrect because it focuses on the stress Kitty's mother felt as Kitty's older daughters got married. Choice C is incorrect because it shows that the French fashion was not accepted; this means that Russian society has not changed to embrace the French fashion. Choice D is incorrect because it shows Kitty's mother is increasingly uneasy but does not show why.

22. A: Paragraph 3 says that Kitty's mother dislikes Levin's shyness. Choices B and C are incorrect because these are the characteristics mentioned in paragraph 4 as positive traits that Vronsky has. Even though Vronsky, the mother's favorite, is very obedient to his mother, Kitty's mother does say that this trait makes him unsuitable for Kitty. She is a little uneasy about this trait, but does not rule Vronsky out as an acceptable husband. Therefore, choice D is incorrect.

23. B: The paragraph shows that the central conflict is Kitty's feelings about Levin and Vronsky. Choice A is incorrect because Kitty's mother does not appear prominently in paragraph 1. Choice C is incorrect because the paragraph only mentions the balls but does not give any details. Choice D is incorrect because the reader only learns details about Levin and Vronsky in the following paragraphs, not in paragraph 1.

24. A: Paragraph 6 explains that the peace that came upon Europe after the battle of Waterloo was still unbroken; the continent was not at war. Choices B, C, and D are incorrect because paragraphs 7-9 explain that these choices were problems. Paragraph 7 talks about the problems in Ireland, paragraph 8 talks about the low, or starvation, wages earned by many agricultural workers, and paragraph 9 mentions the problems with the education system.

25. B: The paragraph talks primarily about the royal family, including George III and Princess Charlotte. This paragraph serves to partially explain how Victoria came to be queen. Choice A is incorrect because the paragraph gives few details about Victoria's childhood. Instead, it talks about her father and other royals. Choice C is incorrect because paragraph 4, not paragraph 3, talks about Albert, Victoria's cousin. Choice D is incorrect because only a portion of the paragraph discusses the Duke of Kent. The paragraph is mainly about the royal family as a whole.

26. C: The paragraph shows that Mrs. Browning predicted that the people would love Victoria and that the people did, ultimately, love her (the paragraph says "there are very few sovereigns of whom it could be so truly said that they *have* been well beloved"). Choice A is incorrect because it is the opposite of how the people felt about her. Choice B is incorrect because the quote does not mention any poets other than Mrs. Browning. Choice D is incorrect because the passage does not state that Queen Victoria had those characteristics.

27. D: The paragraphs give many details about the troubles that faced the nation when Victoria became queen. Choice A is incorrect because they don't describe what Queen Victoria did to address these problems. Choices B and C are incorrect because the paragraphs discuss many problems, not just those specific problems.

28. A: Paragraph 9 states that the "system of poor-relief" was defective, leading to an immense amount of poverty. Choice B is incorrect because the lack of funding for education is presented as a separate problem from the efforts to aid the poor. Choice C is incorrect because it is not specific and could apply to many of the problems described in paragraphs 7-9. Choice D is incorrect because the government had already reformed the poor-relief system in a failed attempt to solve the problems, and we have not yet seen whether new reforms are coming.

29. B: Paragraph 5 says that Victoria did not know how close she was to the throne until she was twelve years old. This supports the author's point earlier in the sentence that her childhood was simple. Choice A is incorrect because the passage never says she spent time with her cousin; instead, paragraph 4 simply describes Prince Albert's lineage. Choice C is incorrect because the author does not indicate that Victoria's independence is related to her simplicity. Choice D is incorrect because the passage does not imply that the education caused her childhood to be simple. Instead, the education prepared her for the throne.

30. C: *Tender years* refers to children, or people who are too young to be working. Choice C is the only answer choice that refers to children. Choice A is incorrect because it points out the suffering but does not define *tender years*. Choice B is incorrect for the same reason; *cruelly long* describes the long work hours without defining *tender*. Choice D is incorrect because it refers to women who had to work too hard. However, *tender years* refers to children who were forced to work.

Writing

1. C: A comma should not be used to separate the sentence's subject (*Paul Revere*) and verb (*ran*). Choice A is incorrect because an apostrophe would make *1760s* possessive, which it is not. Choice B is incorrect because the comma is used to separate a nonessential clause from the rest of the sentence. Choice D is incorrect because the words *busy* and *metalworking* are not merely a series of adjectives. Instead, *busy* is an adjective modifying the noun phrase *metalworking shop*. In this usage, *metalworking shop* as a whole acts like a noun because the type of shop is core to the meaning.

2. C: *British* is a proper noun and should always be capitalized. Choice A is incorrect because the passage is written in past tense; therefore, *got* should remain in past tense. Choice B is incorrect because the sentence is referring to something getting worse, rather than something that is the superlative *worst*. Choice D is incorrect because *Stamp Act* is a proper noun.

3. A: Commas are used to separate independent clauses from nonrestrictive phrases. Choice B is incorrect because it is missing the comma. Choice C incorrectly uses *that* instead of *which*. Choice D incorrectly uses a semicolon because the second phrase is not independent.

4. A: *Were* is referring to the plural noun of *colonists*. As a singular verb form, *was* is incorrect in this case. Choice B is incorrect because *parliament* is the correct spelling. Choice C is incorrect because the comma is required to set off the nonessential phrase that follows. Choice D is incorrect because *that* is used to set off a restrictive clause and should not be preceded by a comma.

5. B: A comma and conjunction are correctly used to separate two independent clauses. Although choice A has the conjunction *and*, it is missing the required comma. Choice C is incorrect because no comma is required when a single subject (*colonists*) is shared by two predicates. Choice D is incorrect because the comma creates a run-on sentence.

6. D: "Sonja works very hard" and "she is tired all the time" are both independent clauses (they contain a subject and a verb and express a complete thought). It is appropriate to join two independent clauses with a semicolon. Choice A is a comma splice. Choice B is a run-on sentence. Choice C incorrectly uses a comma to precede the conjunctive adverb *however*.

7. A: *Answer* (present tense form of the verb) maintains the parallel structure of the sentence and matches the verb tense of the words *get* and *read*. The other answer choices represent the present participle (*answering*), infinitive (*to answer*), and future tense (*will answer*).

8. B: The correct spelling of the word is *deleterious*.

9. D: A stele is a large, upright stone that typically has writing on it. Steles were commonly used as monuments in ancient cultures in the Middle East.

10. B: The correct spelling is *mischievous*.

11. D: This sentence contains a prepositional phrase and an independent clause separated from the main sentence via a semicolon. This is the only choice that uses correct grammar. A prepositional phrase starts with a preposition and usually ends with a gerund, noun, pronoun, or clause.

12. B: A semicolon links two (or more) independent clauses. It can also be used to avoid confusion when listing items. Choice B is listing items and using the semicolon to avoid a misunderstanding. Choices A and C combine a dependent and independent clause. Choice D incorrectly mixes commas and semicolons in the list.

13. C: The word should be spelled *meticulous*.

14. C: The meaning of *lachrymose* is "mournful" or "tearful." The context of the sentence shows that the girls are upset (they are crying and comforting each other) in connection with the unpleasant subject (bad haircuts) of the stories.

15. A: This is an example of a conditional adverbial clause; it acts like an adverb and usually starts with words like *if* or *unless*. This talks about a situation that could happen. The other choices do not make sense in this situation; it's clear from the second part of the sentence that a consequence is coming. Choices B and C are independent clauses, and choice D is a clause of manner.

16. A: A semicolon is used to connect two independent clauses that are closely related. A comma should not be used to separate independent clauses, as a comma is more for a pause in the text. The sentence needs some punctuation, so choice C is incorrect. Choice D uses a colon, which should be used to show a list or provide an explanation.

17. B: This word should be spelled with two *r*'s: *surreptitious*. It means "something that is secret" or "sly."

18. C: *Acrimonious* means "bitter" or "vitriolic" and is very similar in meaning to *rancorous*.

19. B: To defer is to temporarily put off, postpone, or delay an action. To defer a loan is to postpone its repayment with the intention of resuming repayments in the future. To decry means to criticize. To differ means to vary or disagree. *Debtor* is a noun meaning "someone who owes a debt."

20. B: This question deals with being able to identify different meanings or parts of speech through patterns in words. The first and second blanks require nouns; the third blank requires a verb. Choice A provides noun, verb, verb. Choice C provides verb, noun, noun. Choice D provides all nouns.

21. B: The sentence portrays a scenario where it seems as though the floor supervisor has knowledge about everything that is happening and is ready to step in to keep things from going wrong. While the supervisor may also be cautious, eager, or a micromanager, the meaning and use of omniscient in this context is *all-knowing*.

22. A: This sentence offers the most effective revision. The syntax is clearer than the other answer choices. The writer achieves maximum impact by holding Mary Shelley's achievement, the creation of Dr. Frankenstein and his hideous monster in her novel *Frankenstein*, for the end of the sentence.

23. C: Merriam-Webster's Dictionary states that \im-'präm(p)-(,)tü is the correct pronunciation of the word *impromptu*. This pronunciation indicates that the *o* is pronounced *ä*, which is an open vowel that sounds like "ah"; the *p* is optional; and the *ü* is pronounced "oo".

24. B: This is the most effective revision. The syntax is clearer than the original sentence, and it retains the vivid description of *automobile* as a "friend and foe." The other choices either are poorly structured or are missing the figurative language of the original.

25. C: The first statement establishes the idea that repairing Route 211 will have financial consequences for the community. The correct answer choice supports this statement by providing specific figures regarding the amount of money the potholes in Route 211 cost drivers last year. The other answer choices may be relevant in the argument, but they do not follow the statement in the question as well.

26. C: A word's origin, or etymology, can sometimes be guessed by examining the word. The word *malaria* is a combination of two parts: *mala*, which means bad, and *aria*, which means air. *Noxious* and *odiferous* have meanings that are similar to "bad air," but have a different etymology. *Consumption* is an old term for tuberculosis, a disease of the lungs once thought to have been caused by bad air.

27. D: The context of the sentence indicates that Mara would feel great happiness.

28. D: Although the word choices all have similar denotations, the context of the sentence, and especially the use of the word *grudgingly*, indicate that Stanley gave only a perfunctory congratulations to Nathan for his good idea.

29. D: "Hunting down the truth" is a figure of speech that means "determined to learn the truth." This is indicated by the context of the sentence, which references the life goal of a detective.

30. A: This sentence best conveys the information without using too many words or having an awkward construction.

How to Overcome Test Anxiety

Just the thought of taking a test is enough to make most people a little nervous. A test is an important event that can have a long-term impact on your future, so it's important to take it seriously and it's natural to feel anxious about performing well. But just because anxiety is normal, that doesn't mean that it's helpful in test taking, or that you should simply accept it as part of your life. Anxiety can have a variety of effects. These effects can be mild, like making you feel slightly nervous, or severe, like blocking your ability to focus or remember even a simple detail.

If you experience test anxiety—whether severe or mild—it's important to know how to beat it. To discover this, first you need to understand what causes test anxiety.

Causes of Test Anxiety

While we often think of anxiety as an uncontrollable emotional state, it can actually be caused by simple, practical things. One of the most common causes of test anxiety is that a person does not feel adequately prepared for their test. This feeling can be the result of many different issues such as poor study habits or lack of organization, but the most common culprit is time management. Starting to study too late, failing to organize your study time to cover all of the material, or being distracted while you study will mean that you're not well prepared for the test. This may lead to cramming the night before, which will cause you to be physically and mentally exhausted for the test. Poor time management also contributes to feelings of stress, fear, and hopelessness as you realize you are not well prepared but don't know what to do about it.

Other times, test anxiety is not related to your preparation for the test but comes from unresolved fear. This may be a past failure on a test, or poor performance on tests in general. It may come from comparing yourself to others who seem to be performing better or from the stress of living up to expectations. Anxiety may be driven by fears of the future—how failure on this test would affect your educational and career goals. These fears are often completely irrational, but they can still negatively impact your test performance.

Elements of Test Anxiety

As mentioned earlier, test anxiety is considered to be an emotional state, but it has physical and mental components as well. Sometimes you may not even realize that you are suffering from test anxiety until you notice the physical symptoms. These can include trembling hands, rapid heartbeat, sweating, nausea, and tense muscles. Extreme anxiety may lead to fainting or vomiting. Obviously, any of these symptoms can have a negative impact on testing. It is important to recognize them as soon as they begin to occur so that you can address the problem before it damages your performance.

The mental components of test anxiety include trouble focusing and inability to remember learned information. During a test, your mind is on high alert, which can help you recall information and stay focused for an extended period of time. However, anxiety interferes with your mind's natural processes, causing you to blank out, even on the questions you know well. The strain of testing during anxiety makes it difficult to stay focused, especially on a test that may take several hours. Extreme anxiety can take a huge mental toll, making it difficult not only to recall test information but even to understand the test questions or pull your thoughts together.

Effects of Test Anxiety

Test anxiety is like a disease—if left untreated, it will get progressively worse. Anxiety leads to poor performance, and this reinforces the feelings of fear and failure, which in turn lead to poor performances on subsequent tests. It can grow from a mild nervousness to a crippling condition. If allowed to progress, test anxiety can have a big impact on your schooling, and consequently on your future.

Test anxiety can spread to other parts of your life. Anxiety on tests can become anxiety in any stressful situation, and blanking on a test can turn into panicking in a job situation. But fortunately, you don't have to let anxiety rule your testing and determine your grades. There are a number of relatively simple steps you can take to move past anxiety and function normally on a test and in the rest of life.

Physical Steps for Beating Test Anxiety

While test anxiety is a serious problem, the good news is that it can be overcome. It doesn't have to control your ability to think and remember information. While it may take time, you can begin taking steps today to beat anxiety.

Just as your first hint that you may be struggling with anxiety comes from the physical symptoms, the first step to treating it is also physical. Rest is crucial for having a clear, strong mind. If you are tired, it is much easier to give in to anxiety. But if you establish good sleep habits, your body and mind will be ready to perform optimally, without the strain of exhaustion. Additionally, sleeping well helps you to retain information better, so you're more likely to recall the answers when you see the test questions.

Getting good sleep means more than going to bed on time. It's important to allow your brain time to relax. Take study breaks from time to time so it doesn't get overworked, and don't study right before bed. Take time to rest your mind before trying to rest your body, or you may find it difficult to fall asleep.

Along with sleep, other aspects of physical health are important in preparing for a test. Good nutrition is vital for good brain function. Sugary foods and drinks may give a burst of energy but this burst is followed by a crash, both physically and emotionally. Instead, fuel your body with protein and vitamin-rich foods.

Also, drink plenty of water. Dehydration can lead to headaches and exhaustion, especially if your brain is already under stress from the rigors of the test. Particularly if your test is a long one, drink water during the breaks. And if possible, take an energy-boosting snack to eat between sections.

Along with sleep and diet, a third important part of physical health is exercise. Maintaining a steady workout schedule is helpful, but even taking 5-minute study breaks to walk can help get your blood pumping faster and clear your head. Exercise also releases endorphins, which contribute to a positive feeling and can help combat test anxiety.

When you nurture your physical health, you are also contributing to your mental health. If your body is healthy, your mind is much more likely to be healthy as well. So take time to rest, nourish your body with healthy food and water, and get moving as much as possible. Taking these physical steps will make you stronger and more able to take the mental steps necessary to overcome test anxiety.

259

Mental Steps for Beating Test Anxiety

Working on the mental side of test anxiety can be more challenging, but as with the physical side, there are clear steps you can take to overcome it. As mentioned earlier, test anxiety often stems from lack of preparation, so the obvious solution is to prepare for the test. Effective studying may be the most important weapon you have for beating test anxiety, but you can and should employ several other mental tools to combat fear.

First, boost your confidence by reminding yourself of past success—tests or projects that you aced. If you're putting as much effort into preparing for this test as you did for those, there's no reason you should expect to fail here. Work hard to prepare; then trust your preparation.

Second, surround yourself with encouraging people. It can be helpful to find a study group, but be sure that the people you're around will encourage a positive attitude. If you spend time with others who are anxious or cynical, this will only contribute to your own anxiety. Look for others who are motivated to study hard from a desire to succeed, not from a fear of failure.

Third, reward yourself. A test is physically and mentally tiring, even without anxiety, and it can be helpful to have something to look forward to. Plan an activity following the test, regardless of the outcome, such as going to a movie or getting ice cream.

When you are taking the test, if you find yourself beginning to feel anxious, remind yourself that you know the material. Visualize successfully completing the test. Then take a few deep, relaxing breaths and return to it. Work through the questions carefully but with confidence, knowing that you are capable of succeeding.

Developing a healthy mental approach to test taking will also aid in other areas of life. Test anxiety affects more than just the actual test—it can be damaging to your mental health and even contribute to depression. It's important to beat test anxiety before it becomes a problem for more than testing.

Study Strategy

Being prepared for the test is necessary to combat anxiety, but what does being prepared look like? You may study for hours on end and still not feel prepared. What you need is a strategy for test prep. The next few pages outline our recommended steps to help you plan out and conquer the challenge of preparation.

STEP 1: SCOPE OUT THE TEST

Learn everything you can about the format (multiple choice, essay, etc.) and what will be on the test. Gather any study materials, course outlines, or sample exams that may be available. Not only will this help you to prepare, but knowing what to expect can help to alleviate test anxiety.

STEP 2: MAP OUT THE MATERIAL

Look through the textbook or study guide and make note of how many chapters or sections it has. Then divide these over the time you have. For example, if a book has 15 chapters and you have five days to study, you need to cover three chapters each day. Even better, if you have the time, leave an extra day at the end for overall review after you have gone through the material in depth.

If time is limited, you may need to prioritize the material. Look through it and make note of which sections you think you already have a good grasp on, and which need review. While you are studying, skim quickly through the familiar sections and take more time on the challenging parts.

Write out your plan so you don't get lost as you go. Having a written plan also helps you feel more in control of the study, so anxiety is less likely to arise from feeling overwhelmed at the amount to cover.

STEP 3: GATHER YOUR TOOLS

Decide what study method works best for you. Do you prefer to highlight in the book as you study and then go back over the highlighted portions? Or do you type out notes of the important information? Or is it helpful to make flashcards that you can carry with you? Assemble the pens, index cards, highlighters, post-it notes, and any other materials you may need so you won't be distracted by getting up to find things while you study.

If you're having a hard time retaining the information or organizing your notes, experiment with different methods. For example, try color-coding by subject with colored pens, highlighters, or post-it notes. If you learn better by hearing, try recording yourself reading your notes so you can listen while in the car, working out, or simply sitting at your desk. Ask a friend to quiz you from your flashcards, or try teaching someone the material to solidify it in your mind.

STEP 4: CREATE YOUR ENVIRONMENT

It's important to avoid distractions while you study. This includes both the obvious distractions like visitors and the subtle distractions like an uncomfortable chair (or a too-comfortable couch that makes you want to fall asleep). Set up the best study environment possible: good lighting and a comfortable work area. If background music helps you focus, you may want to turn it on, but otherwise keep the room quiet. If you are using a computer to take notes, be sure you don't have any other windows open, especially applications like social media, games, or anything else that could distract you. Silence your phone and turn off notifications. Be sure to keep water close by so you stay hydrated while you study (but avoid unhealthy drinks and snacks).

Also, take into account the best time of day to study. Are you freshest first thing in the morning? Try to set aside some time then to work through the material. Is your mind clearer in the afternoon or evening? Schedule your study session then. Another method is to study at the same time of day that you will take the test, so that your brain gets used to working on the material at that time and will be ready to focus at test time.

STEP 5: STUDY!

Once you have done all the study preparation, it's time to settle into the actual studying. Sit down, take a few moments to settle your mind so you can focus, and begin to follow your study plan. Don't give in to distractions or let yourself procrastinate. This is your time to prepare so you'll be ready to fearlessly approach the test. Make the most of the time and stay focused.

Of course, you don't want to burn out. If you study too long you may find that you're not retaining the information very well. Take regular study breaks. For example, taking five minutes out of every hour to walk briskly, breathing deeply and swinging your arms, can help your mind stay fresh.

As you get to the end of each chapter or section, it's a good idea to do a quick review. Remind yourself of what you learned and work on any difficult parts. When you feel that you've mastered the material, move on to the next part. At the end of your study session, briefly skim through your notes again.

But while review is helpful, cramming last minute is NOT. If at all possible, work ahead so that you won't need to fit all your study into the last day. Cramming overloads your brain with more information than it can process and retain, and your tired mind may struggle to recall even previously learned information when it is overwhelmed with last-minute study. Also, the urgent nature of cramming and the stress placed on your brain contribute to anxiety. You'll be more likely to go to the test feeling unprepared and having trouble thinking clearly.

So don't cram, and don't stay up late before the test, even just to review your notes at a leisurely pace. Your brain needs rest more than it needs to go over the information again. In fact, plan to finish your studies by noon or early afternoon the day before the test. Give your brain the rest of the day to relax or focus on other things, and get a good night's sleep. Then you will be fresh for the test and better able to recall what you've studied.

STEP 6: TAKE A PRACTICE TEST

Many courses offer sample tests, either online or in the study materials. This is an excellent resource to check whether you have mastered the material, as well as to prepare for the test format and environment.

Check the test format ahead of time: the number of questions, the type (multiple choice, free response, etc.), and the time limit. Then create a plan for working through them. For example, if you have 30 minutes to take a 60-question test, your limit is 30 seconds per question. Spend less time on the questions you know well so that you can take more time on the difficult ones.

If you have time to take several practice tests, take the first one open book, with no time limit. Work through the questions at your own pace and make sure you fully understand them. Gradually work up to taking a test under test conditions: sit at a desk with all study materials put away and set a timer. Pace yourself to make sure you finish the test with time to spare and go back to check your answers if you have time.

After each test, check your answers. On the questions you missed, be sure you understand why you missed them. Did you misread the question (tests can use tricky wording)? Did you forget the information? Or was it something you hadn't learned? Go back and study any shaky areas that the practice tests reveal.

Taking these tests not only helps with your grade, but also aids in combating test anxiety. If you're already used to the test conditions, you're less likely to worry about it, and working through tests until you're scoring well gives you a confidence boost. Go through the practice tests until you feel comfortable, and then you can go into the test knowing that you're ready for it.

Test Tips

On test day, you should be confident, knowing that you've prepared well and are ready to answer the questions. But aside from preparation, there are several test day strategies you can employ to maximize your performance.

First, as stated before, get a good night's sleep the night before the test (and for several nights before that, if possible). Go into the test with a fresh, alert mind rather than staying up late to study.

Try not to change too much about your normal routine on the day of the test. It's important to eat a nutritious breakfast, but if you normally don't eat breakfast at all, consider eating just a protein bar. If you're a coffee drinker, go ahead and have your normal coffee. Just make sure you time it so that the caffeine doesn't wear off right in the middle of your test. Avoid sugary beverages, and drink enough water to stay hydrated but not so much that you need a restroom break 10 minutes into the test. If your test isn't first thing in the morning, consider going for a walk or doing a light workout before the test to get your blood flowing.

Allow yourself enough time to get ready, and leave for the test with plenty of time to spare so you won't have the anxiety of scrambling to arrive in time. Another reason to be early is to select a good seat. It's helpful to sit away from doors and windows, which can be distracting. Find a good seat, get out your supplies, and settle your mind before the test begins.

When the test begins, start by going over the instructions carefully, even if you already know what to expect. Make sure you avoid any careless mistakes by following the directions.

Then begin working through the questions, pacing yourself as you've practiced. If you're not sure on an answer, don't spend too much time on it, and don't let it shake your confidence. Either skip it and come back later, or eliminate as many wrong answers as possible and guess among the remaining ones. Don't dwell on these questions as you continue—put them out of your mind and focus on what lies ahead.

Be sure to read all of the answer choices, even if you're sure the first one is the right answer. Sometimes you'll find a better one if you keep reading. But don't second-guess yourself if you do immediately know the answer. Your gut instinct is usually right. Don't let test anxiety rob you of the information you know.

If you have time at the end of the test (and if the test format allows), go back and review your answers. Be cautious about changing any, since your first instinct tends to be correct, but make sure you didn't misread any of the questions or accidentally mark the wrong answer choice. Look over any you skipped and make an educated guess.

At the end, leave the test feeling confident. You've done your best, so don't waste time worrying about your performance or wishing you could change anything. Instead, celebrate the successful completion of this test. And finally, use this test to learn how to deal with anxiety even better next time.

Review Video: Test Anxiety
Visit mometrix.com/academy and enter code: 100340

Important Qualification

Not all anxiety is created equal. If your test anxiety is causing major issues in your life beyond the classroom or testing center, or if you are experiencing troubling physical symptoms related to your anxiety, it may be a sign of a serious physiological or psychological condition. If this sounds like your situation, we strongly encourage you to seek professional help.

How to Overcome Test Anxiety

Additional Bonus Material

Due to our efforts to try to keep this book to a manageable length, we've created a link that will give you access to all of your additional bonus material:

mometrix.com/bonus948/pert

Made in United States
Orlando, FL
16 November 2024

53990540R00150